LAW
ENFORCEMENT

**An Introduction to the Police Role
in the Community**

LAW

ENFORCEMENT

An Introduction to the Police Role in the Community

THOMAS F. ADAMS
Lieutenant, Police Department
Santa Ana, California

Instructor, Orange Coast College
Costa Mesa, California

PRENTICE-HALL, INC., Englewood Cliffs, N.J.

Library of Congress Catalog Card No.: 68-15567.

Printed in the United States of America.

Current printing (last digit):
10 9 8 7 6 5 4 3 2 1

PRENTICE-HALL INTERNATIONAL, INC., *London*
PRENTICE-HALL OF AUSTRALIA, PTY. LTD., *Sydney*
PRENTICE-HALL OF CANADA, LTD., *Toronto*
PRENTICE-HALL OF INDIA PRIVATE LTD., *New Delhi*
PRENTICE-HALL OF JAPAN, INC., *Tokyo*

DEDICATED TO NORA . . .

. . . *my inspiration* . . . *my wife*

Preface

In Shakespeare's *As You Like It* Jacques very aptly expounded his commentary on life by stating:

> All the world's a stage,
> And all the men and women merely players.
> They have their exits and their entrances,
> And one man in his time plays many parts,
> His acts being seven ages . . .

On the stage known as the United States of America more than one quarter of a million of the nearly two hundred million players assume the role of *peace officer*. Although not a leading part, it is an extremely important supporting role in the play called *Life*. As a matter of fact, I seriously doubt that the play would have a successful run without the peace officer.

The police officer wears many caps and assumes many subroles when playing his part. He is a father-confessor to the youngster who has made his first mistake, a referee in a family or neighborhood quarrel, an actor in the drama of a high-speed pursuit and capture of a wanted felon, an investigator at the scene of a crime or accident, and a director of pedestrians and vehicles on the streets. He seldom has the time or the favorable atmosphere to vie for the popular vote of the people he serves, and he settles for at least a little tolerance for himself and the role he fills. Some people learn to respect the policeman, some learn to fear him, and others are taught to despise—and sometimes openly flout—him and his authority. The most significant characteristic of the unique role the policeman plays in the community is that very few people actually know exactly what that role is.

Several thousand years ago, the leaders in whatever passed for civilization at the time recognized the need for regulation of the people to make the community civilized and to keep it civilized. They promulgated laws, prescribed punishment for the violators of those laws, and designated a few of the strongest and most trustworthy men as enforcers of those laws to maintain order in accordance with the laws. Today, the picture is essentially the same. The laws are still present, and so are the enforcers. The primary differences between the past and the present are in the multiplicity and complexity of the laws, and the intellectual level of the enforcers, now known as peace officers. The policeman—or peace officer—of today is not only strong and trustworthy, but he is also intelligent, diplomatic, and charismatic.

In this book, we shall attempt to explain as thoroughly as possible the enigmatic role of the peace officer in the community. The traffic summons, the curfew arrest, and the field interview are just a few of the police procedures that involve a daily confrontation between peace officer and law-abiding citizen. At best, they do not lend themselves to the creation of an atmosphere that would endear the police officer to the people contacted. The purposes of, and the procedures involved in, these citizen-police contacts and a great many others as well, need explanations.

The purpose of a text such as this is twofold: first, to introduce the future or newly employed peace officer to the role that he is now filling, or is about to fill; second, to serve as a guide to the nonpoliceman who wishes to make himself aware of the police role. Teachers, journalists, attorneys, public administrators, and other community leaders should base the opinions and teachings about the police role upon factual information instead of legends and clichés.

Part 1 deals with the actual preparation for the role, including academic preparation and study techniques, and a general orientation to the career in law enforcement. Although an attempt is made to cover the many roles played by most of the major police and investigative agencies in the so-called police system, the major emphasis will be placed upon the local agencies—the municipal police department and the county sheriff's department. These two organizations comprise the backbone of law enforcement in the United States. Local government and local law enforcement are intrinsic to the American way of life. Qualifications for police service, career opportunities, and the selection process will focus primarily upon the local police agencies.

In Part 2, the text moves into the philosophical and historical aspects of the police role. Along with a discussion of the basic characteristics of the human being that call for a regulatory system is a discussion of the various types of criminal behavior: the first offender, career and professional criminals, white-collar criminals, and the phenomenon known as organized crime. The professional criminal makes a business out of crime, while the white-collar criminal may, to paraphrase, make crime out of his business. The white-collar offender may be a pillar of the community or church, the epitome of success who diverts hundreds of thousands of dollars entrusted to him by his customers or clients to his own use.

Organized crime is such a big business in this country, and in many other parts of the world as well, that the astronomically high profits in illicit gambling, prostitution, narcotics trafficking, and other organized criminal operations are almost impossible to comprehend. Organized crime cannot exist without the complicity of public officials at all levels of government. The encroachment upon the American scene by organized crime is no less menacing to the good order of the country than is the menace of communism. In this text it will be possible merely to take the first step toward the eventual control or suppression (to say eradication would be to hope for too much) of organized crime by creating an awareness of the problem.

Part 3 deals with the police system in the United States, which is actually a "nonsystem." Each local jurisdiction at the city and/or county level has its own law enforcement agency. There are also numerous other state and federal law enforcement and investigative agencies, each with its own specific jurisdiction—legal or geographical. Contrary to popular belief, there is no hierarchy or rank order for the many thousands of police agencies in the United States. This concept will be discussed in the text, as well as the jurisdictional responsibilities of many involved.

Part 4 will present a comprehensive overview of the basic purposes and objectives of the major operational units of the average police department, such as the Patrol, Traffic, Investigation, Juvenile, and Vice divisions. It is essential, I believe, to be familiar with the purposes and objectives of a unit prior to learning the actual procedures. It serves as a base from which the student and the practitioner may strike out in his studies of the procedural aspects of those units.

Part 5 deals with police ethics and professionalization. The police agency functions according to the laws, administrative rules and policies, and court-imposed rules of procedure promulgated in the form of interpretations of the rule and intent of the U.S. Constitution, and the various state constitutions. A chapter is devoted to this timely subject, with police power and the Bill of Rights as principal objects of the discussion.

Policemen are citizens of the community too. They are not only restricted by the same laws as are the other citizens, but they are protected by the same Bill of Rights and constitutions. Although their on-duty actions must be impartial and in the best interest of the community as a whole, their personal thoughts and ideals are theirs to zealously hold and guard. Enforcing the *intent* of the law in deference to the *letter* of the law is a responsible task to be performed by intelligent and objective peace officers.

Throughout the book, it is the author's intention to illustrate key factors with examples of actual or hypothetical cases to emphasize the fact that a police department is a living and dynamically changing organism in the community with the basic objective of maintaining order in the community. The members of that agency must be selected on the basis of their intelligence and ability to perform the job as true professionals. We hope that—through the medium of this text— we will have brought about a broader and more detailed understanding of the tremendously important police role in the community.

T. F. ADAMS

Contents

xi

5
POLICE ETHICS
AND PROFESSIONALIZATION

PART **1**

INTRODUCTION

1

Academic Preparation
for the Police Role

The police officer, by virtue of the many-faceted duties he must perform, is probably more intellectually and physically versatile than any other individual employed in an occupation or profession that provides a service to the community. He is responsible for providing a protective service primarily, and his responsibility to the community is most generally described as "protection of life and property." The police officer is many things to as many people, a representative of the community chosen from the community to maintain order and enforce the laws, an enforcer of the rules and a referee in disputes. He is an imperfect mortal rendering a service or a variety of services for other fallible humans who expect perfection from him, while each individual defines "perfection" in his own terms according to his particular and peculiar values and standards.

INDUCTIVE AND DEDUCTIVE REASONING

"Common sense" is an enigmatic and elusive term that has all the attributes of a chameleon. A policeman must possess and exercise a great deal of it, whatever it is. He investigates crimes and complaints and acts upon them in accordance with laws and the many rules that he must follow. He cannot merely accept and act upon all information that he receives at its face value. He must make a value judgment in all situations, dependent upon the facts as they present themselves at any specific moment. Native ability, or natural qualities that are charismatic in kind, enhance the individual's success potential as a policeman, but most of the qualities and characteristics that a police-

Photo courtesy Santa Ana Police Department

man must demonstrate are those that may be developed and improved upon with training and education. Based upon this premise, the processes of inductive and deductive reasoning are included among the skills that the policeman must learn and master. Consider the following illustration.

The investigator reported for work at the usual time in the morning. It was his responsibility to receive cases that involved crimes classified in his specialty assignment—in this instance the specialty was residential burglaries—and to continue investigating them until he reached a logical conclusion. He knew that it was a virtual impossibility to solve all the assigned cases for a variety of reasons, but his percentage of clearances was consistently high and to him the most logical conclusion for any of his assigned cases was a conviction of the guilty party. He was regarded by his fellow investigators as an excellent man with an enviable reputation, but obviously endowed with "a built-in radar system," "an instinct for detecting clues beyond the realm of normal human capabilities," and "a lot of good luck." Two qualities that most of his colleagues did not attribute to him were his capacity for doing a great deal of hard work and his deductive reasoning ability developed by training and experience. He was unquestionably a good investigator.

The hero of our story picked up one of his many newly assigned case reports. He read it carefully. As a matter of fact he read all of his case reports carefully. He asked himself: "Are all of the elements of the corpus delicti reflected in the report to substantiate that a crime has—in fact—been committed?" and "Does the report paint a word picture of how the crime scene appeared to the investigating officer at the time of the investigation, and a reasonably accurate account of how the crime was committed?" He studied the report, drawing on a piece of scratch paper a diagram of the crime scene as described in the report, and outlining the series of events that seemed to have taken place while the burglar was at work. The point of entry was a bathroom window that had been left unlocked by the owners of the house when they left at 7:00 P.M. for the theater. The muddy footprints indicated that the culprit went through the bedroom, stopping to pull open some bureau drawers but taking nothing, and then walked down the hallway into the kitchen. The report indicated that the victims had left the kitchen that evening with all the dishes washed and stored in their proper places, but an empty glass that had contained milk was found on the sideboard when the victims discovered their plight as burglary victims.

The report went on—the investigator making mental and visual notes—and described the general condition of the house and the various bits of evidence that indicated the obvious fact that the burglar was seeking only what cash he could find in the house. In a desk drawer the burglar had moved—but did not take—several expensive mementos, but he did remove several dollars from an envelope that had been between the pages of a checkbook. The culprit, apparently having found what he was seeking, then apparently left the house. There was no evidence to show the point of exit.

The investigator reached into his desk drawer and pulled out a folder containing several of his other assigned cases. He sorted out three or four similar reports: entry through unlocked windows—no forced entry—and the objects of the burglaries were similar in the fact that the burglar would usually help himself to milk or similar refreshments from the refrigerator, and the only object of the thefts was cash.

The next move the investigator made was to look at his map and note the relative locations of the victims in those similar cases.

He discovered, and not particularly to his amazement, that all of those particular burglaries occurred within a six-block radius, and that the time element placed them as occurring some time between 7:00 P.M. and midnight, all on Thursday nights. Still not leaving his desk, the "lucky" investigator picked up his telephone receiver and asked the Records Clerk to search the files for all residence burglaries that had occurred during the previous year on the specific streets that he listed for her, and he asked that she include in her search those burglaries that had been cleared by arrest during the same period of time.

A study of the files revealed a similar series of crimes that had occurred several months prior to the series that he was currently investigating, and that they had been cleared by the arrest of two young men who had been living at that end of town. A few phone calls later the investigator discovered that both youths had been tried, found guilty, had served time for the offenses, and that one of the two was again living somewhere in the city. The investigator now had at least one possible suspect.

Armed with the material gained during the initial few minutes of office work, the investigator then set out on his quest for a solution to his cases for which he had "hot leads." The man worked diligently on the cases for several days, not giving any thought to lunch breaks, coffee breaks, or the end of his normally scheduled work days. He interviewed witnesses and victims, he sorted out and inspected the various bits of evidence and fingerprint smudges, and had numerous consultations with the laboratory and identification personnel. He worked on his other assigned cases, too, but he had something substantial on the particular series of burglaries that caused him to focus his attention on them primarily. After many hours the investigator had compiled sufficient evidence to identify his suspect with reasonable certainty. He apprehended and questioned the suspect, confronted him with the evidence against him, and was successful in solving several of his assigned cases.

The star of our illustration chalked up another high clearance percentage for the month. His friends and colleagues reacted in a variety of ways, some alluding to his phenomenal luck, others crediting him with "just having a natural ability for solving crimes," and still others regarded him as something slightly less than psychic.

The case described above is an exemplification of deductive reasoning. It involves the employment of all the senses and faculties at the disposal of the actor, and his ability to see not only the "big picture" of the situation as a whole, but to also see it as a collection of many individual bits and pieces, to analyze and evaluate them individually, and to act upon his observations and conclusions in such a manner as to consider all factors in their respectively proper perspectives and to bring the case to a logical conclusion.

Conversely, the process of inductive reasoning must be executed with equal proficiency. The police officer who is first to arrive upon the scene of what is suspected of being a criminal law violation must collect and categorize all of the bits and pieces of evidence and information. He then assigns relative priority and importance ratings to them, evaluates them in relationship to the overall situation, and acts upon them in accordance with the results of his value-judgment decisions. The officer sifts through all of the statements of witnesses and victims for the true facts, and he inspects the evidence to determine whether a crime had actually occurred. He ascertains whether all of the elements are present to constitute a crime. In many cases, his judgment is the determinant in whether he shall deprive a person of his liberty or even his life whenever a specific set of circumstances presents itself to the officer, sometimes when such a decision must be

Photo courtesy Orange County Sheriff's Department

A GREAT DEAL OF AN INVESTIGATOR'S TIME IS DEVOTED TO
A CAREFUL STUDY OF POLICE RECORDS.

made in a fraction of a second. As opposed to the deductive reasoning factor, induction involves taking all of the many individual parts and assembling them in a logical manner so that they may be considered as a whole.

PRESERVICE EDUCATIONAL PREPARATION

Graduation from high school is generally considered an acknowledgment that the student has been reasonably well prepared for his social role in the community. Although frequent exceptions are encountered during the civil service selection process, completion of high school should be likewise considered as adequate preparation for entrance into the world of business and the majority of occupations open to the high school graduate. The police officer must be able to express himself to others both orally and by means of the written word in such an efficient manner that everyone with whom he has any verbal contact can adequately understand him and the true meaning of what he has to say. Although he should excel in all academic subjects and take an active part in physical education activities, there are certain subjects and extracurricular activities that later prove valuable to the embryonic police officer.

Spelling and English grammar are nuisance courses to some high school students, but they are most important to the man or woman who chooses to enter a profession in which the principal function they perform is communicating with others. Speech and drama prepare the student for speaking before audiences of more than one with confidence, and journalism disciplines the student to transmit his observations and impressions into report form. Extracurricular activities should include active membership and officeholding participation in school clubs and student government. The police officer is a community leader in his occupational role. Leadership qualities can be learned through properly directed training and actual experiences of trial and error. All forms of physical activities should be on the required list for the future policeman and policewoman.

"After high school, then what?" the student may ask. The universal entrance age for police officers, investigators, and virtually all full-time law enforcement personnel in America is twenty-one years. The average high school graduate is eighteen to nineteen years old. The interim period provides for the aspirant to law enforcement an excellent opportunity to further prepare himself academically.

The two-year college program fulfills the needs for basic introduction to the skills and knowledge required for the entering law enforcement officer. The general academic subjects and liberal arts electives round out the individual in the broad sense, and the "tool and technique" police science or criminology courses prepare the student for efficiently executing the mechanics of the job for which he is preparing. The baccalaureate and higher degrees further enhance the candidate's desirability and eventual promotability.

As professionalization of the entire field of law enforcement and criminal justice evolves into reality, the academic requirements will doubtlessly increase. It is a means to an end, however, not an end in itself. Knowing a job and knowing *about* a job are two different situations. You don't learn to swim without getting into the water, nor can you learn the job of *being* a policeman without "getting into the water." During the past several years, various police agencies and colleges have cooperated in a variety of programs that provide to the preservice student practical on-the-job training while still attending college. Two of the more popular programs are internship and cadet training.

How to stimulate and maintain the interest of the young high school graduate during the interim between graduation and his twenty-first birthday has always been a problem. Rather than leave a young man's decision to enter law enforcement to chance, it is more desirable to help him make his choice while still in high school through career guidance programs. It is then necessary that we encourage him for the next few years. The ultimate goal would be entrance into the ranks of law enforcement as an officer, a deputy, or an investigator. But there must be some intermediate goals that are attainable along the way. Without these goals, there is frustration, and in many cases a redesignation of goals. Internship and cadet training provide those intermediate goals, and emotional satisfaction as well. Additional incentives may be provided in the form of assured acceptance into the sponsoring agency at the completion of the training, and financial assistance in the form of nominal pay on an hourly basis.

Internship, or work experience programs, have been in operation within two-year and four-year college programs in California and elsewhere for many years. The student is usually required to attend on at least a half-time school schedule and to take a major in the law enforcement program. Some schools include young ladies in their program, but their utilization by cooperating agencies is on a much more limited basis. The student enrolls for the internship, or work experience, course for a specific number of credits (or units) and is required to work and/or observe at a specified cooperating agency for a minimum number of hours. This particular type of course usually does not involve financial remuneration for the student.

Approval of the intern is dependent upon successful completion of a series of entrance examinations and a thorough background investigation conducted by some agencies, and other agencies call for little more than a brief oral interview. In exchange for his hours of work observation, the student receives the credits and grades characteristic of all other college courses. He may be required to prepare periodic reports to both the agency and the college professor in charge of the program, and to the agency intern coordinator.

The cadet training program is similar to the internship program, but there is usually an employer-employee relationship between the student and the agency for which he performs. On-the-job supervision in a cadet program is usually the primary responsibility of the employing law enforcement agency. It is possible to assign the cadet to a wide variety of duties throughout the agency in nearly every area except actual enforcement or investigative assignments. Although not operable at the time of the preparation of this manuscript, it is possible that the cadet program could be extended to include the duties of the public service officer in the three-step policeman levels described by the President's Crime Commission and the administration of justice report released in early 1967.[1]

A student attending classes on a full-time or three-quarter schedule may be scheduled for a twenty-hour week during the school year and a full schedule during school vacation when the officers would be taking their vacations. The most practical method of selection of cadets is to have them go through the identical series of exams and the entire selection process as if they were applying for the policeman position. Later, when the cadet reaches the age of twenty-one and/or completion of his college education and he becomes a candidate for a full-fledged law enforcement officer, only a new medical exam and an oral interview would be necessary. An advantage to completing the selection examination process at the beginning of the cadet's employment in that capacity is that the individual who obviously will not gain eventual employment as a law enforcement officer will know it at that time rather than having the misfortune of

[1]This three-step entrance program as presented by the President's Crime Commission will be discussed in more detail in Chapter 14.

spending four years in college only to find out—with degree in hand—that he is not qualified for the job.

Although most of the cadet programs currently in operation are conducted by municipal law enforcement agencies, there is no reason why it should not be extended to include sheriffs' departments, state police, highway patrols, and many state and federal law enforcement and investigative agencies. In order to assure the agency that the program is actually going to produce officers or agents for that agency instead of professional student-cadets, the cadet could be required to sign an agreement that he will apply for the officer or agent position within a reasonable time (specifically stated in the agreement) after he reaches his twenty-first birthday or completes his college training, whichever occurs first, and that his failure to do so will result in his termination as a cadet. This technique would assure a turnover of cadets, limiting their membership to future policemen or investigators only.

Supplementing a paid internship or cadet training program, some colleges use their police science students in a variety of paid police-type activities. Some of those activities include on-campus traffic control, crowd control, and general security. Still another incentive to the future police officer-student is the requirement that they wear distinctive uniforms while in class and on campus. *Esprit de corps* runs high when the students are well trained and strictly disciplined. Entrance into this select group of students should be difficult, with summary expulsion for those who disobey the rules or fail to perform as required.

TEXTBOOK STUDY METHODS

Study is a way of life for the modern policeman. His formal education at the college or university is supplemented by continuous home study and in-service training. A few years ago there was a common agreement among professional-minded law enforcement men and women that books and literature in the field of law enforcement were simply not available. There was a dearth of information. The situation has been remedied considerably as the drive for law enforcement professionalization has gained momentum, and the chief concern for the serious student is in careful selection of material. In this section, we will discuss a few basic techniques in the art of textbook study. The choice of *what* to read is the student's. A few pointers on *how* to read a textbook will undoubtedly prove valuable to the professional policeman-student.

1. *Selection of the text.* If the book is designated by the instructor, there is no choice, only the confidence in the instructor that he has made a wise choice. If the selection is left to the reader, one of the first steps in the selection procedure is to determine if it actually covers the subject matter that the title and advertising purports that it does. For salability, the author and publisher will attempt to title the book so that it corresponds with the contents. Look for the date of the copyright, and consider the timeliness of the material at that time as compared with the present. Who is the author and what are his qualifications, including his experience as well as his educational achievements? The last question at this stage of the selection process is to determine what other books have been written on the same subject, and to compare them if possible.

2. *Preparation for study.* Schedule a regular study time so that you may form a study habit. After determining a time, exercise self-discipline and stick to the schedule, utilizing the time for serious and uninterrupted study. Selection of a suitable place for study is also very important.

3. *General rules for textbook study.* Get to know the author by reading his preface and introduction; and get a feel of the purpose for writing the book, the message—if any—the author intends to get across, and a summary of the material contained in the rest of the book. Make a cursory review of the entire book, giving attention to the broad outline presented by the table of contents, the glossary for definitions, the bibliography for sources, and the introductory and summarizing paragraphs in each chapter for general content. Study the charts and diagrams.

Now that you have completed a cursory review and are oriented to the book, go back to the beginning and study it carefully, chapter by chapter. Underline key points that you wish to augment with your own emphasis or refer to in later review, or that you consider questionable. Make marginal notes and footnotes, including not only information that you have to support the text, but also conflicting arguments of your own or other authors. Take notes as you proceed, recording both impressions and verbatim quotations that you will use later. Record sufficient information in your separate notes to identify the source, using quotation marks when quoting directly. A very effective but time-consuming study technique is to prepare a precis outline on each book that you read, paraphrasing and rewriting the chapters in tightly condensed form, condensing entire chapters into approximately a paragraph each.

COLLECTION AND CLASSIFICATION OF INFORMATION

Selectivity is more important than sheer volume in the compilation and retention of information for the student and practitioner in law enforcement. Although a great variety of methods have been suggested by a corresponding array of experts, I have found only three of these systems practical from the work input standpoint as well as reference value. One of the most valuable files for the instructor is a clipping file indexed into as many categories as time and space will allow. Illustrations can be documented with actual news stories and photographs, and they have a greater effect than vague "once upon a time" stories. A three-by-five card file of sources of information proves quite effective if cross-indexed as to subject matter and source. The key to success with this type of file is brevity, and it works quite well in conjunction with a clipping file and the third system on our list: a looseleaf notebook. The notebook is a compilation of all source material, separated into categories by dividers, and adequately indexed for easy reference.

CLASSROOM NOTE-TAKING AND OUTLINING

About 11 percent of what we learn is through the sense of hearing. About 83 percent of our learning is through sight, including what the student sees on the paper he keeps at the end of his poised pencil during the lecture. Retention varies also. An individual retains about 10 percent of what he reads, 20 percent of what he hears, and a total of 50 percent of what he sees and hears. The point is that by merely reading a book or listening to a lecture without actually becoming involved in the material, the student is not likely to get the maximum benefit from the lesson.

The student will assimilate and retain a great deal more if he actually studies what he reads, making marginal notes, underlining, and generally digesting the text material; and if he gets involved in the lecture through the media of visual aids, discussions, and a collection of well-prepared notes. The notes need not be—nor should they be—slavishly recorded verbatim reproductions of the entire lecture in parrotlike fashion but, rather, carefully selected quotations and impressions of the material covered as interpreted by the person recording the notes.

There are a few problems in effective note-taking that have to be overcome as much as possible by the student. One of the most serious problems is that some lecturers are not adequately prepared, and as a result they ramble and mumble. I suggest that if such a lecturer is encountered the actual value of what he has to offer is subject to question. Other lecturers are brilliant speakers and are literally held in awe by their students, but—aside from being impressed—they learn nothing. Such instructors are suspect for about the same reason as the mumbler; he does not accomplish his purpose: to express and instruct. The one problem that the listener does have control over is his own inattention. If he is to take notes, he will have to give his full attention to the lecture and make a deliberate effort to take notes continuously while listening.

There are many advantages to note-taking, and just a few of them are listed here. One of the principal advantages is that it forces the listener to seek out key points and significant ideas in the lecture, and to utilize his own thought process in restating those impressions in his own words. The information gained through lecture is often more current than even the most recently published text, and the lecturer's information may not be recorded elsewhere—or if it is it may not be as understandable as it is when presented in a lecture, when there is an opportunity for feedback between instructor and student.

The instructor frequently emphasizes his evaluation of the material he presents in rank order by writing certain information on the blackboard, presenting it in numerical order, and repeating for emphasis. The direct contact with the instructor and a good set of notes enhances the possibility of the student's later being able to organize and write the information in his own words. The value of such notes as these is much greater than a verbatim transcription of direct quotations of the instructor. Retention is also enhanced considerably, because the student both sees and hears the information presented in the lecture.

Outlining is a matter of personal choice if it is to prove of actual value to the user of the form. It disciplines the user to think in organized fashion, to relegate points and facts to their relative positions of importance, and it provides a means by which the user may arrange a logical sequence of events and ideas. There are many excellent sources for the student who is not familiar with the general outlining procedure.

Classroom notetaking, outlining, and formulation of good study habits provide a substantial foundation for development of skills in field notetaking, and in the collection and evaluation of information. Crimes are solved as a result of orderly collection of data and deductive reasoning. Learning to separate the essential from the nonessential, the important from the unimportant, and the meaningful from the meaningless is a skill that can be learned in the classroom and transferred to future police work. Skill in probing, scanning, studying, and evaluating contribute to attainment of the "common sense" qualities of a policeman that are vital to effective decision-making in the police role.

Here are a few suggestions to follow when taking notes:
1. Write impressions, not verbatim statements, except when specifically necessary.
2. Use your own language instead of the lecturer's.
3. Record the examples and anecdotes as well as the straight lecture material.
4. Abbreviate, write fast, and transcribe your notes as soon as possible after the lecture while it is still fresh in your memory.
5. Indicate emphasis in your notes to correspond with emphasis by the instructor. Use underlining, asterisks, numbers, checkmarks, colored pencils, and other means at your disposal.
6. Leave liberal spacing for later editing and additions.
7. Define your terms as defined by the lecturer.
8. Add your own thoughts and ideas, but identify them as your own, and do not confuse them with those of the lecturer, particularly if they conflict.

Exercises and Study Questions

1. Now that you have completed reading this chapter, close the book and write a summary of the chapter from memory.
2. Prepare a precis outline on this book, or one of similar size.
3. Look into a department store window and write a word picture of the contents and arrangement of the window. Leave the scene and, from

your description, draw a diagram of the display. Return to the window and compare your sketch with the display.

4. Write an illustrative example of "inductive reasoning."

5. Write an illustrative example of "deductive reasoning."

6. Describe the duties of a cadet, or intern, as discussed in this chapter.

7. What percentage of learning is accomplished through the sense of hearing?

8. According to the author, what three systems of collection and classification of information are most effective?

9. When taking notes, is it better to transcribe *impressions* or *verbatim* statements made during the lecture?

10. *Recommended Semester Project*: Poll the police agencies and colleges in the state in which you live to determine which ones participate in an intern or cadet program. From your research, write a paper on your evaluation of such a program.

Suggested for Additional Study:

Smith, Samuel. *Best Methods of Study* (New York: Barnes & Noble, Inc., 1966). This is an excellent book in the College Outline Series that comprehensively covers the various techniques of reading, note-taking, outlining, writing, and the several other aspects of serious study.

2

Orientation to a Law Enforcement Career

The actual role that a policeman plays in the average city in the United States is both enigmatic and contradistinctive. Citizens and policeman alike are not quite sure as to exactly how this armed protector, a carryover from medieval days when most of the world was a savage wilderness, fits into our modern society, which claims to be at an advanced stage of civilization. The fact of his continued existence throughout the ages, and the apparent need for his service and protection today, bear mute testimony to the fact that the policeman has been an integral part of the pattern for this civilizing process. Force has historically been necessary for nations to win and retain their freedom, whether used or merely threatened. The policeman is a welcomed protector when the victim is under attack or is in danger of unlawful deprivation of his property. He represents that imminent force that is charged with the responsibility for enforcing the laws and maintaining the public peace. But he is less popular when he happens to catch an otherwise law-abiding resident of the community in the act of violating a traffic law, or perhaps engaging in a pleasurable experience that the offender's peers have seen fit to proclaim unlawful. The would-be policeman often finds himself in a position of being antipolice under a certain set of circumstances, and strongly propolice when everything is going his way. The trick in orienting the actual and potential law enforcement officer is to create within him a justifiably acceptable self-image.

Several years ago the author prepared a hand-out introduction to the police service entitled "So You Want to Be a Policeman." The introduction of the paper, intended for high school seniors, started like this:

17

"Wouldn't it be swell to have a job doing nothing but chasing around town all night long playing a tag match with law breakers and drinking coffee and cokes at the drive-in restaurants?" you might ask yourself when you see a black and white car speeding down the street with red lights flashing and the siren wailing with that tone of urgency and authority that has no equal. Unfortunately, this is too often the average young man's opinion of the life of a "cop."

Recall, if you will, your own impressions of the actual job that the policeman performs. Did you ever wonder what he was doing between traffic tickets, or when he was not engaged in a match of skill with an obstreperous protagonist? Did you look to the policeman as a man respected as any other professional man, or did you hold suspicion and contempt for him?

The life of a policeman is of such a character that it requires a man of unusual character and selflessness to fill the position. The professional policeman must subjugate his own personal desires and strivings in deference to the needs of others. Even when he is not actually on the job, he is devoting many long hours to study and other types of preparation for that job. His work day and work week usually begin when other people head for the comforts of home and family, and leisure-time recreation. The majority of policeman work during the night, on holidays, the Sabbath, vacation time, and—of

Photo courtesy Santa Ana Police Department

course—at all other times. There is a certain element of romance and excitement in the life of a policeman, and that is the part that we usually read about and see dramatized on television and at the movies. There are many other aspects of the work that would seem dull and monotonous to the thrill-seeker, such as walking for hours down the deserted streets of a business district protecting the property against burglary, staking-out in the used car lot huddled among the automobiles waiting for the sneak thief to make his nocturnal appearance to compile another statistic in the property crimes category. The thrill of the high-speed chase is often overshadowed by the most undesirable task of pulling an injured child and his mother out of a mass of twisted metal at the scene of a traffic collision.

What kind of a man does it take to fill the position of policeman? In the next section, let's take a look.

QUALIFICATIONS FOR POLICE SERVICE

The candidate must be an excellent specimen in all respects: physically, mentally, emotionally, and morally. He must be capable of protecting the public peace in many ways, and he must meet the following standards.

Age. At least 21 and not more than 31 to 35. Although he may be recruited and appointed to a position with the agency in some category other than policeman at an earlier age, the man does not become a policeman until he reaches the legal age of majority. The maximum age is for many reasons; one is that the man has a longer span of productive years during which he can perform before he retires. Other reasons include a natural one that the younger man is usually in better health and has greater stamina and endurance. The retirement age for police officers is usually lower than for other occupations, therefore, the lower entrance age is more desirable. It is also easier for a man in his twenties to return to college to resume his studies for a new career than it is for a man approaching forty.

Height. The minimum height for policemen is usually set at 5′ 8″ to 5′ 9″. Maximum height, if any, varies from 6′ 5″ to 6′ 7″. The height limitations are usually stressed most rigidly by municipal and county law enforcement agencies that assign all entering members to uniformed service. A key factor in this requirement is the appearance that the officers present when in uniform. It plays a part in the make-up of his "image" or "charisma" that is so essential to an officer's ability to gain and hold the respect of the many people he confronts daily, particularly groups of belligerent or noncooperative persons. Being too tall is just as much of a handicap as being too small. For many of the Federal, state, or private investigative and enforcement agencies, the height of the candidate is immaterial.

Weight. Minimum weight is approximately one hundred and forty five pounds with a variable maximum. Military charts for weights to correspond with heights are usually used.

Eyesight. Color-blindness is a disqualifying characteristic. Near-perfect eyesight without corrective lenses is a must. Visual acuity may deteriorate as the individual grows older, but the officer on patrol during the hours of darkness is at a great disadvantage with visual defects.

Other physical requirements. Additional medical and physical considerations will be discussed during the section of this chapter dealing with the medical examination.

Educational requirements. Graduation from high school is an absolute minimum for some police agencies, and should be for the others. Although successfully passing a high school equivalency examination may be accepted by some agencies, they usually require the high school diploma that can be earned by meeting certain requirements established by the various school boards. Some college is most desirable, with a few municipal and county police agencies requiring two to four years of college. The state and federal agencies usually require two to four years of college, while the Federal Bureau of Investigation requires an additional degree in law or accountancy. The basic training academy is college level training, and continued attendance at nearby colleges in the police science or criminology departments is encouraged, if not required.

Mental-emotional condition. Psychological testing will determine that the successful candidate possesses the mental adaptability, capability, and emotional stability to perform his duties in a mature and intelligent manner under all sorts of circumstances.

Background. The candidate must be free from any felony conviction record, but certain misdemeanor records may be allowed if explainable and if they do not include acts of moral turpitude, such as a limited number of traffic citations. A history of laziness, inability to get along with employers or fellow-employees, dismissal from a job, military disciplinary action, asocial behavior, and many other undesirable characteristics will disqualify the candidate. This will also be covered in more detail later in the chapter.

Just a few of the many requirements have been covered. Others are that the candidate must be a citizen of the United States; some agencies require residence in the state and/or jurisdiction in which the candidate seeks employment either prior to making application or shortly afterward. Each agency is part of an autonomous government, and entrance requirements are individualized to meet the needs or whims of local officials. Throughout this chapter it must be borne in mind that the federal and state law enforcement and investigative agencies vary somewhat, depending upon the nature and scope of their duties and responsibilities.

CAREER OPPORTUNITIES

Opportunities for both men and women in the police service seem to be almost without limit at the time of the writing of this chapter and for many years to come. This is particularly true of the large cities, where urbanization continues, and in Southern California where similar megalopolis-type areas are forming. As the community grows, so does the law enforcement agency that serves that area, and there is no end to the growth in sight. Although the greatest need in law enforcement is for police officers and clerical personnel, there are endless other possibilities. Following are partial lists of the many positions that are available to people who wish to work for a modern police in either a peace officer or "civilian" status, each requiring a different individual with a distinctly different background of experience, ability, and education.

For Men

Correctional officer or jailer, animal controlman, identification technician, photographer, fingerprint classifier, examiner of questioned documents, chemist, criminalist, polygraph expert, mechanic. Other opportunities include property clerk, radio dispatcher, communications technician, and many others. Agencies related to law enforcement departments may have openings for many of the foregoing, in addition to crime studies analyst, office manager, special investigator, state policeman, claims adjuster, parole and probation officer, recreation director.

For Women

Parking control checker, key punch operator, data processing programmer, tabulating equipment operator, typist, file clerk, stenographer, secretary, communications operator, statistician, matron. Laboratory technician, nurse, correctional officer, teletype operator, duplicating machine operator. Many male and female jobs are listed in one or the other category, although many are interchangeable and open to either or both sexes.

These lists have been randomly compiled and the order in which the various positions are listed does not rank them as to relative importance or pay scale. Law enforcement is undergoing some dynamic changes. In many cities, the police agency is actually the largest single employer. Although the operating units comprise the bulk of the personnel, there is considerable diversification even in the smaller agencies. About the only limitation on the employment possibilities in law enforcement are the ingenuity and creativity limits of the individual administrators.

THE SELECTION PROCESS

Posting the Examination

Usually two to three weeks prior to giving an examination, the department personnel division or the central personnel agency announces that applications are being accepted. The announcement lists the title of the position and the pay scale. Minimum physical, educational, and experience requirements are stated so that the interested candidates may compare their own qualifications to determine if they need to continue with their applications.

The bulletin briefly describes the typical duties of a policeman, such as: "Under general supervision patrols an assigned area in the enforcement of laws, maintenance of order, prevention of crime, and protection of life and property, and performs investigative work in the prevention of crime."

On the bulletin, the candidate may find such additional information as a list of instructions on how to proceed with the application, an explanation of the step procedure in employing a new candidate, and a list of the employee benefits offered by that particular jurisdiction. A deadline for filing the application is established, and the machinery for the recruitment process is set into motion.

The Application Form

The personnel agency and the police department personnel division may actually use two separate forms. The original application form used by the personnel agency consists of only one or two pages requiring basic information about former employment, education, places of residence, and vital statistics to show qualification for the position, and is actually the only "application" form. A second document is a personal history statement used by the department; it is usually quite lengthy, asking for an autobiography of the candidate. It provides the information that serves as a basis for a thorough background investigation. A typical personal history form will be dissected later along with a discussion of the background investigation procedure.

Some agencies interview all candidates when they submit their applications. They are questioned about any prior criminal records, dismissals from places of employment, poor driving records as indicated by excessive traffic citations and/or accidents, and any other factors that may actually disqualify the candidate. Once the application has been filed and the accompanying screening completed, the next step is the written examination.

The Written Examination

The basic test in a battery of psychological tests for police officers is a general intelligence inventory. At this point it is more important that the candidate have a capacity to learn than have knowledge about the job. Most candidates have had no prior police experience or training—although that trend may someday not be true —and it is generally understood that the candidate will be trained if accepted for the job. The policeman must be able to assimilate the greatest amount of information in the shortest possible time, and to mix that information with a liberal amount of common sense and native ability in getting along with people.

Supplemental exams in the battery may include any or all of the following: Memory, reading comprehension, spelling, police adaptability, and specific tests to determine whatever qualities the particular jurisdiction wishes its policemen to possess.

The Oral Examination

Those candidates who successfully complete the written exams are scheduled for an oral exam. The test usually lasts from thirty to forty-five minutes, and the most important features of the test are (1) the initial impression the interviewee makes upon the interviewers, and (2) his ability to handle himself well in an oral exchange with three or four expert interviewers. There are basically three types of interviews: unstructured, nondirected, and structured. The unstructured interview is usually under control of the interviewers, but has had no advance planning and varies from interview to interview. The nondirected interview is the type that is controlled by the interviewee and takes whatever course the person desires. The structured interview is—in my opinion—the most valid and reliable one of the three. A series of specific questions are asked of all candidates and not only are their individual answers evaluated, but they are compared between candidates. The interviewers are also in control throughout the interview and a preplanned course is followed.

Although they do not necessarily appear in the following order, these are some of the questions one might encounter when being interviewed for a position as a police officer:

Why do you want to be a policeman?

When did you first develop such a desire? If you could not be a policeman, what would you most like to do for a living?

Name three attributes of personality that you consider most essential to police work.

Do you believe that you possess any of these attributes?

What is your strongest asset?

What is your greatest weakness?

What do you like to do for entertainment?

Whom did you respect most as a teacher in school? Why?

Were you in the military service?

Of all your military or work supervisors whom did you respect most? Why?

Is there anything in your past that you believe will disqualify you from the service?

What weaknesses do you have that you think may interfere with your effectiveness if you are accepted for the job?

What is your ultimate goal in life?

Do you think you will ever attain that goal?

Another type of question that the interviewee will meet will be the hypothetical question or series of questions during which the interviewer will attempt to ascertain the values and standards of life possessed or held by the interviewee. The honesty, morality, integrity, and other personality traits are evaluated. Questions such as "What would you do if you observed another policeman steal a pack of cigarettes?" and "What would you do if you saw another policeman break into an appliance store and steal a television set?" would be asked. If there is a variation in answers, then an exploration will no doubt follow to determine why there is a difference—why the double standard. An endless variety of avenues may be explored in this fashion. The interviewers will include experienced police officers, usually sergeant or higher, personnel specialists, civic leaders, clergymen, public officials, and any other persons the personnel director may choose to select the best-qualified candidates. A board may consist of any number of people, but is usually limited to three or four.

Physical Agility Qualification

Brute strength is not as important to the policeman as is agility and endurance. The deliberate antagonist and the individual who physically resists arrest are occasionally encountered during the normal tour of duty, and they must be properly handled with dispatch. A well-trained police officer can usually handle the situation efficiently, provided the odds against him are not too great. At the time he is being considered for the position, the candidate must be in excellent physical condition as determined by both medical and the physical agility examinations.

The agility test usually starts off with a few basic tests to determine muscular development and coordination, which include a rope climb, sit-ups, and push-ups. It is then followed—or preceded—by an obstacle course with a realistic maximum time limit.

Every part of the course has a realistic counterpart in actual street police duties. Picture the following examples taken from actual experiences: (1) The petty thief captured in the act outside the stadium during a sporting event who ran when an attempt was made to handcuff him. He disappeared among the long row of parked automobiles. (2) The escaping armed robber who alighted from his wrecked car, vaulted a cinder-block wall, jumped upon another, ran along the fence, then jumped off into another yard before finally being captured. (3) The car thief who jumped out of the car, dropped down into a drainage ditch, crawled through a culvert underneath the freeway, and escaped across an open field. (4) The frightened juvenile who—for fear his parents would punish him for being out after curfew—sprouted wings and "flew" as though his feet were not touching the ground. In all of these situations, what must the police officer do? Subdue them? Shoot them? Fire warning shots into the air? No. In most cases, the officer is justified only to the extent that he may chase and capture them, then use only what force is necessary. The problem is catching them. Success in passing an agility test serves to predict the candidate's ability to take part in chases such as those described.

Medical Examination

Whenever a new employee goes to work, the employer assumes legal responsibility for his physical well-being while actually on the job. He is obligated to provide safety training and safe devices with which the employee must work. The nature of police work involves certain hazards that cannot be avoided by safety equipment as in a shop. The gun-crazed madman bent upon killing everyone who gets in his way, the high-speed chase of the traffic violator, and many other situations that involve emotional traumata take a heavy toll even from the healthy policeman.

The man who has high blood pressure (hypertension) or ulcers prior to entering the police service is a liability who will certainly worsen as a result of the emotional stresses attendant to even the routine aspects of the work. No matter how badly he may wish to become a policeman, or how favorable he may look otherwise, an

Photos courtesy Orange County Sheriff's Department

THE PHYSICAL ABILITY AND ENDURANCE TEST IS DESIGNED TO DETERMINE A CANDIDATE'S STRENGTH, ENDURANCE, AND AGILITY.

early medical retirement must be expected. Therefore, the decision must be in favor of the agency and he must be passed over.

Every agency having its own autonomy in many respects, has— or may have—different medical requirements. The following is an example of a typical list of medical standards for a policeman.

1. Height. 5′ 8″ or 5′ 9″ or no maximum.
2. Height-weight ratios:

Height	Minimum	Maximum
5′8″	140	170
5′9″	145	175
5′10″	150	180
5′11″	155	185
6′0″	160	190
6′1″	165	195
6′2″	170	200
6′3″	175	210
6′4″	180	220
6′5″	185	230

3. Vision and eyes: 20/30 each eye, corrected. Color vision must be normal. Reject for: Impaired depth perception, impaired eyelids that interfere with vision or do not protect eye from exposure, and other impairments, such as ulcers, corneal scars, or cataracts.

4. Hearing and ears: Ability to hear a whispered voice at fifteen feet with each ear.

5. Nose, sinuses, and mouth: A variable minimum amount of teeth, with some requirement as to appearance and ability to masticate properly. Rejection for speech impediment, deformity of mouth or lips, pyorrhea, acute or chronic sinusitis, enlarged tonsils and adenoids, or nasal obstructions.

6. Skin: Must be free from gross disfigurements or blemishes. A candidate may be disqualified for obscene tattoos.

7. Extremities: Must be in excellent condition. Disqualification for recurring dislocations, loss of joints from certain fingers, particularly the thumb and index finger. Healed fractures of bones must not inhibit or limit the strength or use of any limb. X-rays may be ordered.

8. Cardiovascular: Pulse limits 50 to 90. Blood pressure should not exceed 140/90. Candidates will be rejected for history of heart disease or heart damage, past or present syphilis.

9. Respiratory: Chest x-ray and skin test for tuberculosis is recommended. Any acute or chronic disease of the respiratory system will disqualify.

10. Gastro-Intestinal: Rejection for any acute or chronic disease of stomach, including existing or history of ulcers. Other disqualifying features are diseases of the intestine, liver, pancreas, spleen, and gall-bladder, or hemorrhoids—other than minor—until repaired.

11. Genito-urinary system must be free from acute or chronic disease.

12. Disabling disease or deformity of the bone structure will disqualify the candidate. Of particular interest to the medical examiner are the spinal structure, the feet, and any presence of arthritis.

13. Neurological and psychological: The candidate will be rejected for any acute or chronic organic disease, or history of epilepsy, vertigo, or paralysis.

14. General: Upon completion of the medical examination and the accompanying chemical analyses that the doctor may order, he may pass the candidate as qualified for the position, or he may reject the candidate for any cause or defect that he believes would impair the health or inhibit the usefulness of the candidate, if accepted.

Psychiatric Tests

This phase of the selection process is generally conducted by a licensed psychologist or psychiatrist. The police officer must be free from any psychological or emotional problems that will interfere with his ability to function properly and effectively. There is no place among the police ranks for the homosexual, sadist, masochist, or the coward. Certain fears—or phobias—may be so great as to make it impossible for the police officer to function effectively. Some of those fears may be of high places, pain, being in a closed place, or fear of fear. The psychopath, sociopath, or person suffering from any other mental or neurological disorder should be screened out, and such a screening process cannot be accomplished exclusively by a pencil and paper test. Therefore, only an expert can handle this phase of the selection process.

The psychiatric exam usually consists of a battery including the Minnesota Multiphasic Personality Inventory, the Rorschach Ink Blot Test, another test containing of a free-hand drawing that is later evaluated by the psychiatrist, and the final test in the battery is usually a personal interview.

It is the responsibility of the psychiatrist to recommend the candidate as qualified—or not qualified—for the position. Even this method of psychological selection is not perfect, as many latent tendencies are not identified, but it is considered an invaluable tool in the selection process because the *obvious* misfit is obvious only to the psychiatrist in many cases. As an example of the value that the psychiatric test may have is the candidate who is passed as acceptable and later becomes disgruntled with the department's policies. In one Southern California city several "hate" letters were given to the psychiatrist who had originally examined all of the policemen then on the job. From his files, the doctor collected several samples of written material from previous tests and compared them with the writing style of the anonymous letters. He provided the Chief of Police with a list of possible suspects, which later was narrowed down to the true culprit. Although the latent personality trait involving anonymous letter-writing did not reveal itself at the time the officer was admitted into the ranks, it did later and the end result was removal of an unfit policeman. There are many other examples, both positive and negative, but the one cited was nearly unique.

Fingerprints

Any time a person applies for a position with any governmental agency he is fingerprinted, and sometimes photographed. Whenever a person is arrested for any offense he *may* be fingerprinted, but when a person is "booked" into jail for any offense, he *usually is* fingerprinted. Whenever a person is committed to any state or federal penal institution he is fingerprinted. Private corporations involved in sensitive productions involving government contracts fingerprint all applicants. Whenever fingerprints are taken by any of the foregoing agencies, they are classified by the individual agencies for their own files, then one set is mailed to the Federal Bureau of Investigation central clearing house and another set mailed to the respective state clearing houses. At each of the many clearing houses, each set of fingerprints is classified and a record of the prints' owner added to a cumulative file maintained on each individual. As there are no two sets of fingerprints alike, the prints are more positive means of identification, and a single individual may have a fingerprint record under more than one name.

Whenever an agency submits a set of fingerprints to a clearing house, such as the FBI, that agency sends back by return mail the cumulative list showing all the times that individual has been fingerprinted for any reason under any name. For example, a "rap sheet" (a chronology of the times and places a person has been fingerprinted) on a single individual may read as follows: At age 14, Jerome Ford was committed to a farm for delinquent boys in Virginia for a series of delinquent acts. At age 17, Jerry enlisted in the U.S. Navy at Bethesda, Maryland. At age 23, our subject was arrested for auto theft in Chicago and used the name Jerry F. Queensbury. At age 27, Mr. F. changed his name in a lawful court procedure in Seattle to Jerrold Fillmore Quick. Finally, our subject—true name Quick—applied for a job as a policeman in San Francisco under his true name. As far as we know from the information furnished in this account, the subject has been fingerprinted in Virginia, Maryland, Illinois, and California under three different names. Although his name has been changed, his finger-prints have not. When the San Francisco Police Department sends the candidate's fingerprints to the FBI and the California Bureau of Criminal Identification and Investigation, they will receive replies from both of those agencies. The "rap sheets" will show the dates, the reasons for the taking of prints, plus the name given at the time, and the disposition—if provided by the contributing agency—of each particular incident, such as "released, no complaint filed."

In addition to what we already know, the information sheet from CII may also show Mr. Quick as an applicant for the position of policeman in San Diego and Eureka. He had either forgotten, or deliberately failed to mention when making his application in San Francisco that he had applied at the other two agencies. A check with those two agencies might possibly reveal that Quick actually did become a member of one of those departments, and was dismissed two months later for the use of excessive force.

In the case of some juvenile arrests, individual agencies maintain fingerprint files but—because of the tender ages of the children—do not submit them to state or federal agencies. In an actual case worked by the author, one young candidate's background checked perfectly except for a lapse of about three years, during which time the candidate's mother was married to one of her several husbands in one of the Southern states. Although the FBI reported no fingerprint record on the candidate, a copy of his fingerprints was mailed to police departments in the two largest cities where the candidate had lived during that specific three-year time span. As a result of those inquiries, one of the two agencies reported that the candidate had been arrested under another name as one of the leaders of an auto theft ring that had operated in that state for several months until they were apprehended transporting one of the cars across the border. Had the check not been made, the candidate would—no doubt—have been appointed to the ranks of the police department.

Polygraph

Polygraph operators theorize that virtually everyone has at least one skeleton in his closet. Verified deceptive patterns are noted in replies to such questions as "Did you ever steal anything in your life?" or "Did you ever cheat on a test in school?" or "Did you ever tell a deliberate lie to hurt someone else?" Doctor Kinsey's reports on the sexual behavior of the American male and female further bears this theory out with respect to our social mores. If this device—the polygraph—is utilized as a part of the police selection process, a great deal of discretion and good judgment must be exercised. Indiscriminate use of polygraph files could be devastating. The examiner must be absolutely above reproach and there must be no question as to his professional competence. His examination should pertain only to those character traits that directly relate to the applicant's suitability for the police service.

When preparing a set of questions for polygraph examination for pre-employment screening, it is first necessary to determine exactly what type of person the chief administrator wishes to employ. Sexual promiscuity or immorality cannot be condoned in the police employee. There is absolutely no place in the organization for a burglar, a robber, or a thief. Many other traits must be identified and evaluated. The examiner must determine whether a single act of theft or a single act of moral indiscretion at some time in the candidate's lifetime makes him a thief or sexual deviate. Individual departments utilize their polygraph examination phase of the selection process differently. A personal inquiry of each department's personnel division would be necessary in order to ascertain their specific utilization of the polygraph.

The Background Investigation

The initial application submitted by the candidate is usually relatively brief compared with the personal history statement required by the Police Department Personnel Division. The form is actually an autobiography in question and answer form, and it is used as the basis for the background investigation. The investigation is primarily conducted for the purpose of screening out the undesirable applicants who have derogatory personal histories. Secondarily, the investigation provides the administrator with a complete biography of each employee. Typical questions asked in the Personal History Statement form will be listed in the following paragraphs, along with a discussion of the background investigation, and how they are related. The order of the investigation may not necessarily coincide with the order of the form, but they will be discussed in that order in this chapter.

1. List all other names you have used or been known by, including nicknames, maiden name, adopted name, other. State during what period(s) of time each other name was used. School attendance and work records often reflect a variety of names for many reasons. Married women have all used at least two names: maiden and married.

2. Description of your automobile(s). As a matter of routine, automobile license numbers may be checked against hit-run wants. Another purpose for this question is that an individual's automobile sometimes reflects his personality, such as the brightly colored convertible as opposed to the conservative black vintage model that appears to have been under wraps for fifteen years before being driven on the streets. Some neighborhood service station operators, who are good sources of information, know their customers only by their automobiles.

3. Education record. This category includes high school, college, vocational, and trade schools. Personal visits to these institutions are made by the investigators, if possible, or mail inquiries made to determine scholastic records in addition to sociability, participation in sports and other school events, and citizenship records. Scholastic grades are naturally of interest to the background investigator. When compared with the intelligence quotient of an individual, it is often possible to determine something about the drive and perseverance he may or may not possess. An individual with an extremely high IQ who made C's and D's may prove less desirable as a potential employee than the average IQ with a scholastic record of A's and B's attained by the student who diligently applied himself and made the best of what he had in the way of natural ability.

4. Degrees, credentials, certificates you hold. Pilot's licenses, radio licenses, teaching credentials, special certificates, and degrees reflect both the training and capabilities of the individual.

5. Disciplinary action while in school, including scholastic probation. This information aids in determining behavior patterns.

6. Employment record, including all places of employment during the candidate's lifetime, and periods of unemployment. Name and address of employer, type of business, dates of employment, high salary, position and duties, name of immediate supervisor, and reason for leaving. The police agency is another potential employer and naturally wants to know something of the candidate's work history. When possible, the investigator makes a personal contact with all previous employers (out-of-town employers are questioned by mail) for the purpose of talking with fellow workers and supervisors, and looking through the candidate's work records. Rating while on the

job, sickness histories, and all other relevant data is collected and evaluated.

7. Military record, if any, including duty assignments, rates or ranks held, any disciplinary action, and type of discharge as well as the actual dates of service. Another employer, of course.

8. List relatives, their names, places of residence, occupations, and additional information that will sufficiently identify them. Criminogenic personalities in a candidate's family may have sufficient influence over him that he might possibly be placed in an untenable position of having to yield to social pressures to take preferential actions for family harmony, such as "clearing" criminal records by removing or altering records from the files, or possibly exerting official influence to gain special favors. Community reputation of the entire police agency also depends upon the individual reputations of all of its employees.

9. References. Some agencies require only four or five references. This is of no value to the investigator, because the candidate invariably lists the family physician, a clergyman, an attorney, possibly a so-called influential citizen, and perhaps a casual acquaintance who works as a policeman. None of these people are likely to condemn or negatively criticize the candidate; most are no more than slightly acquainted. Some agencies require ten to fifteen references who have knowledge of the candidate's reputation, who know him socially, and who have knowledge of his professional or occupational capabilities. Armed with this list of people who have personal knowledge of the candidate's personal and occupational characteristics, the investigator attempts to find out as much as he can about exactly what the candidate is "made of." He also inquires as to the identity of other people who may know him. Out-of-town reference letters are usually mailed to the references and a few confidential questions asked in an effort to glean from as many sources as possible the maximum amount of information that can be amassed.

10. List all surgery or serious illnesses during the candidate's lifetime. Nature of illnesses and/or purpose for any surgery, and the names of hospitals and doctors are required. These items are checked out very carefully because the employer assumes liability for the candidate once appointed. Some permanent disabilities are discovered that otherwise may have been overlooked by the medical examiner, or omitted from the original application by the candidate. Along with this question there will usually be others pertaining to sick leave history, and any history of the candidate's having been a recipient of any disability allowance for sickness or injury.

11. List additional sources of income, such as earnings by spouse. At first glance, an individual's expenditures may appear to be in excess of his income, and the investigator may draw the conclusion that the subject is on the verge of having his wages attached or going into bankruptcy. Good credit is mandatory for the police employee, and the candidate must have the self-control to live within his means. The total income presents a true picture of the candidate's fiscal status.

12. List outstanding debts and credit references. Other questions along the same line may call for a statement regarding whether the candidate has ever been refused credit and any other data relevant to the candidate's credit record.

13. List all places of residence during the candidate's lifetime. Out-of-town places of residence are checked out by the local police having that particular jurisdiction, if the agency's investigator cannot drive the distance and conduct his own investigation. All cities and counties in which the candidate lived are either visited in person by the investigator, or a letter of request for investigative assistance is sent to those that are too far distant. Police, court, and school files are searched for any record of the candidate, the local credit bureaus' records checked, and personal contacts are made with former employers, teachers, neighbors, friends, and anyone else who may have known the candidate. Personality and character traits of the candidate are the object of this phase of the investigation. Many police agencies have established such a favorable working relationship that a request sent by the Santa Ana, California, Police Department Personnel Division to another police department even as far away as New York City or Houston results in the initiation by that agency of an investigation that yields as comprehensive a report as is required.

14. Marital status, name of spouse and children, if any, and vital statistics on all aspects of the marital and familial situation of the candidate, including former marriages.

15. List all traffic citations and/or traffic arrests (not including parking tickets), *including* those received while under the age of eighteen. The questioner calls for the date and place, charge or violation, and the disposition (fine, forfeited bail, jail, or the like). The driving record of a potential policeman is most essential, because virtually all police agencies require their officers to possess a valid driver's license and their normal duties include driving department vehicles under both routine and emergency conditions. A poor driving record will disqualify the candidate who has proved to be an insurance liability, accident-prone, or citation-prone. Police officers who violate the traffic laws are subject to the same treatment—citation or arrest—given the nonpolice violators.

16. Other than traffic (covered in 15 above), have you ever in your lifetime been arrested, held by the police for investigation or questioning, or otherwise been under investigation by the police? Complete details are required, including the nature of the incident, time, place, and disposition. The background investigator secures copies of all reports, if available, and he looks into the nature of the charge, including recontacting victims, and interviews the original investigating or arresting officer. In many cases, deliberate omission of information that should be included in response to this question is sometimes a serious matter. As an example of deliberate omissions or falsification of the personal history statement is the case of the twenty-five-year-old candidate who listed that he had never been questioned by the police under any circumstances. His background investigation revealed that he had been caught stealing some items from an automobile at the age of fourteen, was severely reprimanded by the police officer, and was released to his parents. Other than the one incident when he was arrested and released as a child, the candidate's background was excellent. When the Personnel Investigator later questioned the candidate about the incident, the candidate denied anything of that nature ever taking place. He was given an opportunity to refresh his memory and make any changes on the form that he wished to make before being considered for the position. He chose to continue his denial of the act, even when the investigator suggested that it had occurred when he was about fourteen and in a specifically named city when he lived at a certain address in that city. The candidate continued to adamantly maintain that he had never been contacted by the police for any reason, and finally conceded with a great deal of reluctance that such an incident had taken place when he was confronted with a copy of the arrest report. He was disqualified— not for the act of theft at age fourteen, but for *falsifying his personal history statement.*

17. If you have applied for employment with any other police agency, list the date of application, name and location of the agency, and the status of the application (accepted, not accepted, pending, or the like). The purpose for this question is to aid in the investigation and evaluation of the subject. Another agency may already have conducted a thorough background investigation and some duplication will be avoided, and the opinions of other qualified police practitioners will help in what amounts to a re-evaluation of the candidate for a similar position.

The final part of the Statement is an agreement by the candidate that he understands the terms of the probationary appointment procedure, that he also understands a thorough background investigation will be conducted, and that he will be disqualified for any deliberate falsification or omissions.

Selection Interview

Following the background investigation, the next step in the selection process is to schedule the candidate for a selection interview. The interview is usually conducted by at least one staff officer charged with the responsibility for selecting only the best-qualified candidates. In all but the largest departments it is most desirable for the Chief of Police, the Sheriff, or other department head to take an active part in the selection interviews. In any event, the final decision and responsibility is his. The successful candidates are appointed and launched on their careers. Their first six months to one year is on a probationary status, a trial agreement.

Oath of Office

Administration of the oath of office as a peace officer is relatively simple when compared with the public trust and responsibility that goes along with assumption of the role. Preservation of the public peace, maintenance of order, and enforcement of the laws of the United States, the state in which the officer is to serve, and the local ordinances are his responsibility as long as he fills the role. He must zealously protect the rights and property of everyone within his jurisdiction, and be equally zealous in his own strict adherance to the laws and the mandates of the federal and state constitutions, and the courts.

Probation

Public agencies that provide their employees with the protection and many other benefits of a civil service system have a six-months-to-one-year probationary period that precedes attainment of permanent status, or tenure. The purpose of the probationary period is to give the employee a breaking-in period during which he determines whether he and the job are suited for each other and to serve the employing agency as the final—and most important—part of the selection process. During the new officer's probation, he may be terminated by the agency for unsuitability with no right to appeal his dismissal. The decision of the department head in the case of any probationary termination is final.

WOMEN IN LAW ENFORCEMENT

Sharron

The police agency is similar to any service organization that carries on daily business operations, including telephone switchboard and secretarial services that accompany these operations. Men and women fill these various "housekeeping" positions, dependent upon their abilities and job classification. But there is another job classification that calls for a woman to fit the qualifications: Policewoman. She is a regular part of most major police departments in the country, including such federal agencies as the Bureaus of Customs and Immigration and Naturalization.

At the Workshop for Policewoman held by the International Association of Chiefs of Police at Indiana University in early 1966, Lois Higgins[1] recounted a brief recapitulation of the history and significant evolution of women police in the United States. She reported that women were first employed as police matrons as early as 1845. The need was apparent. Women criminal law violators who were sentenced to serve terms of imprisonment in jails, prisons, and workhouses had to be searched, guarded, and supervised while in custody and the utilization of male custodial personnel was unsuitable for a variety of reasons.

The earliest reported appointment of a woman to actually perform police officer duties in the United States was in 1893 when the mayor of Chicago appointed a policeman's widow—Mrs. Marie Owens —to the position of "Patrolman." Mrs. Owens worked in that capacity for thirty years, and her "patrolman" duties included "visiting the courts and assisting detective officers in cases involving women and children."

According to Doctor Higgins, subsequent appointments of women to various policeman-type jobs took place throughout the country, including Portland, Oregon, and Grand Forks, North Dakota, in 1905 and 1910, respectively. The first woman to be hired for the specific job titled "policewoman" was Mrs. Alice Stebbins Wells. She was employed by the City of Los Angeles, California, in the year 1910, and her duties were defined pretty much the same as those of the policewoman of today: ". . . supervision, and the enforcement of laws concerning dance halls, skating rinks, penny arcades, picture shows, and other

[1]Executive Director, International Association of Women Police, Chicago, Ill. Doctor Higgins' presentation at the workshop was published in Nelson A. Watson and Robert N. Walker (eds.), *IACP Proceedings of Workshop for Policewomen* (1966) .

Photo courtesy Chicago Police Department

SOOTHING THE FEARS OF A LOST CHILD IS JUST ONE OF THE
MANY DUTIES PERFORMED BY CHICAGO'S POLICEWOMEN.
TACT AND UNDERSTANDING ARE AMONG THE MANY QUALI-
TIES REQUIRED OF THOSE OFFICERS WHO WORK IN THE
YOUTH DIVISION.

similar places of recreation." She searched for missing persons and provided information to women and girls on matters within the scope of
her police duties.

The cause of getting policewomen accepted as an actual, working
part of the police department has been—and still is in many cities—an
upstream swim in a strong current of traditional dogma. Women doing a man's work? Or is it exclusively man's work? Mrs. Wells thought
not. Obviously, neither does Lois Higgins or the many hundreds of
other women of her timbre throughout the United States.

In 1966 Doctor Higgins reported that there were more than three
thousand policewomen serving in at least two hundred cities, and two
thousand serving as sheriffs' deputies and in federal service with police
duties. Equal-opportunity provisions of civil rights legislation may
well open up the field even wider.

Entrance requirements for policewoman match those for policeman, except the natural differences, including height and weight, and a variety of other factors dependent upon the needs of the respective hiring jurisdictions and the availability of qualified personnel. In many cases, the educational and experience requirements may be more stringent for women than men simply because the recruiting department can afford to be more selective in choosing from among many more qualified candidates than it actually needs.

DEPARTMENT REGULATIONS CONCERNING THE DUTIES OF POLICEWOMEN

The policewoman is primarily charged with the investigation of cases and situations involving women, girls, and children. Her duties shall include frequent visits to all public places that may be frequented by women and girls with a view to locating any conditions that may contribute to vice and delinquency, and shall take appropriate action regarding any violation of the law that comes to her attention.

She shall handle cases of delinquent girls, dealing with them in a manner that will result in the greatest good for the subject and society, and protecting them from the older and more experienced offenders. She shall make a study of the environment and any other contributing factors with a view to correction.

She shall cooperate with officers of all divisions, as may be consistent with her work assignments, furnishing them with information and assisting them particularly in the arrest and prosecution of female offenders. She shall investigate vice complaints and alleged prostitutes, take proper police action, and prepare the necessary reports concerning such action.

She investigates cases involving neglected, abused, or delinquent children, and conditions likely to encourage delinquency or criminal behavior among women and children.

She searches female prisoners or suspects for contraband or weapons they may be carrying on their persons, and accompanies females when they are transported in police vehicles. She interviews female suspects or is present during interviews as necessary.

She performs other duties as may be consistent with her divisional assignment, or as required by a superior officer.

The foregoing paragraphs reasonably represent the duties of the average policewomen, and there will be such other material as may be related only to specific departments.

Exercises and Study Questions

1. Visit or write to the police agency you intend to join, and secure a detailed list of qualifications for the position you hope to fill. Compare yourself with those qualifications. Do you qualify?

2. Interview a policewoman. Determine the qualifications for the job and the actual duties that she performs. Compare work assignments of policewomen and policemen.

3. List two reasons why the maximum age is as low as it is for entrance into law enforcement.

4. List five different positions for men and five for women that are available in law enforcement outside of the classifications of policeman and policewoman.

5. What are the most important features of an oral examination?

6. If you are actually planning to enter law enforcement as a policeman or policewoman, list three good reasons *why*.

7. What type of persons should the psychiatric test screen out?

8. Which federal agency serves as a clearing house for fingerprints from agencies throughout the country?

9. Why is it necessary to investigate a candidate's background? Illustrate one hypothetical situation that could occur without a background investigation.

10. *Recommended Semester Project*: Contact at least two local police agencies and secure all the information you can about their background investigation process. Prepare a paper describing and evaluating the procedures as they perform them.

PART

PHILOSOPHY AND HISTORY OF THE POLICE ROLE

3

Law Enforcement,
a Community Need

INTRODUCTION

A utopian society is virtually impossible. By definition, such a society is "impossibly and impractically ideal." A citizen's "pursuit of happiness" is manifested in as many ways as there are people pursuing it in a free country. Competition and conflict are intrinsic to a society that is characterized by dynamism, materialism, individualism, fierce loyalty to special interest groups, strong social pressures for prestige and affluence, and differences of opinions and moral standards. Absolute conformity to unrealistic mores of a nonexistent "perfect" society is neither desirable, nor is it possible.

The human maturation process includes a learning pattern. Behavior is governed to some extent by physical, psychological, and social needs, and the manner in which the individual seeks to satisfy those needs. The basic physiological needs are hunger, thirst, sexual satisfaction, rest, comfort, and pain avoidance. While learning how to satisfy those needs, the individual learns the many taboos of his own culture that frequently frustrate the drives involved in seeking his goals of satisfaction. The child learns that the pain of punishment may be avoided by minding his parents. Sexual satisfaction is gained by reciprocating for the satisfying experience by assumption of the responsibilities of supporting a wife and children. Basic sustenance is reasonably achieved with little effort or conflict, but certain minimum requirements must be met, such as work to earn money to spend.

The psychological needs are secondary needs that are not *absolute*, but many of them are *essential*. The psychological needs are love, recognition, "belonging," prestige, popularity, self-confidence, a feeling of well-being, security, and a general freedom from mental and emotional pressures.

The social needs are less essential than the preceding two types, but the individual learns to develop them as real needs that must be satisfied. Those needs include, luxury and comfort, better homes, newer automobiles, more and better clothing, and more money to buy the items that serve to give the individual a feeling of social prestige. The advertiser-created "American way of life" is a quest for more of everything.

As the child matures to childhood and on to adulthood he progressively develops his own combination of needs and his own methods for seeking satisfaction of those needs. He learns by doing, by watching others, by studying the methods written and taught by others, and by trial and error. The individual learns to share, to be patient, and to go about satisfying those needs in an orderly manner in keeping with the customs and mores of the particular society in which he holds membership.

Frustrations are experienced by the individual and he learns that he will never satisfy all of his needs. What he must learn is self-control and compromise. He learns to work for his money, study for his education, and to respect the rights and property of others if he is to have them respect his rights and property. He learns that some actions are right and other actions are wrong. There are laws, rules, customs, taboos, regulations, bans, and a variety of agents and agencies to enforce them. Through interaction with others, and with respect to all of these laws and regulations the individual has to obey, the majority of the population somehow manages to develop into law-abiding, socially acceptable members of society.

There has always been a need for laws and a body of men charged with the responsibility and authority for enforcing those laws. The ultimate authority rests with the people—the governing body—in the United States. More than four thousand years ago the Babylonian ruler Hammurabi recognized the need for a code of laws in order that he might perpetuate his civilization. He codified a list of social rules "so that the strong oppress not the weak, that the widow and orphan be protected." Hammurabi's Code is recognized as the oldest known law code in the history of the world.

The imminence of crime and criminal behavior in the United States or in any other country has been explained quite fluently by Emile Durkheim in his *Rules of Sociological Method*.[1] He states:

> There is no phenomenon that presents more indisputably all the symptoms of normality, since it appears closely connected with the condi-

[1]Emile Durkheim, *Rules of Sociological Methods* (Glencoe, Ill.: The Free Press, 1950).

tions of all collective life. . . . What is normal, simply, is the existence of criminality, provided that it attains and does not exceed, for each social type, a certain level, which it is perhaps not impossible to fix in conformity with the preceding rules. . . . To classify crime among the phenomena of normal sociology . . . is to affirm that it is a factor in public health, an integral part of all healthy societies.

Whether to accept or reject Durkheim's point of view is a matter of personal choice. The fact is that his statement has been borne out for at least four thousand years to date, and at the time of this writing there appears to be no spectacular change in sight.

THEORIES OF CRIME CAUSES AND EFFECTS

Classical School

Cesare Beccaria (1738?–1794), held that the occurrence of crime was based upon a theory of "pain avoidance." Beccaria postulated that a would-be violator of the law weighed the pain or penalty of punishment in comparison with the benefits that he might gain from committing the crime.

In Beccaria's home—Italy—his ideas were not very warmly received. In England the theory "caught on" and for a time the classical theory was most prevalent there. There was no provision in punishments prescribed for crimes committed in error or as a result of extenuating circumstances, such as some degree of culpability on the part of the victim. The notable points of the Classical School theory were:

1. Commission of crime was a matter of free choice on the part of the wrongdoer.
2. Hedonism exists in that every individual seeks a maximum of pleasure, and he avoids pain.
3. Punishment for crimes was to satisfy the need for retribution or vengeance, but also to serve as a threat of punishment as a deterrent to crimes of a similar nature being planned or considered by others.
4. The laws and their punishment had to be published for uniformity, and for their deterrence value.
5. The length of sentences were fixed by law and were uniformly applied in accordance with the violations.
6. Children and the insane could not be charged as criminals.

The Lombrosian Theory of Criminality

Cesare Lombroso (1836–1909) was another Italian who focused his attention on the individual when attempting an explanation of crime. His basic premise was that a person was a "born criminal," or a criminal by heredity. Lombroso classified criminals by physical characteristics, and he applied scientific methods by devising a system for taking head measurements for his criminal classification. Although this theory is invalid, a common lament heard from a victim may include: ". . . but he had such an honest face. He just was not the criminal type." Lombrosian criminal characteristics included the flat nose, deep-set eyes, specific cranium configurations, and red hair, all of which he alleged had some direct correlation to criminality.

Economic Theories

Marx and Engels classified crime as a side-effect of economic pressures. Although there was some validity in the premise, there was no attempt at an explanation of morality in the poor noncriminal.

Other Explanations of Crime

Some theoreticians attributed crime to mental retardation, or psychosis, epilepsy, emotional disturbances, or "moral insanity." For several hundred years the approach was to study crime causation or explanation by formulating a theory by which the criminals could be categorized and their behavior explained on the basis of such categorization. The trend during the past several decades has been to study each person as an individual rather than as a unit in a category.

There is no battery of tests that will identify a "born" or a potential criminal, which further negates a variety of hypotheses about propensities for criminality. Studies to date have shown that there is nothing substantial to report when comparing known criminals and persons who have no arrest records in several areas of study where such comparison has been attempted. There is no correlation in temperament, physical maturity, emotional maturity, and only a slight correlation indicated when the entire personality is surveyed by means of the Rorschach (ink blot) test. It has been found that the sociopath, or psychopathic personality, has a greater propensity for the formation of criminal behavior patterns if the individual so identified is allowed to develop those patterns.

The sociopath is described as extremely self-centered, impulsive, aggressive toward society, and with an attitude of omnipotence. He has no feelings of conscience and he lacks what Freud defines as superego, which consists of a combination of conscience, fair-mindedness, empathy, and social sensitivity. To the true sociopath, only those laws that are agreeable to him and that he chooses to obey seem to restrict him in any way. Although not all sociopaths are criminals—or all criminals sociopaths—there is a predisposition to the formulation of criminal behavior patterns.

The sociologist's point of view regarding criminal behavior is that many factors with a variety of combinations go together to cause a person to commit a criminal act, and then go on to live his life as a criminal. Some early criminologists attempted to prove that single traits were determinants of criminal behavior. Some of the factors they attempted to authenticate with well-chosen source material were:

1. *Heredity.* Specific families with extensive criminal histories, such as the "celebrated" Jukes family, were used to illustrate the point. Out of twelve hundred family members studied by Dugale in 1877, one hundred and forty were criminals, seven of whom were convicted murderers, some sixty were thieves, and the balance were prostitutes. This study shows better than 10 percent criminality in one family. The prognosis was "heredity," and no explanation was attempted for other factors such as environment, group pressures, or any other factors involved in such a family situation.

2. *Phrenology.* Phrenologists attempted to correlate criminality with blindness, deafness, ugliness, physical deformities, and other physical and psychological defects as determinants of criminality. Some theoreticians attempted to classify the offender by body build, and such a somatype explanation has been attempted as late as the 1930's and 1940's.

Ecological Theory

In some of the larger cities in the United States it became apparent that criminal behavior was more prevalent in some neighborhoods than in others. One of the pioneers in the study of crime ecology was Clifford K. Shaw, who studied the city of Chicago the first time for the period 1934 to 1940. By the use of pin maps, he located the residences of nearly 56,000 delinquent children and adults. His findings were reported in *Delinquency Areas* in 1927, and later in *Juvenile Delinquency and Urban Areas*, with Henry D. McKay in 1942 (published by the University of Chicago Press).

The studies by Shaw and others showed that certain neighborhoods housed disproportionate percentages of delinquent children and criminal adults. Those neighborhoods were characterized by disorganization and congestion, and "anomie," an absence of social influence or controls. The neighborhoods were in the centers of town, adjacent to industry and commerce. During the Industrial Revolution and the accompanying mass migration to the cities, the people who worked in the factories had to live nearby. The factories depended upon centralized steam power and transportation, and the result was an industrial community of low-priced housing for the laborers. The residential zone immediately adjacent to the factories served as a transition zone. As each new migrant group moved into the city, they resided in the area called Zone I in Shaw's study (a series of concentric circles starting at Zone I and numbered progressively higher as the zones moved out). As the people became more successful, they moved to better neighborhoods, then the next migrants moved in.

Shaw's study showed a succession of seven minority groups: Swedish, German, Polish, Irish, Jewish, Italian, and Negro. Other studies showed similar trends, with New York's most recent immigration of Puerto Ricans. In each of these decadent neighborhoods, a delinquent subculture was developed and has been perpetuated throughout the years by the current residents. There has been a succession of conflicts between the cultures of the newcomers and the dominant groups already in residence. The newcomers have never been welcome, but the "street culture" has continued to be perpetuated and passed on from group to group, although there is conflict between the groups.

Differential Association Explanation of Crime

The late Edwin H. Sutherland postulated his genetic explanation of crime, commonly known as his differential association theory and discussed in depth in *Principles of Criminology*.[2] The theory involves environmental influences, ecology, psychological considerations, and sociological principles. The principal premise is the theory that criminal behavior is learned through interaction with others by means of the same mechanisms that are involved in any other learning process. In capsulated form, the explanation is summed up: "The specific direction of motives and drives is learned from definitions of

[2]E. H. Sutherland and D. R. Cressy, *Principles of Criminology* (5th ed.; Philadelphia: J. B. Lippincott Company, 1955), pp. 77–79.

the legal codes as favorable or unfavorable. . . . Differential associations may vary in frequency, duration, priority, and intensity, . . . and a person becomes delinquent because of an excess of definitions favorable to violation of law over definitions unfavorable to violation of law."

Reference Group Theory

Dr. Martin R. Haskell, eminent criminologist at California State College, Long Beach, introduced a socio-psychological explanation of crime that he calls the reference group theory.[3] He offers six propositions as an explanation of this theory.

1. The family is the first personal reference group of the child.
2. The family is a normative reference group (the norm conforms to the larger society).
3. Prior to his participation in a delinquent act the delinquent boy adopts a street group as a personal reference group.
4. The street group that becomes the personal reference group of the lower class boy in New York City has a delinquent subculture.
5. A boy for whom the street group is a personal reference group is likely, in the dynamic assessment preceding a delinquent act, to decide in favor of the delinquent act.
6. The individual tends as a member of a personal reference group to impart into its context attitudes and ways of behaving which he is currently holding in sociogroup life.

ADDITIONAL CRIME INCIDENCE FACTORS

This chapter is merely an attempt to synthesize a vast variety of principles, theories, and explanations for crime and criminal behavior for the purpose of arriving at a common ground of understanding by the reader and student that there is more than one point of view. The serious student should carefully study the subject of this chapter in additional courses and texts in order that he may more effectively understand and cope with the problem of crime and its causes. For further elucidation, some additional factors should be considered.

[3]M. R. Haskell, "Toward a Reference Group Theory," *Social Problems* (Winter 1960–61).

Age and Crime

The national statistics show a direct correlation between youth and crime. It is a young man's folly, so it would seem to the observer of crime statistics. Commission of crime by the young, as shown by the statistics, is not new, and it seems to be related to the physical condition, amount of leisure time, and the economic dependence of the young offender. On a line graph, the crest would appear between eighteen and thirty years with a sharp rise and decline between nineteen and twenty-five. The drop is gradual to about thirty-five, then a sharp decline to age forty-five and above.

Sex Ratios

In the United States women enjoy virtually the same freedom as men, while in other countries there are some women who enjoy no freedom at all. The crime rates for women in the United States are also higher. The ratio of women arrested compared to men is about one to ten, and the types of crimes they commit have about the same ratio, except for those offenses that are associated with the sex difference.

Racial Differences

The nonwhite criminal versus the white shows a disproportionate ratio, with the highest rate of arrests per thousand population appearing among the Negro. Attempts to show atavistic traits of the Negro offender have demonstrated no correlation, which indicates that the higher rate should be attributed to such factors as economic and environmental influences more than any "throwback to barbarism" or other expression of bigotry.

Climate and Unusual Weather Conditions

The opportunity for more frequent people-to-people contacts will arise more often in the warmer climates than in the Arctic. Unusual "hot spells" are also related to the greater incidence of crimes of violence. Consider also the many factors other than heat that are involved, such as more personal interaction among people and more opportunities for conflict, increased leisure time, and greater amounts of alcoholic beverages consumed during the very hot days and nights.

Composition of the Population

Age, race, and sex ratios in a community are directly related to crime rates. A homogenous community of long-standing stability will have less conflict than the dynamic community with a wide variety of racial, ethnic, and cultural differences. The younger population will have had less time to attain the stability level of the older members of the community.

Relationship of the Police to the Community

The method of selection and retention of the police officers has a direct relationship to the image of the entire department, and the attitudes of both the citizenry and the police officers themselves. The number of policemen per thousand population has a direct bearing upon the effectiveness of the police. Enforcement policies as articulated by the chief have a similar impact on the community.

Social Attitudes

Contempt or disregard for the law has been a trend in many communities. One has only to read a newspaper to see that flagrant acts of criminal behavior occur under the guise of some so-called peaceful demonstrations or similar affairs. A vocal minority is involved in such lawlessness, but they are capable of being a troublesome minority. The general attitude of the community will be reflected in the actions of the juries and the courts in such cases when arrests are made. "Moral holidays" occur when certain acts that would otherwise be considered crimes are sometimes allowed to occur because of the "temper of the crowd" or the spirit of the occasion. Halloween has been regarded by many people as a moral holiday when certain minor acts of vandalism may be considered "in the spirit of the day."

Bookies and operators of houses of prostitution may earn hundreds of dollars a day, and sometimes considerably more, but they may receive suspended sentences or be required to pay small fines when found guilty of their crimes. The action is explained by a statement such as "they didn't hurt anyone," or "their victims were just as guilty as they were," or "it's only a minor crime." All of these factors are directly related to the incidence rates of all crimes in any given community. The community with a consensus that indicates a desire for a corruption-free government will reflect that attitude in the people who hold office in that community.

Economic and Social Crises

Personal acquisition of property and vigorous business practices perpetuate an attitude of competition. Personal prestige is gauged by many people on the basis of personal wealth. Some people cannot acquire such wealth by legal means, and will cheat, steal, and amass great fortunes in other unethical and illegal ways. White collar criminals use their businesses and professions as a means to acquire wealth by criminal means, and the professional and career criminals make a business or a profession out of crime. Many criminals in all three categories of crime—white collar, professional, and career—have been eulogized. Witness the influence peddlers and politicians who have been staunchly defended in spite of their flagrant criminal acts, and hailed as heroes.

Contrary to what one might believe would occur during an economic depression, the rates of property crimes do not rise. Instead, they go down. One reason for this downward trend may be that there is a less significant difference between the relative wealth of the classes. In times of affluence, the gap is greater, and the crime rates go up.

There is a correlation between the economic stature of the arrested criminal and his crimes, although the fact that he is impoverished is not a sure predictor that the poor man will commit crimes. Most criminologists theorize that the correlation is more likely to be the result of the living patterns of the poor and their environment of frequent contacts with the delinquent subculture that exists in impoverished areas.

Mobility

The basic family group is not static in most of the growing urban communities and no longer serves as the primary reference group for many individuals. Mass communication and transportation has caused the individual to become a part of the larger society in general instead of his own family and neighborhood. He seeks entertainment, employment, and recreation wherever he chooses, and he may move away from home with no provocation. He moves to a city where he is comparatively free from the social and ethical pressures imposed by his peers and those who have exercised authority over him. Community responsibility is lacking in the transient. Although he may not become a criminal, the transient has no social ostracism to face if he does.

ORIGIN OF CRIMINAL LAW

What is criminal law? Although a legal dictionary will go into much greater detail, a working definition of criminal law is: A rule regarding human conduct that requires or prohibits a specific act, that has been enacted by political authority, that applies to all persons to which the rule refers, and is enforced by punishment prescribed and administered by the local, state, or federal government that has legal jurisdiction. No matter how reprehensible or amoral the act or omission may seem, there are certain factors that must exist before the rule can legally classify an act or omission as a crime: (1) It must be specific, (2) it shall have been enacted by a political authority, (3) it must be uniform in its application, and (4) it must be accompanied by penal sanction.

The United States is a nation of laws. The entire system is regulated by laws, all of which must be specifically written. The student errs enormously, however, when he seeks to determine what is—and what is not—law by seeking his answers only in the legal code books. The legal code is the basic document and the principal source of the law, but there is another source of law that cannot be overlooked: the courts.

Although the legislative branch of government is charged with the responsibility of introducing and passing.the laws, the final determination of how they shall be applied—if at all—is made by the courts. The law may remain the same as originally written, but it is subject to human interpretation that may change with the general public opinion and the personal philosophies of the judges and Supreme Court Justices. The courts hear the testimony, examine the evidence, then hear the attorneys' arguments, and study the precedents set by previous cases of similar nature. By determining what is law with regard for prior cases with identical sets of circumstances, the process is known as *stare decisis,* or "adhere to the decisions."

Criminal jurisprudence in the United States is fashioned after the English system, with a few exceptions. Notable among those exceptions is the difference in the basic law of each system. The codified law as enacted by legislature is the basic law in the United States, and it is modified and changed by a series of court decisions. The British basic law has been the Common Law, or the decisions of the courts themselves. The laws were made as each case was adjudicated, and were court-made laws. When each case came to court, the Common

Law was researched for a similar case upon which to base the current situation. If there was no precedent, the case at hand became the precedent for subsequent cases. This was the origin of *stare decisis.*

Specificity is very essential to our legal system. The law must be clearly understood—it must specifically state what it is intended that it state. Auto theft involves the taking of an automobile with the specific intent to deprive the owner of his property. The uniformity principle is applied somewhat at variance with the theory, as may be witnessed by the student of jurisprudence or the casual observer. But the principle in theory is to attempt to apply the law to all its violators on an impartial and equal basis.

Punishment must be prescribed in order for the law to meet all the "legal" requirements. To merely require or prohibit a certain act is not sufficient. What to do if the law is violated must be planned and written into the law. The punishment distinguishes between the felony and misdemeanor. The threat of punishment as prescribed in the law may serve as a deterrent to the would-be offender. This attitude is based upon the classical theory. By prescribing the punishment in the code, there is a greater likelihood that it will be more uniformly applied.

The exact origin of criminal laws vary from law to law. There are basically two types of crimes: *malum in se* and *malum prohibitum.* The former is interpreted as including those crimes that are "evil in themselves," and the latter is "made evil by law." The *malum in se* crimes are those against the person and certain property offenses that violate the rules of common decency, the various religious tenets, and those that pose a threat to the health and safety of the community. The *malum prohibitum* crimes are those that the legislative representatives of the society make illegal, and they include such offenses as overtime parking or other minor vehicle code laws, gambling, betting on horse races off the track when betting at the track is legal, and a variety of others.

Some criminal laws originated with personal wrongs. Acts of personal violence, or ravishment, of theft of another person's property were a personal matter for the victim or a member of his or her family to seek retribution. The original theory was "an eye for an eye and a tooth for a tooth" or similar attitudes.

The avenger was not always capable of taking action with the desired results. He sometimes suffered additional injuries of person or loss of property. He was forced to seek aid, sometimes from "vigilante" groups of his peers who organized for their own self-protection. At other times the avenger was obliged to employ professional soldiers of fortune or other professional enforcers to handle his job with dispatch.

The next step in the evolving process was for the people to call upon the government to provide law enforcement and protective services. The professional government law enforcement agents are trained and capable, and they investigate the alleged violations, identify and apprehend the offenders, and hail them before the courts for appropriate punitive action. This system is currently in existence.

Retribution through the criminal courts is in the form of fines, or imprisonment, or both. The fine money goes into the public funds, because a violation of criminal law is a wrong against the state, or the people as a whole. If the victim wishes to seek personal financial recompense, he must then go to the civil courts and institute a tort action, a personal matter. The goal in a tort action is to receive financial retribution, or for the court to order the wrongdoers to perform, or to refrain from performing, a specific act.

Some criminal laws have been created because of an emotional reaction to indignities foisted upon helpless and unsuspecting victims. Other criminal laws had their origin in the religious and social mores of the community. These offenses are largely those that would be found in the *malum in se* category. Similar rules or laws are found listed among the basic doctrines of the many religions, such as the Ten Commandments. They include such offenses as criminal homicide, child molestation and similar sex offenses, burglary and theft, and criminal assault.

Another category of offenses are those that arose out of a conflict of interest among different special interest groups, or those that are legislated to fulfill a basic need to aid in expediting the smoother function of government rules and regulations. These laws most frequently fall into the *malum prohibitum* type of offenses. Tax and licensing regulations, reporting requirements, import and export laws, some traffic laws, and similar laws establish certain acts as crimes by stating that they are crimes.

TYPES OF CRIMINAL BEHAVIOR

When one studies crimes, their causes, effects, and all of the many related aspects, it is also necessary to study the types of criminal law violator. The most distinctive method used to study the criminal is to study him as an entity unto himself, an individual who commits an act or is guilty of an omission that is defined in the legal codes as a criminal offense. This individualistic approach is not invalid, but for the busy police science student and police practitioner this method is too time-consuming. A less exacting but still valid method for studying the criminal is by category, not losing sight of the fact that the subcategories vary with personal differences.

The categories that we shall consider in this chapter are the "circumstantial," or first offender, the career criminal, the professional, the white-collar criminal, and those persons who are involved in organized crime. One other category shall be designated as "exceptional offenders." They include the sex offender, narcotics-users, and the various other persons who violate the laws more frequently than accidental offenders.

The Circumstantial Offender

Traffic law violations are classified as crimes in most instances. They are prohibited or required by law and are enforced by penal sanctions of fine and/or imprisonment. Some of the offenses listed in the traffic codes are classified as felonies. Except for such offenses as those felonies, and which may involve some deliberate act, the traffic violator generally falls into this category. The vast majority of criminal law violators other than traffic are also classified in this category.

Although probably less than 1 percent of the entire United States population has a record of formal charges for nontraffic criminal violations, the number still adds up to millions. The exceptional criminal may have been detained as a juvenile or arrested as an adult, or both. He is usually a first offender, or "first arrest," and his first official *recognized criminal act* becomes a matter of record.

The circumstantial offender may have committed any of a thousand or so offenses, such as one of the following. (1) A young man is several miles from home and has just lost his bus fare. His parents will be expecting him in a few minutes and his dinner will be waiting. As he walks along—despondent and frustrated—he sees a bicycle on the sidewalk. The young man knows that stealing is wrong, but he rationalizes that he is not going to steal the bike. He's just going to ride it a few blocks and drop it, just enough to get him home on time. A criminal? He may repeat the action two or three times before his misdeeds come to the attention of the police and, subsequently, the Juvenile Court. (2) A young man is goaded into defending the honor of his charming female companion by striking an antagonistic "loud mouth." As the police officer arrives on the scene he sees only the physical attack and did not witness the disturbance of the peace. (3) And one of the most common of all "accidental offenders": the shoplifter who commits a theft on impulse because of the combination of temptation and opportunity.

The circumstantial offender is one who usually commits his crime without premeditation or design prior to the act, but, because of the circumstances as they occur at the time, all of the elements of the crime are present and the violator becomes another statistic. Because of the larger number of circumstantial, or accidental, offenders, they give the police the greatest problems. They often commit one offense and never repeat. Many of them do not develop patterns that lead to their identification and they are not discovered. When they are apprehended their cases are appropriately adjudicated. Unless they develop asocial or criminal behavior patterns they are seldom heard from again, but there are thousands more who take their places on the court calendars and "police blotters." Their offenses are unpredictable and there seems to be little the police can do to prevent them except by maintaining a constant and vigilant patrol.

Career Criminals

The career criminal is a failure. He spends a lifetime in custody and out of custody. Although the offender who falls into this category may be difficult to distinguish from the professional criminal, specialists do make the distinction on the basis of individual personalities of the violators rather than their crimes.

Crime is a way of life to the offender in this category and it usually starts at a very early age. Exactly where and when he was indoctrinated into a life of crime varies, but it is usually during adolescence. The "street culture," or "delinquent subculture" is part of the child's environment, and if the child's activities and attitudes are not directed toward lawful and socially accepted activities and attitudes, his life of crime usually begins.

The career criminal is in the lower levels of the criminal class structure. He is a misfit in the law-abiding community. He develops and maintains social and "business" relationships that help him eke out a living in his own parasitic way and to protect himself from discovery and apprehension as long as possible.

The career criminal is usually found in the category of "property" offenders, if he were to be identified by his crime specialty. Since he is not willing or able to consistently make a living by lawful means, he must make a profit out of his crimes. The individual who commits murder for a living may be classified in this category, but he is not likely to continue such employment for as long a period of time as other criminals because of his particular specialty. The career criminal is usually a burglar, a robber, petty thief, a dealer in stolen cars, or he may be a check man. Whatever his crime, the career criminal is a specialist and his arrest record will generally reflect a series of similar offenses.

Professional Criminal

There are a few factors that distinguish the professional from the career criminal, the most significant of which is the comparable degrees of success. The career criminal's record usually shows a long series of arrests and delinquency since childhood; the professional criminal's record is free from such a pattern. The professional can be so classified on the basis of his comparative proficiency and success. Any arrest record that he may have will show comparatively lower frequency and—in all probability—a lower percentage of convictions for those arrests.

The professional criminal does not consider himself a criminal and he is not likely to associate with other persons who are criminals. He is an assimilationist, blending himself into the total community in a respectable middle-class environment, and his friends and associates are respectable citizens, frequently leaders in business and government.

A police officer may refer to a frequently arrested shoplifter, pickpocket, or burglar as a professional thief. Actually, it may be largely a matter of semantics to attempt to distinguish between the two, but for the sake of keeping the two classes apart in this chapter, I suggest that you consider the professional as one who is more apt to commit the more sophisticated crimes of theft by fraud, embezzlement, and confidence games, and such burglaries as those involving the "cracking" of safes and high-value losses that require skill and planning. The professional is more difficult to identify as a criminal because he is usually prepared to register surprise or indignation when found out and will make apologies or restitution because of "this terrible mistake." He may have influential friends who make excuses for him and whom he uses—probably without their awareness of the fact that they are being used—to get him out of his troubles. The professional criminal is also prepared for his defense, and it is not unusual for him to buy witnesses and to be represented by high-priced attorneys.

White Collar Crime

As a contrast to the professional criminal, who makes a business out of his crimes, the white collar criminal makes a crime out of his business. This category includes the business and professional who violates the criminal statutes during the normal course of their business. Crimes by employees committed against their employers may be regarded by some experts as white collar crime, such as the bank official who is finally indicted for embezzlement of hundreds of thousands of dollars of the bank's money over a period of several years.

White collar crimes as referred to in this chapter include such offenses as price-fixing by so-called "competing" corporations, making false statements in income tax claims, making fraudulent advertising schemes, selling food supplement and vitamin pills or energy potions that do not do what they are purported to do for the body. Other white collar crimes include adding water to frozen food products, false labeling and packaging by butchers and grocers, and many fraudulent practices carried on by virtually every type of business and profession in existence. Some lending institutions manage to collect more than the legal interest rate; some attorneys charge for investigative services that are never performed, and some doctors charge their patients for drugs that are not actually administered, and some politicians keep their well-oiled machines running on their constituents' gasoline. Most of these crimes are not detected, and in the case of those that are detected, relatively little punitive action is taken.

"How is it that in this community the white collar criminals can get away with their offenses, sometimes flaunting violations with what appears to be absolute impunity, and get fat off the naiveté of the public?" the observer may ask. To put this problem in its true perspective, it is first essential to point out that the number of observers who would ask the question are obviously in the minority. It is simply a matter of fact that a generally accepted attitude is one of detached passivity. The term *caveat emptor* (translated as "let the buyer beware") has been applied in the attitudes of many agencies, including the courts, toward the victims of white collar crimes. Although they are in the statutes as crimes, the white collar crimes are not prosecuted or otherwise handled in the same manner as those of burglars and robbers.

Although there have been some notable exceptions, the president of a law-breaking corporation is not likely to be sent to jail for a violation of the Sherman Anti-Trust Law. Many studies have been made of this subject, and the consensus of the criminologists who have studied white collar crime is that a preponderance of the larger corporations in the United States in nearly every category, including banking, manufacturing, mining, securities, mercantile, and numerous others have not only been guilty of criminal offenses and sustained little or no punitive action, but they have been constant repeaters over a period of several years.

White collar criminality is deleterious for the entire community. It enriches the pocketbooks of the people who commit the offenses, but common knowledge throughout the community that such a situation exists and that the violator is not impugned or punished in any manner because of his political or monetary power, or because of a lack of sufficient evidence to prove the offense, or for any other reason, causes the people in the community to develop their own standards and ethical values accordingly. The "guy who cheats a little bit" is really not too bad, when he has the biggest house, the biggest cars, the most money, and the greatest social prestige in town. The white collar law violator, people rationalize, is not *really* committing a *serious* crime. Nobody is getting hurt. The man is a good citizen otherwise and, therefore is not a criminal but a shrewd businessman. Other side-effects of "turning the other way" when it comes to white collar crimes are that it reduces respect for the law ("laws are only for fools" or "laws are made to be broken") and for the entire system of the administration of justice.

One example of the general attitude of the lawmakers toward one type of white collar crime is the Sherman Anti-Trust law. Offenders may reap millions of dollars in profits while their punishment —if handled as a crime—is merely for a misdemeanor. Three methods for enforcement of that particular law are (1) criminal prosecution (the last resort although the first alternative), (2) cease and desist orders by the courts upon appeal by the U. S. Attorney General or a state District Attorney, or (3) the victims may sue in civil court for damages. Although the offense is a criminal matter, it is most frequently handled as a tort with no penal sanctions involved.

Strange bedfellows—career criminals, professional criminals, and white collar criminals—who all, for their own peculiar reasons, express contempt for the laws, for government, and for government "bureaucrats." They are all criminals who pose a menace to the peaceful pursuit of happiness in any community.

Organized Crime

Prostitution, gambling, illicit liquor production and distribution, and narcotics trafficking are all "big money" to the underworld. Whenever any of these vice enterprises extends beyond a "single agent" operation it takes on the characteristics of organization. But it may not be as simple as it appears. Organized crime has its tentacles sunken deeply into virtually every type of criminal operation in the United States, into many legitimate businesses that are used as a "cover" to explain the wealth of the organized crime operators, and their presence in locations where they can get "a piece of the action" in vice operations.

In his book *Police Administration*,[4] O. W. Wilson defines organized crime as: ". . . the combination of two or more persons for the purpose of establishing, in a geographic area, a monopoly or virtual monopoly in a criminal activity of a type that provides a continuing financial profit, using gangster techniques and corruption to accomplish their aim."

In the summer of 1963 a small unobtrusive-looking man of Sicilian descent made a television debut. His name was Joseph Valachi. His act was neither music nor sleight of hand; it was more of a monologue. The story-teller's tale was an awesome one that he presented before the television audience via a U. S. Senate subcommittee hearing and it was all about the machinations of an evil subculture in the United States and other countries that he called "Cosa Nostra," or "our thing," more commonly known as the Mafia.

The Mafia had its early beginning in 1282 in Sicily, when the townspeople of Palermo formed a vigilante group that roamed the countryside killing French soldiers to avenge the rape-slaying of a young bride. The cry of the people was *Morte alla Francia Italia Anela* or "MAFIA," translated "Death to the French is Italy's cry." Since that time the Mafia has continued to exist under a variety of conditions. For hundreds of years the predatory band of renegades consisted of heroes to the people of Sicily in the form of an "underground," who harrassed the French oppressors. As it exists now, the organization was formed in the eighteenth century as an underground organization to combat the French oppression of the Sicilian people. The Mafia very effectively plundered, robbed, and kidnapped for ransom, and the movement's members and leaders were respected by the citizens as the Robin Hoods of Sicily. After the island was unified as a part of Italy, there was no longer a need for the Mafia underground and they were out of a job. But the band of pirates on the highways and the mountains continued to operate. Their method was the same, but their victims became their own countrymen. The champions became, as a result of political transformation, an organization of notorious criminals.

4O. W. Wilson, *Police Administration* (2d. ed.; New York: McGraw-Hill Book Company, Inc. 1963) , p. 299.

Many distinguished experts on organized crime in the United States, including Director Harry Anslinger of the Federal Bureau of Narcotics, Chief of Police Edward J. Allen of Santa Ana, California, and Captain James Hamilton of the Los Angeles Police Department have known of the Mafia in the United States and of its insidious purpose. It was first exposed in this country by New Orleans Chief of Police David Hennesey in 1890 and it is still in existence. Joseph Valachi's testimony concerning the existence of the Mafia, or Cosa Nostra, as he called it, was not as spectacular in its content as it was in its character. The revelation by Valachi was a breach of the code of silence, or "Omerta," by one of the organization's own members.

Although the details of an organization can be carefully laid out in orderly fashion, and committee reports and documents prepared by eminent specialists provide incontrovertible proof that organized crime exists, the direct testimony of one of the co-conspirators had a greater impact and a more convincing type of proof. Whatever Mr. Valachi's accomplishments may have been in his lifetime, they were eclipsed by his testimony about the Cosa Nostra. It was a most dramatically convincing vehicle, one that provided the millions of television viewers a glimpse at the true story of the Mafia and organized crime.

Organized crime has a bureaucratic structure, and is similar to a large corporation with a franchise system in many respects. Two significant differences are the types of businesses involved, and the manner in which the business is conducted and the company rules enforced. There is considerable involvement of organized crime in legitimate business, but their principal money-making ventures are gambling, narcotics, prostitution, business and labor racketeering, boxing, bootlegging of liquor, and murder. In each of the major metropolitan areas where organized crime flourishes there is a leader who rules by force and fear. There are no formal organizational manuals or charts, but the members know what areas "belong" to whom, and which of the many operators is in charge. The organization is secret and the secrets are carefully guarded, with death a punishment for their revelation.

A capsule look at organized crime may provide some insight into the scope of the problem. Heroin traffic is estimated to cost users in the United States more than $300 million each year. "Lucky" Luciano is alleged to have made a profit of approximately $10 million per year from prostitution and narcotics smuggling prior to his imprisonment and eventual deportation to Italy, from which he continued to operate as a worldwide Mafia leader. Al Capone, a smalltime procurer from New York, moved to Chicago and failed to gain admittance into the Mafia but did manage to muscle his way to the top of an organization that yielded for him an annual estimated income of $20 million. In the ten years from 1920 to 1930, one estimate of Capone's earnings showed that he had amassed at least $25 million from gambling, $10 million from prostitution, $10 million in narcotics, and $50 million from the illicit liquor and beer industry that thrived during prohibition.

The Eighteenth Amendment to the U. S. Constitution provided fertile ground for organized crime and its principals. Prohibition was an attempt to change human behavior by legislation, and the people who wished to partake of alcoholic beverages were forced to violate the law to satisfy their wants. Organized crime readily, willingly, and capably provided for the needs of those people who were willing to violate the law to avoid changing their behavior patterns. Organized crime thrived because of the need for a powerful organization that could sustain such an illicit operation in defiance to the law. Organized crime exists when the following factors are present: (1) there is a need for a product or service by a large number of people, (2) society is failing to provide such a product or service by lawful means, and (3) there is an organized group ready and willing to provide the product or service.

There have been many investigating teams and committees established and sustained for the purpose of studying the problem of organized crime. Local, regional, and nationwide intelligence units investigate and disseminate to other agencies information concerning organized crime and the many people who comprise its ranks. Varying degrees of success are met in combating organized crime, but it continues to thrive in our society.

In 1951, at the conclusion of an exhaustive study of organized crime by Senator Estes Kefauver and the Senate Committee to Investigate Crime in the United States, the committee's findings and conclusions coincided with those of its predecessor committees, and the same conclusions have been echoed by many that have followed. This is a partial quotation from the Kefauver Committee's report:

> The most shocking revelations of the testimony before the committee is the extent of official corruption and connivance in facilitating and promoting organized crime. Nevertheless, it should not be assumed that our revelations cast doubt as to the integrity of the great preponderance of law enforcement and other officials. On the contrary, our findings and conclusions relate only to a small but disturbing minority of such officials. The committee found evidence of corruption

and connivance at all levels of government—Federal, State, and local. . . . The evidence of corruption and connivance with government officials on the state and local level with organized crime is present in four different forms:

1. Direct bribe or protection payments (juice) are made to law enforcement officials, so that they will not interfere with specific criminal activities.
2. Political influence and pressure of important officials or political leaders is used to protect criminal activities or further the interests of criminal gangs.
3. Law enforcement officials are found in possession of unusual and unexplained wealth.
4. Law enforcement officials participate directly in the business of organized crime.

Exercises and Study Questions

1. What are the "psychological needs" listed in the first part of this chapter?
2. What is the theory of Emile Durkheim?
3. List the basic concepts of the theory of criminal behavior advanced by Cesare Beccaria.
4. What was Lombroso's theory of crime causation?
5. Define and discuss a "sociopath."
6. Contact your local police department and ask to see their latest year's Uniform Crime Report statistics. Compare the ages of the persons arrested for the crime of auto theft, burglary, robbery, and thefts of property valued over $50. Can you make any conclusions as to the relationship between certain age groups and specific crimes? From your analysis of the statistics, can you form any opinions as to what factors are involved in the commission of property crimes?
7. Discuss the general attitude of the people in your community towards crime and criminals.
8. What factors are essential to constitute a criminal law?
9. How does the circumstantial offender compare with the career criminal? The professional? The white collar thief?
10. *Recommended Semester Project*: Collect newspaper and magazine clippings and articles that deal with organized crime or white collar criminality. Write a paper defining and discussing the subject of your choice based upon the file that you have collected and your additional study on the subject of your choice.

Suggested for Additional Study:

Sutherland, E. H., and D. R. Cressey. *Principles of Criminology* (6th ed.; Philadelphia: J. B. Lippincott Company, 1960). This is an excellent text and a must for every criminology student. Sutherland's theory of differential association is one that attributes criminal behavior to a number of factors rather than a single characteristic. Prior to Sutherland, the latter explanation was popular with sociologists. Later scholars have improved upon similar theories, but Sutherland should have the credit for pioneering an idea that was unique when he presented it.

Taft, D. R., and R. W. England, Jr. *Criminology*, (4th ed.; New York: The Macmillan Company, 1960). A well-written textbook on crime as an expression of our general culture. The three major sections of the book are (1) Background of Criminal Behavior, (2) The Explanation of Crime, and (3) Treatment of Offenders.

4

A Brief History of
Law Enforcement Services

INTRODUCTION

Historical records dating back to the time of Hammurabi show evidence of some sort of controlling, or law enforcement, body wherever any semblance of civilization existed. Someone, or a group of persons, whether self-appointed or chosen by some other means, at the head of the government has traditionally found it necessary to establish and enforce laws to assure order in the community. Self-regulation by all the members of the masses has not yet been successfully accomplished. Ground rules, or laws, governing the behavior and customs are essential ingredients in a civilized community to assure adherence to those laws for the protection of the weak, the helpless, and the innocent. The history of law enforcement is synonymous with the history of civilization. Simple logic proves that statement to be true. Civilization is possible only through *order,* and order is maintained by law enforcement officers. Even today, when we have presumably attained a state of advanced civilization, chaos would reign if our local law enforcement agencies were to be rendered impotent.

The task of enforcing the laws has traditionally been delegated to the most capable and most trusted men available to handle the job. The role is one of sacred trust, and has never been intended as a vehicle or platform from which an officer can gain great personal wealth or notoriety, or as a license for abuse of power to the detriment of others.

Law enforcement in the United States has its origin primarily in England. The purpose of the text is to explain the mechanics and

Photo courtesy Police Science Department, Orange Coast College

BRITISH CONSTABLE ALAN JONES, CENTER, DISCUSSES SIMI-
LARITIES IN POLICE ADMINISTRATION WITH CHIEF OF
POLICE GEORGE SAVORD, LEFT, OF CYPRESS, CALIFORNIA,
AND POLICE SCIENCE COORDINATOR DERALD HUNT OF
ORANGE COAST COLLEGE.

philosophies of the police agencies of the United States, not to ex-
pound on the vices or virtues of ancient history. However, it does
give one a more comprehensive understanding of the present when he
has at least a speaking acquaintance with the past.

ANCIENT HISTORY

Some historians have written that there have been laws and some
sort of police enforcement as long ago as 4000 B.C. in China and
Egypt. It is only logical to assume this if there was any form of civilization. The first permanent record of any sort concerning law enforcement to which we can refer with any authority are the Codes of
Hammurabi, the Babylonian ruler who lived about 2000 B.C. His
codes were inscribed on stones of black diorite, found by modern
archaeologists, and are still legible. They prescribe and proscribe
rules of conduct and provide for specific methods of punishment for

the violators. They have been called one of the greatest contributions to mankind.

Other evidence of ancient law enforcement is the ephori of Greece, a body of five ephors elected each year at Sparta and given almost limitless powers. They possessed the highest executive power in the country, and there were no controls over their personal conduct except the influence and authority of the other members. They were a combination of investigator, judge, jury, and executioner. An ephor presided over the Senate and Assembly, carried out its decrees, supervised education, levied fines, and inflicted other forms of punishment, arrested and tried other ephori for suspected transgressions, and performed all other types of regulation. This type of law enforcement naturally spawned the corrupt enforcer and enriched the greedy because there was no control over them by the people, except to vote against them at election time, if they dared.

THE ENGLISH BACKGROUND OF OUR U. S. POLICE SYSTEM

The police role as we know it in the United States is to serve as the enforcement arm of the executive branch of government. The powers and limitations are established by law, and are generally limited to the protection of life and property, and the enforcement of written laws only. The judging and punishing of offenders is the responsibility of other branches of our constitutional government. Although the origins of the many peoples in this country are in almost every part of the world, the United States police system is principally based upon the English system. "System" is actually a misnomer, because the so-called system is more like a "nonsystem." Federal, state, and local law enforcement agencies operate independently within their own spheres of jurisdiction without any semblance of hierarchy. As we discuss the historical evolution of English law enforcement, the similarities will be readily apparent.

During the latter part of the Anglo-Saxon period in the ninth century, King Alfred established what was to be one of the most significant police roles in English history. Recognizing the need for stricter adherence to the rules of society by the people, Alfred established a "tithing system" in each county, or "shire." The chief judicial and law enforcement officer in each shire was the "shire-reeve," an appointee of the crown. He was the local government, representing the State in all matters of nation-wide or local importance. He served at the pleasure of the king, and his tenure was dependent upon order within his own jurisdiction as well as profits to the king.

Law enforcement under the broad, general control of the shire-reeve was accomplished by means of the tithing system. Each head of a household would be responsible for his own family's conduct, as well as that of the other tithings, or members within his group of ten families, under the direction of one of their number designated as chief tithingman. The philosophy of this method was to make neighbors responsible for each other, compelling them to bring the wrongdoer to trial or else suffer the consequences themselves. It was an honor system on a national scale. The tithings were grouped into larger units known as "hundreds"; the hundreds in the shire, or county, comprised the major structure of the political organization within the shire. All able-bodied men in the shires were usually armed, and were always ready to form the *posse comitatus,* or "power of the county" wherever and whenever the "hue and cry" was sounded by the shire-reeve or one of his lieutenants—the chief tithingman— that a wrongful act had been committed by someone within the shire. The shire-reeve and his posse would seek out the violator and bring him to trial and punishment. Everyone within this system was involved in the enforcement of the laws and edicts of the land under the guidance of the shire-reeve.

The Norman king, William the Conqueror (1027–1087), kept the tithing and shire system during his reign, but reinforced its strength by giving the shire-reeve a military rank in addition to his already powerful civil position. He was usually selected from the landlord baronage, and the position was frequently passed along from father to son to son for several generations. The shire-reeve served at the pleasure—or displeasure—of the king and usually retained a firm grip on that office as long as he was instrumental in gaining a profit or advantage for the crown.

The prototype of our American county sheriff maintained his role as chief law enforcement officer in the shire for several hundred years. Sometime early in the Norman period (1066–1285) the *Comes Stabuli* (constable) appeared on the scene. Constables were hired on a full-time basis to aid the shire-reeve in carrying out his duties, thereby giving some continuity to the task of law enforcement. The *Comes Stabuli* were not much unlike the modern American town constable, or chief of police.

In 1072, the *Vicecomes,* or traveling (circuit court) judges were introduced to the English scene, and the law enforcement powers of the sheriff and constables were separated from their judicial powers.

The jury by the peers of the accused was started in the year 1166, and the grand jury was also originated the same year. The grand jury was charged with the responsibility to make inquisitions into facts of crimes, and render *Vere Dictums* (verdicts), called indictments or "true bills" when rendered by our American grand juries today.

Prior to the year 1166, there were many different types of private policemen hired by the citizens and merchants to protect their persons, their homes, and their shops. The shire-reeves and the assistants, the *Comes Stabuli*, were more concerned with the more important matters of the crown, such as land and tax problems, and crimes against the populace as a whole rather than crimes against individual victims, such as burglary or assault. But during the year of 1166—a significant one for the history of law enforcement—King Henry the Law-Giver issued his *Leges Henrici*, which made criminal law enforcement a public matter. He separated offenses into felonies and misdemeanors by defining the felonies and leaving all other offenses in the category of misdemeanors. His decree stated: "There will be certain offenses against the King's peace, arson, robbery, murder, false coinage, and crimes of violence. These we deem to be felonious."

Magna Carta was signed under protest by King John in 1215, and was an agreement that the people would be provided "due process of the laws," protecting the individual against unnecessary infringement upon his rights and liberty by the crown. Governmental organization was changed so that there was more local control, with a separation of state and local governments. Article 13 of Magna Carta stated in part, ". . . the city of London shall have all its ancient liberties and free customs . . . and all other cities and villages shall have all their liberties and customs." Another article in that wonderful document concerning due process read: "No freeman shall be taken or imprisoned or disposed or outlawed or banished or in any way destroyed except by the legal judgment of his peers or the laws of the land."

In Westminster, then capital of England, King Edward I established a curfew in 1285 by ordering that the city's gates be closed so that the undesirables would be locked out of the city at nighttime, and the residents and other occupants locked in. In order to enforce the curfew, a night watch was created. The night watchmen were called bailiffs. Their duties included guarding the gates to the city between sunset and sunrise, checking on the security of all places within the city, and keeping track of all "persons and lodgers." Members of the night watch were selected from the ranks of able-bodied men in the community on a compulsory basis and were paid for their services. They carried lanterns and staffs while on patrol and were virtually ineffective, according to historians. One branch of the night watch of that time was the *Police Desmour,* charged with the responsibility for regulating streetwalkers and prostitutes and keeping them in their designated districts.

It was not until about the fourteenth century that policemen were actually trained for their jobs. The office of justice of the peace was created to replace the shire-reeve, and to more efficiently handle the duties of his office. Each shire, or county was provided three or four men "learned in the law" with full authority to "pursue, arrest, chastise, and imprison." They were assisted by the constables, who had previously been under the control of the shire-reeves. The justice of the peace retained his role of policeman and judge for about seventy-five years, when the office evolved into a strictly judicial role.

The years 1500 to 1800 are called the Period of Watch and Ward. Several different police systems were inaugurated during these years in England. There were basically three new systems: the merchant police or Ward and Watch, the parochial police, and the military police. The merchant police were private watchmen employed by the bankers and merchants to protect their property. They guarded the places at nighttime, and also worked as private detectives for the purpose of locating and recovering stolen goods. One of those detective forces was the Bow Street Runners, a colorful cutthroat group of bounty hunters for criminals and their booty. The second type of police force to appear during the Watch and Ward period was the parochial police, who were employed by the religious parishioners for the protection of their members and their property. The third police force was the government operated military police, under the direction of the provost marshal and the crown.

In 1655, Oliver Cromwell divided England and Wales into twelve police, or military, precincts. He placed a marshal in charge of each precinct, and maintained control of the people by means of this system during his reign. The rule was military, and the law was Martial Rule, which superseded all forms of local governmental control. Magna Carta and the Bill of Rights were disregarded under the guise of military expediency.

In 1829, Sir Robert Peel, a Member of Parliament, introduced a bill to found a centrally controlled system of law enforcement in the Greater London Metropolitan area. He based his conclusions as to the need for the new police system upon a study completed by Dr. Patrick Colquhoun. The various police agencies, both public and private, were ineffective. Peel labeled the Ward and Watch the "shiver and shake watch." He stated that the men comprising the watch spent half the night shaking from the cold and the other half shaking from fear. Sir Robert's bill was passed, and the entire world watched the creation of one of the first truly professional police agencies. The police departments in the United States were patterned after the London Metropolitan Police, as we shall see in this and succeeding chapters in this book.

Sir Robert first divided the London Metropolitan area (not the City of London, which is a small and separate entity) into sectors, or districts, and replaced the existing police systems with his new organization, one sector at a time. He personally interviewed and selected all candidates for the new department, and out of twelve thousand who applied, he selected two thousand. Tenure was dependent upon ability and production, and candidates served a probationary period. Turnover during the first few years of operation was enormous, and Sir Robert stated: "The securing and training of proper persons is at the root of efficiency." By 1835 the entire department was organized and operational, with headquarters at Scotland Yard. The exact origin of the name Scotland Yard is subject to debate, but the ancient buildings and grounds bore the name until 1890, when the department moved to New Scotland Yard.

The new force was organized along military lines, and police agencies have since been considered paramilitary in nature. Numbered police badges were issued to identify the men as individuals as well as officers of the law. The salaries of these new officers were dependent upon their effectiveness in reducing crime, and they were assigned to shifts that rotated around the clock. The reporting system was improved so as to provide statistics on the crime picture in the area as well as to provide *modus operandi* information to assist in the identification and apprehension of offenders. A detective bureau was established for the purpose of conducting investigations under circumstances in which the appearance of the uniform would hinder investigation. The organization numbered about three thousand in 1835 and has since grown to more than twenty thousand.

We have devoted a great deal of space to the English police system because it is apparent that the American "system" (actually, an absence of a system is more descriptive of the potpourri of police agencies in the United States) developed along the same general lines in techniques and traditions. The various law enforcement officers who appeared in England have their American equivalents, as we will see in subsequent chapters. These include the modern American sheriff, marshal, constable, justice of the peace, jury, grand jury, and the many other police officials who comprise American law enforcement, as well as the municipal police agencies. We will now examine the evolution of the police in the United States.

THE EVOLUTION OF LAW ENFORCEMENT IN THE UNITED STATES

In 1833, the City of New York was so impressed with the efficiency of the Metropolitan Police Department in London that a delegation was sent to that city to study the department with a view to adopting some of their ideas. The result was the formation of the New York City Police Department in 1844 along the general lines of Scotland Yard. The department in New York was the first of its kind in the United States, followed by Boston in 1850, and many other cities since then. The major difference between the two systems is the form of control. The American police forces are comparatively free from any federal or central control; each autonomous community is responsible for the establishment, maintenance, and administration of its own police department.

But let's go back to the earlier beginnings of law enforcement in the United States. When the settlers came to this country, they brought with them their various traditions and customs. As a body, the new residents of this country were suspicious and contemptuous of a strong central government; local autonomy was fiercely defended. The law enforcement bodies were no exception in this trend toward local control. Although the systems of the Old and New World were similar, the controls were diametrically opposed. The control of the local police in most European countries was by strong central governments. The English customs had the greatest amount of influence on our police systems, so the offices of the shire-Reeve and constable in England became the Sheriff and Constable in the populated areas of this country, and the U. S. Marshal was the law enforcement officer in the Territories and unpopulated areas. The local sheriffs and constables were elected for short terms by the people whom they served instead of being appointed by any central authority. This was, of course, after the settlers had emancipated themselves from English rule and formed an independent government.

New England became a land of settlements and villages centering around industry and commerce. The municipal type of government was formed, and the municipal police officer—the constable—

was elected into office. In the South, agricultural, and more rural, the county form of government and the county sheriff were adopted as most suitable to fill the needs of the people.

Many other types of law enforcement were tried in various parts of the New World, usually holdovers from the native countries of the residents of the different communities. For example, in New Amsterdam, later New York, the police patrol officers of the night watch for many years were called the "rattle watch" because they carried with them larger versions of the rattles now used as party toys, with which to warn would-be offenders of their presence. Boston had an organized night watch as early as 1636, whose purpose it was to patrol the streets to combat larceny. Philadelphia had a similar night watch, and other cities of any size had some semblance of night patrols. Most of them were vigilante, or volunteer, groups that poorly supplemented the sheriffs and constables and their few assistants.

A Day Watch, organized to combat crime when the Night Watch was not operating was created about 1800 in New York. This was the first daytime, paid police force to appear in America, and the two separate watches—night and day—continued to operate independently for many years. Other communities followed the lead of New York by hiring full-time, paid policemen, but there is no record of there ever having been a round-the-clock police force in the United States until 1844, when New York City combined the Day and Night Watches into a single police force fashioned after the London Metropolitan Police Department. Boston followed in 1850, and the modern non-civilian police force as we know it today made its appearance on the American scene. It is interesting to note that it was not until the year 1855 that the police were allowed to wear uniforms. Prior to that time, it was considered un-American for civilian police officers to wear any clothing that would give them a military, or "uncivilian" appearance.

Since 1844 the police service in the United States has remained pretty much the same in some respects, and has changed drastically in other respects. Let's take a look at some of the landmarks in the progress of law enforcement in the cities and counties of the United States. Many systems which originated many years ago appealed to the residents and became so much of a part of the communities that they are still in existence today throughout the country.

The sheriff and constable are constitutionally elected officers, and are usually designated as the chief law enforcement officers in their respective areas of jurisdiction. The sheriff is generally the title assigned to the officer for the county, and the constable is usually responsible for a smaller area, such as an unincorporated township. Their terms of office are usually for two to four years, and in many states they cannot succeed themselves in office. The philosophy behind this law is that within a short period of time in office, an individual cannot gain too much control over the people who elect him. The office of constable is slowly fading into oblivion, but the sheriff is pretty well ensconced in county government in many parts of the country with little likelihood that he will disappear from the scene for many years to come. We will discuss the duties of the office of sheriff later in this book, but a cursory glance at the comparative roles of the sheriff of the past and present will show that there is actually little difference.

Election of municipal chiefs of police was quite common when local departments were first established. Public suspicion of government officials was prevalent, based upon actual experience with the corrupt officials who served for life at the pleasure of the king. Short terms assured the people that their police administrators were new to the job and would not have time to become corrupt or too powerful in office. This system was found to be an illusory concept however. Not only were the chiefs not able to gain control of the community, but they hardly had sufficient time to gain control of their own officers or to acquire sufficient experience to perform their jobs efficiently. Their terms were so short that they did not give up their civilian occupations while in office. The artisans, shopkeepers, and businessmen had their futures to consider, so they were policemen on a part-time basis only, seldom devoting their full energy and resources to the important task of running a police department.

Because of this lack of professionalism that resulted in election of politicians as police administrators, the trend has been for many years to permanent appointments of administrators qualified by experience and ability instead of popularity at the polls. Tenure is based upon continued good performance and substantial results in the reduction of crimes and traffic accidents, and clearance of crimes. The elected police chief system remains in only a few cities.

In the mid-1800's, administrative police boards were established. The chief of police was a professional, and retained his job on a continuous basis, but the theory of the board system was to maintain civilian control over the police department to assure responsiveness to community needs. The boards were composed of judges, mayors, and private citizens, and the police chiefs served at their pleasure. This system lasted many years, but it was found that there were many major disadvantages, including the prevalence of political corruption, and at best the board members often proved themselves bungling, inexperienced, meddling amateurs.

The next step in the evolution of police administration was state control of the local agencies. This system was a reaction to the politically corrupt local boards, and the theory was that the new system would be free from local partisanship, and that the citizens throughout the state would be assured of adequate and uniform law enforcement. After all, they argued, the state laws were promulgated for the entire state, and the state could best determine how those laws should be enforced. Except for several cities which still operate within the framework of this type of administration, most states and cities found that this system was not the answer to the problem. Control reverted to the local governments. The reasons for failure were that the laws were *not* uniformly applied. They were completely disregarded in some areas and overenforced in others. Fiscal support and police protection in some sections of the state were disproportionate. There was too much absentee administration and a lack of responsiveness to local demands and needs.

The next system of police administration to appear was the commission government charter. The elected commissioners were charged with various branches of city government, and the public safety commission (police, fire, and sometimes health and sanitation departments) was one of those commissions. This system was found inadequate, as was the administrative police board comprised of amateurs. It, too, is on the decline.

The mayor-council and council-city manager types of municipal government are now the more prevalent and efficient local systems. The former type of government is quite efficient when the mayor is a full-time official and a capable administrator. The latter type assures more continuity in the business administration and executive control of the overall operations because a professional nonpolitical administrator is managing the affairs of the community. Under either system, the chief of police is usually selected on the basis of education, experience, and demonstrated ability, and he continues to serve as administrator of the police department as long as he continues to perform the job efficiently and effectively.

SUMMARY

We have cursorily reviewed the evolution of police administration, bringing us to the present. From the favored appointee, to the politically popular, to the professional police administrator, we now have progressed to modern law enforcement standards and techniques, although we still cling tenaciously to some remnants of antiquity. In the next several chapters we will examine the processes of modern law enforcement.

Exercises and Study Questions

1. What country in Europe had the greatest influence upon the development of the American police "system"?

2. What was the contribution of Hammurabi to civilization?

3. Discuss the sheriff in the county where you live with the shire-reeve in England. How do they compare?

4. What was Magna Carta, and what influence did it have in relationship to modern law enforcement?

5. What was Sir Robert Peel's contribution to law enforcement?

6. What is the major difference between the municipal police forces in the United States and the local forces in England, if any?

7. What was the purpose for limiting the tenure of police chiefs and sheriffs to short terms?

8. Discuss the various methods for selection of police chiefs, and which of those methods seem to you to be best to assure the community of the most efficient police department.

9. In the history of American law enforcement, have chiefs of police ever been selected by popular election? Do you believe such a method is good, or bad? Why?

10. *Recommended Semester Project*: Conduct a thorough study and write a more detailed history of American law enforcement than that which is presented in this chapter.

Suggested for Additional Study:

A good encyclopedia. Study the history of law enforcement in general, and the various types of law enforcement officers, including the sheriff, marshal, constable, justice of the peace, and the vigilante groups.

PART

THE MODERN UNITED
STATES POLICE "SYSTEM"

5

Police Agencies and the
Nonsystem Concept

INTRODUCTION TO THE POLICE "NONSYSTEM"

When one thinks of a system such as a "police system," the first thought that comes to mind is of a well-arranged series of agencies and departments of a large bureaucracy. Each has a specific area of responsibility and reports to a command unit through a hierarchy of command. A police system—if one were to exist—in the United States would be a rank ordering of all the local police agencies in sequence, according to their relative importance, then higher up the scale would be placed the many state agencies, and finally a rank ordering up through all of the federal agencies to a single head or committee. Such a system does not exist in the United States.

The "system" of police agencies is actually a façade. The average observer assumes a system because he observes several agencies working together. Police officers and agents of the many agencies have a common purpose—preservation of the peace—and they are homogeneous in respect to work requirements and qualifications. There is a general spirit of cooperative teamwork, an attitude of "I must help him if I want him to help me."

Each type of law enforcement agency had a different origin. Of all the types of police organizations, the municipal police force is the most common, and one of the most essential branches of local government intrinsic to an orderly civilization. Some police forces or investigative agencies have been created to fill a specific need, as you will see as you read of the various agencies in this chapter. Law enforcement agencies have been created at state and federal level for the purpose of enforcing taxation, licensing, and other revenue laws.

Others have been formed to meet particular needs on a state-wide or national basis because of the lack of efficiency of the local police, or the dilemma caused by the inability of local police departments to carry out certain duties beyond restrictive jurisdictional boundaries. Such organizations as the narcotics bureaus and alcoholic beverage control departments, highway patrols, and similar departments have state-wide jurisdiction. Federal agencies are able to cross state lines and cooperate with the police of foreign countries because of their nation-wide jurisdiction. Still other agencies found at all levels of government have been created and perpetuated because they serve as convenient instrumentalities of special interest groups. These little "empires" may convince their supporters that only they are capable of performing the specific investigations required of them, and that any other arrangement would be catastrophic. Other special enforcement bureaus or divisions of various governmental agencies have arisen as a result of distrust of certain local police agencies due to the real or imagined inefficiency of those agencies. Except for the local city and county police agencies, the majority of police forces, particularly federal and state forces, are of relatively recent origin. The

Photo courtesy of Federal Bureau of Investigation

TRAINING CLASS FOR FINGERPRINT TECHNICIANS, TECHNICAL
SECTION, FBI IDENTIFICATION DIVISION, WASHINGTON, D.C.

first state police agency—the Texas Rangers—was not created until 1835. The first federal police agency was the Secret Service and it was founded in 1865.

Another type of police agency that should be included in a discussion of the police system is the private police department. Private police forces are generally formed by large corporations because of their need for more concentrated protective services than can be provided by the government police. Many private police agencies are very capable and efficient. An example of a very well organized and efficient private police force is the railroad police of the United States and Canada, the largest privately supported police agency in the world. The force is composed of several thousand agents stationed throughout the two countries, supported by approximately four hundred separate railroads.

Many other very efficient private police agencies exist to perform all types of protective and investigative duties. As a matter of fact, industrial policing is a highly specialized police function that requires a great variety of skills. There are other organizations, however, that have been composed of hoodlums and troublemakers. A vivid example of such a force was the Coal and Iron Police in Pennsylvania, created by several mine operators for the purpose of forcibly breaking up labor strikes. That particular organization was outlawed by the Pennsylvania State Legislature in 1935.

When studying the police system, consider first the various local police forces, each responsible for policing its own respective political subdivision of the state, the cities protected by the city police and the unincorporated and rural areas policed by the constable, the marshal, or the sheriff. Each jurisdiction could be related to the other jurisdictions as interlocking pieces in a jig-saw puzzle. The many state and federal agencies have similar jurisdictional relationships with the emphasis placed on division of responsibility as opposed to geographic allocation of jurisdictional boundaries. There are overlapping pieces in the system's jig-saw puzzle, however, and there are jurisdictional disputes and conflicts. The conflicts are probably more evident in the federal jurisdictions because they all have no geographic boundaries within the United States, whereas the local departments are separated by city limits and county lines.

There is considerable overlapping of federal police and investigative responsibilities, and also to a lesser extent with the state agencies. Rivalry, distrust, and intrigue have been the products of jurisdictional conflicts, although the trend during recent years has been toward a greater amount of cooperation and more professional attitudes. Three alternatives to the existing interforce conflicts of federal agencies with overlapping jurisdictions have been advanced by observers of the problem. One alternative is to retain all of the existing agencies, but to redefine their respective jurisdictions systematically to assure a minimum of conflict. The second alternative is to establish a central bureau by consolidating all of the existing agencies. The third alternative is to retain the present system, or "non-sytem," and to establish an interdepartmental committee as a single coordinator to direct the efforts of the many agencies with a minimum of duplication and conflict. Similar proposals could be applied to the many agencies of the states. At the local level, there should be no displacement of the existing arrangement of having police departments in each separate political subdivision which are directly accountable to the people of that jurisdiction. The first proposal of the preceding three that were presented with respect to the federal agencies—retention of the existing agency but redefining the jurisdiction—already applies to local police agencies. The second proposal —consolidation of all agencies—is not practicable nor desirable at the local police level. The third proposal—that of coordination of several agencies—is feasible. Coordination of such operations as records keeping, training, laboratory, and similar functions placed at strategically located positions in the state and operated jointly by the many contributing and participating agencies would result in a greater amount of uniformity in procedures, greater efficiency, and would assist the progress of police service toward eventual professionalization.

There are nearly one-half-million officers and agents working for approximately forty-thousand separate agencies in the United States with law enforcement and/or investigative responsibility. Such a non-system of cooperating agencies has room for improvement, but a great deal of credit must be accorded to the many thousands who perform their duties as capably as they do. Such is the police non-system.

THE LOCAL POLICE

The Municipal Police Department

The entire police and policing picture centers around the city or township police department. They are charged with crime prevention and repression, traffic law enforcement, protective patrol services, arbitration in neighborhood and family disputes, apprehension and arrest (or citation or warning) of criminal law violators, and recovery of stolen property. The local police officers perform a multitude of nonenforcement tasks, such as providing information and assistance to visitors and tourists, as well as residents, vehicular and pedestrian traffic control, safety education, crowd control at sporting events and other public gatherings, and the general task of maintaining order and peace in their respective jurisdictions.

The city police departments comprise a large portion of the more than forty thousand law enforcement agencies which employ nearly one-half-million men and women in the United States to provide for the protection, comfort, assistance, and maintenance of a moral conscience for the nearly two-hundred-million people in their jurisdictions. The organization of the municipal police department will be outlined in the next chapter. The entire Part 4 of this book is devoted to the primary police functions that are performed by the local law enforcement agency. The local agencies—although not specifically mentioned in those chapters—include the municipal police departments, the town constabulary, township and borough police, and the county law enforcement agencies.

The federal and state law enforcement and investigative agencies have limitations on their scope of authority, which usually restrict their officers and agents to the investigation and enforcement of only those laws and other matters that specifically relate to their specialties. The municipal police department is charged with the responsibility for taking an active part in both investigation and enforcement of federal and state laws as well as the ordinances of their own specific political subdivisions. The extent to which they become involved varies with the nature of the offenses and the working relationship with the various other agencies.

The city policeman may arrest a common thief and uncover a cache of smuggled tax-unpaid liquor and a kilo (roughly two pounds as packaged by smugglers) of marijuana. The jurisdictions involved in these violations include the local department, of course, but also a few other agencies. The Alcohol and Tobacco Tax Unit of the Treasury Department is responsible for "bootleg" alcoholic beverages, and the Bureau of Customs has a jurisdictional interest in the liquor as well if it came across a border. The illegal narcotics in such a case may involve additional agencies. The Bureau of Customs would have a legal interest because of the smuggling violation, although there is no legal means for the smugglers to possess the marijuana because it has been outlawed in the United States since 1937. In addition to the local police department's legal interest in effecting the arrest for the state law violation for possession of the illicit drug, the state agents would be concerned because of the significance of the drug's presence and the state-wide narcotics problem, and the federal agents would be concerned because of the violation of a tax law involving marijuana and also the nation-wide implications of smuggling the drug. The agency that would handle the case initially would be the local police department.

In the hypothetical case at hand, the local department would take custody of the evidence and properly preserve it for later presentation in court, the concerned agencies would be notified, and the appropriate reports prepared and disseminated. The suspect would be interviewed by representatives of all involved agencies and follow-up investigations initiated as a result of those interviews. But what of the initial arrest and prosecution? The local agency would, in all probability, be the one which would make the formal charges for the state violations of theft and unlawful· possession of marijuana. Any additional charges would be initiated by the agencies having specific jurisdiction, and separate trials for those offenses would be held later.

In some situations there are offenses which are subject to concurrent jurisdiction, such as bank robbery, interstate transportation of a stolen vehicle, taking a kidnaped victim across state lines, and hundreds of others. Those offenses are likewise investigated and enforced by agents of more than one agency. They cooperate effectively to their mutual advantage. The prosecution is usually at the initiative of the agency in whose jurisdiction the original violation occurred, and the product of the efforts of the other agencies are added to the weight of the prosecution.

The County Sheriff

In the majority of counties in the United States, the sheriff is the principal law enforcement officer with his jurisdiction primarily limited to the unincorporated areas of that county. In his duties as officer of the court, and in the execution of his nonenforcement duties, his jurisdiction includes the entire county. In the state of Louisiana the political subdivision in which the sheriff performs his duties is called the parish, but in nearly all other respects their roles are the same.

The sheriff fills his office by popular election in nearly all jurisdictions of the United States, and his term of office is for two, three, or four years. Rotation of the office is almost universal, because legislation either limits the tenure of most sheriffs to a single term, or a limited number of terms. The theory behind such a limitation on tenure is to prevent the man in office from acquiring too much power while holding that office, an atavistic attitude of early Americans, who suspected the motives of anyone in public office.

Throughout the United States the multifaceted responsibilities and duties of the sheriff vary from state to state and from county to county within the individual states. In virtually all areas, the sheriff is responsible for the service of civil processes and maintenance of the county jail and custody of county prisoners. In some jurisdictions the sheriff is "overseer of the highways." In parts of the South and Southwest the sheriff serves as tax collector, and as public administrator for the property of persons who die intestate. In the state of California the county is the principal political subdivision of the state and the sheriff is the principal law enforcement official in each county. He is so designated because he maintains the county jail, serves as bailiff to the Superior Court, and in times of an insurrection or major disaster involving more than one city and parts of the county he may be designated as the coordinator of all of the concerned police agencies, as designated in mutual aid agreements between the various communities. There is no hierarchy of command in this arrangement (except during special emergencies by prior agreement), and during normal times and conditions, the various law enforcement agencies are completely autonomous under the direction of their respective chiefs of police.

The sheriff and his deputies have a variety of duties, some of which are listed as follows:

1. Execution of civil and criminal processes throughout the county, including various writs of execution and attachment, warrants of arrest.
2. Keep the county jail and its prisoners.
3. Keep the peace in the unincorporated areas of the county. In order that he may accomplish this objective, the sheriff and his deputies may take whatever preventive and enforcement action that he deems necessary, including arresting and taking before the magistrate people who have committed, or have attempted to commit public offenses.
4. The sheriff attends Superior Court, and obeys and carries out all lawful orders of the court, also acting as court crier and bailiff.
5. Attend all meetings of the Board of Supervisors (the governing body in California) to preserve order and serve notices, subpoenas, or other processes directed by the Board.

6. Investigates public offenses that have been committed and cause those who have been identified as violators of the law to be prosecuted.

The sheriff is the county officer who is charged with the authority to command as many able-bodied male inhabitants of the county to assist him in carrying out his duty to preserve the peace and to maintain order. This power is called the "power of the county," or *posse comitatus*. In some jurisdictions, the sheriff may also fill the role and the office of Marshal, as described in the next paragraph.

The Marshal

The role of the marshal is similar to that of the sheriff, in that he serves as an officer of the court, but the marshal serves in the Municipal Court while the sheriff serves the Superior Court. He serves subpoenas and civil papers, warrants of arrest, and may serve as escort for the prisoners who must be taken from the jail to the court for trials and hearings. The marshal is elected in some jurisdictions, and appointed in others. Except where the marshal's office is incorporated by the local jurisdiction to include the duties of the chief of police as town marshal, his duties are usually restricted to those enumerated in this paragraph. It is no small task, but it is comparatively limited in scope.

The Constable

The constable is recognized by the constitutions in approximately twenty states, particularly in New England, the South, and the West. Selection of the constable is usually by popular election. He serves a township and his duties are primarily to maintain the peace and serve processes for the local Justice Court. He may also serve as a tax collector or poundmaster, and whatever other duties as may be described by the government in his own state and county. Constables collect fees and mileages for execution of arrest warrants, search warrants, and transportation of prisoners. In some jurisdictions, the constable may be under the direction of the sheriff.

Miscellaneous Local Police Forces

At various times in history, and for various purposes, different types of policing organizations have been formed. Some of those organizations formed for specific purposes, then disbanded when the need no longer continued to exist; some of the organizations continue to exist at the present time.

Vigilante committees have been formed at various locations, usually at times when the residents found that the local police were ineffective either because they were overwhelmed by the incidence of crime, or they were inefficient. Cattle rustling in the West during the 1800's was a sizeable problem that the people attempted to solve by vigilante procedures. During the late 1920's, prior to the FBI involvement in protection of banks against bank robbery and other crimes, a bankers' vigilante was formed in the Mid-West for the purpose of apprehending bank robbers. Law enforcement today calls for greater efficiency than can be accomplished by a vigilante group, and without proper guidance and training an organization of this type could promote anarchy.

Park police have been created by some of the larger cities to provide protection and informational services to the visitors to their parks. Parkway police may be found on the parkways and boulevards in some of the large metropolitan areas. Other agencies may be formed for the specific purpose of guarding public buildings or monuments.

STATE POLICE AGENCIES

At the state government level in the police non-system most law enforcement and investigation agencies are specialized in nature. Their jurisdictions vary with their specific needs, but they usually have statewide authority to perform those police duties—however limited in scope they may be. Highway patrols, for example, uniformly enforce state traffic laws on the highways, and alcoholic beverage control agents enforce licensing and other liquor laws in the entire state.

Each state is different from all the others with respect to their state police agencies, depending upon its history and evolution of policing needs. Starting with the Texas Rangers in 1835, and continuing to the present, new agencies are being formed and old agencies reorganized to meet the changing requirements of the evolving community. Massachusetts employed state constables in 1865 for the purpose of suppressing commercialized vice. The Arizona Rangers were created in 1901, and New Mexico founded its State Police in 1905. Both agencies had local police powers at their inception. The former organization is still active.

Connecticut organized a state police agency in 1903 with a primary objective of investigating and suppressing commercialized liquor and gambling violations. They now examine operators' license applicants and are involved in arson investigations. The Pennsylvania, New York, West Virginia, and New Jersey State Police also double as Fire, Fish, and Game Wardens. The New York State Police officers serve as court officers for Justices of the Peace on Indian reservations.

California's State Police are limited in jurisdiction to state buildings and grounds throughout the state, including the state college and university campuses. In addition to the State Police, there are many other investigative and law enforcement agencies, each with a specific agency or bureau to which it reports, and a specific list of laws and rules with which it is to be concerned.

There is no uniformity in state police and investigative agencies, but there is some similarity. With that premise in mind, let's look at some of those agencies.

State Adjutant General

The National Guard and Air National Guard provide a military force with dual federal and state status, and they are available to both the federal government and the state in the event of a national or state emergency. Their organizations are set up in accordance with the laws of the states, and the regulations of the Army and Air Force. The governor is the commander in chief. Under his direction, and in his name the adjutant general is the chief of staff and commander of all state military forces.

Military control is the initial force of government and the ultimate power of government. It is defined as the "initial force" because it overcomes the enemy and establishes the government in the beginning. It is the "ultimate force" in that the state militia is the governing authority when all other powers are ineffective to protect the state against invasion, insurrection, disaster, or unlawful disturbances.

Some form of military control is a traditional and obviously essential part of every government. Under normal conditions, this control is exercised by the local law enforcement agencies and the control is basically exerted in subtle form by the presence of the officers throughout the community, who take whatever enforcement action is necessary as the need arises. When the military force in the form of the police is ineffective, then it becomes necessary to invoke the more powerful force of the government: the National Guard.

The problem of when to call upon the services of the National Guard is serious and the responsibility for making the decision should not be underestimated in a free country such as the United States. The entire judicial system is suspended under martial rule. The habeas corpus and due process provisions of the Constitution and the Bill of Rights are suspended. Martial rule is proclaimed by the governor, and it is in existence only when the state militia supersedes one or more local police agencies by his proclamation. It is a form of executive control that arises in self-defense of the state. There must be a very real need for such martial rule before the governor may proclaim its existence. Its objective is to preserve the public safety and good order of the community. The governor has the responsibility and authority to determine the need for martial rule and to suspend it at the earliest possible moment when its need no longer exists.

Under all but exceptional circumstances, the state militia will act "in aid of the civil authority." While acting in such a capacity, the militia's aid to local law enforcement agencies is limited. There is no suspension of local control or any of the judicial or legal processes. Objectives and missions are assigned by the local civil authority and the military power shall be subordinate to civil authority. A military situation justifies the use of military force equal to the situation. This attitude toward martial rule provides the military force with more power than that of a peace officer.

The greatest difference between martial rule and civil rule is in the arrest and detention process. Ringleaders of a mob may be detained without formal booking procedures and held throughout the entire disturbance, then later released without trial. Such a detention is considered *preventive* and not *punitive*. In some cases when the military assists local police and when martial rule has not been proclaimed, but when the public safety demands that such processes as preventive custody be used, the courts have ruled that such action was necessary and has refused writs of habeas corpus and denied claims of false imprisonment. In such cases the condition is defined as "preventive" or "qualified" martial rule.

The governor activates the militia, as mentioned earlier, and if necessary, declares martial rule whenever the need for such action is called to his attention in any acceptable manner. Normal channels usually provide for such notification to be made by the chief executive officer of any city or county, or any Justice of the Supreme Court, or Judge of the Superior Court, or any sheriff. The request shows cause for action and a statement to the effect that the civil power is not sufficient to cope with the problem. Some states provide that martial rule may be utilized in any situation of great need, except when any such condition results from a labor controversy.

Highway Patrol

Highway patrol organizations are charged with the enforcement of state traffic laws and all laws governing the operation of vehicles on the public highways throughout the state. The primary purpose for the organization is to provide for the safety of all motorists. Although a state highway patrol has principal enforcement jurisdiction on the highways in the unincorporated areas of the state, some states provide that the highway patrol officers have full peace officer authority and they may enforce traffic laws upon any public highway in the state. In times of civil disturbance or disaster it is the responsibility of the highway patrol to keep traffic lanes moving and open.

Because of the large area to be covered, the state highway patrol is divided into geographical districts, with a ranking staff officer in charge of each district. The districts may be further divided into squads or other smaller units, depending on the needs of the agency and the size of the state. Enforcement activities are accomplished by patrol officers in uniform and distinctively marked patrol cars and motorcycles to (1) enforce the laws regulating the use of vehicles, (2) maintain preventive patrols on the highways, (3) regulate traffic movements and relieve congestion, (4) investigate traffic accidents, and (5) make surveys and studies of accidents and enforcement practices for the purpose of improving traffic safety.

Some state highway patrol organizations maintain a traffic safety section that coordinates traffic safety programs throughout the state to assure uniformity in adherence to the many traffic laws. They assist all organizations, both public and private, in planning and operating effective safety programs. They may assist local agencies by providing intensive enforcement training for traffic personnel. Auto theft records may be maintained more efficiently by a state agency such as a highway patrol because of their statewide jurisdiction, and they may provide laboratory and investigative personnel to assist local agencies in the investigation of hit-and-run cases and auto theft.

In addition to those functions listed in the preceding paragraphs, some highway patrol agencies coordinate the activity and maintain records on commercial vehicle enforcement, maintains public scales on the highways, inspects all school buses and investigates accidents involving school buses throughout the state. Licensing or registration of official smog control device or headlight or other safety equipment installation and inspection stations may also be a function of the state highway patrol, as it is in California.

Department of Motor Vehicles

A state motor vehicle department is a service agency that has three major functions: (1) registration of motor vehicles, collection of fees, and maintaining registration records; (2) licensing drivers, collecting fees, and maintaining files on licenses; and (3) administration of financial responsibility laws. Investigators assigned to this type of agency are involved in investigation of thefts and unlawful transfer of ownership of vehicles. Other investigations will include cases of altered license plates; forged or counterfeit auto registration certificates or drivers' licenses; and a variety of suspected law violations by auto dealerships and auto wreckers.

State Bureau of Narcotics

State narcotics agents are responsible for the investigation and enforcement of violations of the state narcotics laws. Their involvement with the lone users of narcotics and the peddlers of the drugs on the streets is usually through their cooperation with the many local law enforcement agencies and their vice officers. They are principally engaged in the investigation of alleged infractions of the law by persons who are in lawful possession of the drugs but may unlawfully or negligently dispense them. They investigate pharmacies, hospitals, and the offices of doctors, dentists, and veterinary surgeons for illegal sale and use of narcotics. State narcotics agents also seek out manufacturers and distributors of illicit drugs, and generally enforce the legitimate use and dispensation of the drugs.

Alcoholic Beverage Control Agencies

The state department of alcoholic beverage control in many states has licensing authority concerning the manufacture, importation, and sale of intoxicating liquors. The agency has statewide jurisdiction over the administration and enforcement of the state alcoholic beverage control laws that provide for the licensing and regulation of the alcoholic beverage industry in the state. In some states such an agency may also be given the responsibility to assess and collect excise taxes on the manufacture, importation, and sale of alcoholic beverages. The latter responsibility may, however, be handled by a taxing agency instead of by the department of alcoholic beverage control.

The agents assigned to control state liquor laws are primarily involved in the investigation of applicants for licenses to sell alcoholic beverages and to report on the moral character and fitness of the applicants, and the suitability of the premises where the sales are to be conducted.

Violations of the laws that are most frequently encountered by the investigators of an agency of this type are sales to minors, consumption and possession by minors, sales after hours, conduct of the premises as disorderly houses, sales to obviously intoxicated persons, and failure to "fair trade" or post prices. Investigators of the alcoholic beverage control are peace officers in most states, and they have the authority to make arrests at any place in the state. They confiscate evidence, prepare reports, and testify in court in the prosecution of criminal law violators. Because all dealers in alcoholic beverages are licensees, the department handles many disciplinary matters of licensees administratively. Punishment may consist of a written notice to comply with the regulations to a permanent suspension of the license and forfeiture of the fees.

Fish and Game Wardens

Game wardens enforce and prevent violations of laws and other regulations that relate to the conservation and protection of fish and wildlife. The duties of a warden include effecting arrests and issuing citations and warnings to the violators. They investigate wildlife crop damage complaints, advise landowners on the control of wildlife, and issue kill permits. Other duties include the feeding of game birds and animals during unusual weather conditions, assisting in the planning of controlled hunts, and operate checking stations in controlled hunt areas. The Department of Fish and Game and its agents are responsible for assisting in safety programs for hunters and fishermen, for securing assistance from various organizations in planting of fish and rescue operations, and generally assisting in the maintenance of hunting and fishing areas in the state to assure both wildlife conservation and perpetuation of the outdoor sports.

Labor Law Enforcement

The division of labor law enforcement of a state's department of industrial relations or similar agency is particularly responsible for enforcing regulations assuring ideal working conditions for the workers in the state. The laws enforced by such an agency include those that relate to the payment of wages, employment of women and children, private employment agencies, ventilation and sanitary conditions of places of employment, weekly day of rest, hours of work, and general conditions of work. Agents assigned to a labor law enforcement division or bureau are responsible for the additional duties of assuring compliance with the law in labor disputes, investigate industrial accidents and industrial safety, and to maintain labor statistics.

State Fire Marshal

The state fire marshal is a peace officer in most states. He has the primary responsibility for preventing fires by performing the following functions:

1. Studying and eliminating fire hazards.
2. Establishment and enforcement of fire and panic safety regulations in institutions that fall within state or local jurisdictions.
3. Investigation of fires resulting from crime, or in connection with any crime.
4. Development of uniform fire and panic safety laws pertaining to any public or commercial building.
5. Conducting continuous fire prevention and educational programs.
6. Establishment and enforcement of minimum safety requirements governing the manufacture and sale of inflammable clothing, circus and tent show operations, and the treatment of drapes and curtains used in public institutions or assembly places to make them flame resistant.
7. Regulation of the sale, discharge, and display of fireworks.

Horse Racing Board

In states where there is pari-mutuel betting, the horse racing board or a similar agency administers laws governing horse racing, and supervises the conduct of racing at all race tracks in the state. It allots dates for racing, supervises pari-mutuel betting, licenses associations conducting the meetings and to persons connected with the meetings.

Investigators assigned to the horse racing enforcement agency are responsible for routine enforcement of the horse racing laws and rules, and for inspectional duties around the tracks. They watch for violations in the stable area, such as tampering with the horses, or the presence of unauthorized and unlicensed persons. In the public areas, such as the grandstand and the clubhouses, the investigators look for, and take appropriate action (consisting of arrest or ejection) when they come into contact with bookmakers, pickpockets, and other undesirables. Away from the tracks the investigators check out rumors and information concerning "fixes" of races, they search for lost parimutuel tickets, and investigate license applicants and the various people who frequent the race tracks.

"Generalist" Agencies

Various licensing commissions and boards, usually at the state level, establish and administer the many laws related to their respective professions and services. The board members are usually appointed from the ranks of their own professions and serve for specific periods of time. They act to maintain minimum ethical standards of their professions. They employ staffs of investigators, or they may make use of an investigative "pool," that provides investigators when the need arises. Investigation is the primary role of the agents assigned, but they may be designated as peace officers for specific law enforcement responsibilities. Just a few of the boards and commissions involved with this type of investigative responsibility are insurance agents, investment specialists, real estate brokers, chiropractors, medical doctors, pharmacists, dentists, athletes, accountants, engineers, beauticians, private detectives, funeral directors, nurses, social workers, and barbers.

Civil Defense

Disaster acts enacted during World War II and the years following enabled legislation for the provision of mutual aid among the varous political subdivisions in times of major disasters and civil disturbances. According to the laws of many states, the mutual aid is voluntary when the emergency is not extreme, and mandatory when the emergency is extreme. When he determines the need for assistance in accordance with this act, the chief of police or sheriff may request the assistance under these conditions: natural disaster, riot, flood, earthquake, or similar occurrence that taxes the capabilities of the police agency beyond its ability to effectively handle the situation. Police reserves may be called in.

As a partial solution to the problem of their additional manpower needs in times of major disaster or other emergency that may arise with no advance warning, some police agencies utilize a Police

Auxiliary, or Reserve Corps. These "citizen policemen" are usually unpaid volunteers who donate a specific amount of time each week or month to classroom and field training in the various areas of law enforcement. They may comprise search and rescue teams or aero squadrons, or they may be used to supplement the patrol force. In some jurisdictions, reserves have actually been employed on a part-time basis, although such a practice is not advisable.

FEDERAL POLICE AND INVESTIGATIVE AGENCIES

The federal government has no single law enforcement or investigative agency that has unlimited jurisdiction. As pointed out in the first part of this chapter, the various city and county police agencies are responsible for enforcement of the basic state and local laws that provide for the public health, safety, and morals. The federal agencies have been created for the purpose of investigating and/or enforcing specific laws and to cope with specific problems that extend beyond the jurisdictional boundaries of state and local forces. One agency was created to protect the President (Secret Service), and another for the purpose of enforcing federal tax regulations (Alcohol and Tobacco Tax Division of the Treasury Department). These are just two of the many agencies. In the next few pages let's look at some of the police and investigative agencies of the federal government. When reading of these agencies, keep in mind the fact that there is no rank order, no hierarchy of command or responsibility. Each operates within its own sphere of responsibility and authority, and reports to a specific department or bureau to which it is responsible.

DEPARTMENT OF THE TREASURY

The Secret Service

The Secret Service is the oldest of all federal police agencies, created in 1865 for the purpose of providing protection of the President of the United States, his family, and the President-elect. The Secret Service is also responsible for enforcement of laws concerning coins and currency of the government, and for a long list of criminal laws affecting several other federal agencies.

The Internal Revenue Service

The Internal Revenue Service has two enforcement arms with distinctively different jurisdictions, the Intelligence Unit and the

Alcohol and Tobacco Tax Division. The Intelligence Unit is concerned with the enforcement of laws concerning internal revenue and income taxes. The Alcohol and Tobacco Tax Division has primary responsibility for the tax law enforcement relative to alcoholic beverage production and certain weapons. The enforcement agents of this unit enforce the National Firearms Act, which regulates the possession of automatic weapons and defines certain firearms that are illegal to possess.

The Bureau of Customs

Customs agents are responsible for enforcement of the laws involving illegal importing and exporting, customs, and navigation. Customs enforcement men and women guard baggage enclosures, ships, motor vehicles, aircraft, railroad cars, and patrol docks and airfields. They prevent unlawful loading or unloading, or delivery of merchandise, smuggling, or other unlawful acts against the laws of the United States.

Federal Bureau of Narcotics

Narcotics agents have principal jurisdiction over enforcement of federal laws regulating the legal traffic in narcotics in the United States and in monitoring such traffic at both international and national levels. The Bureau of Narcotics is responsible for enforcing the federal laws regulating the production, sale, and transportation of narcotic drugs. The agents of this bureau work very closely with state and local law enforcement agents because of the need to work as a team to cope with the problems of the unbelievably efficient underworld organization of narcotics traffickers which nets fantastic profits throughout the world.

DEPARTMENT OF JUSTICE

The Attorney General

The Attorney General of the United States is the chief officer for the federal government, and his office is responsible for criminal prosecution of all violators of federal laws throughout the country. The Justice Department, under the direction of the Attorney General, has two primary operating units with responsibility for the investigation and enforcement of certain federal laws: the Immigration and Naturalization Service, and the Federal Bureau of Investigation.

Immigration and Naturalization Service

The Border Patrol is the enforcement arm of the Immigration and Naturalization Service. Its principal jurisdiction is the enforcement of the laws regulating the legal entry of aliens into the United States. Their places of assignment are generally at the ports of entry into the United States, but they may be assigned to work in any part of the country. They check people entering the country for their authority to do so, and for the purpose of enforcing the laws against illegal entry they maintain random or fixed check points, which may be located at any place within a few miles of the national border.

The Federal Bureau of Investigation

The FBI of the Department of Justice is not a police agency, but an investigative agency with jurisdiction over all matters in which the United States is or may be a party in interest. Mr. John Edgar Hoover assumed leadership of this agency in 1924, and set about the task of making it the professional organization that it is today.

The Federal Bureau of Investigation has broad investigative jurisdiction encompassing all federal law violations, but limits its scope to about one hundred and sixty federal laws, including all of those federal statutes not specifically assigned to another agency.

Photos courtesy of Federal Bureau of Investigation

AN EXAMINER IN THE FBI LABORATORY COMPARING THE
HEEL OF A SUSPECT'S SHOE WITH THAT OF A CAST MADE
AT THE SCENE OF A CRIME.

Among those matters that are within the primary jurisdiction of the FBI to which its investigators direct the major portion of their attention are the following: administrative investigations, admiralty matters, anti-trust laws, civil rights violations, Atomic Energy Act investigations, bankruptcy violations, bribery, copyright violations, crimes on the high seas, crimes on Indian or government reservations, espionage, Federal Kidnapping Act, Federal Reserve Bank Act, frauds against the government, illegal wearing of service uniforms, interstate transportation of stolen vehicles or stolen property, killing and assaulting federal officers, location of escaped federal prisoners, mail fraud, National Bankruptcy Act, passports and visas, patent violations, robbery and burglary of National FDIC insured and Federal Reserve System banks, unlawful flight to avoid prosecution or confinement, White Slave Traffic Act, and others.

In addition to the investigative functions of the agents of the Federal Bureau of Investigation, that agency provides assistance to local law enforcement agencies with training of its officers and it maintains a criminal laboratory that is available for assistance in local investigative matters. Since 1930 the FBI has been the central clearing house for the most complete file on fingerprint and arrest files, and the agency serves the majority of all the country's law enforcement agencies by maintaining criminal statistics and by disseminating the information on a regular basis in its Uniform Crime Reports.

OTHER FEDERAL POLICE AGENCIES

The State Department Office of Security is another of several agencies that investigates the backgrounds of critical personnel. Their principal duty is to investigate visa and passport applications.

The Coast Guard is a division of the Treasury Department that is responsible for port security, maritime safety, and maritime law enforcement.

Under the Department of Defense, the military services operate both criminal investigative and intelligence units. In the Air Force, the Office of Special Investigations (OSI) handles both types of investigative and enforcement duties.

The Post Office Department has its own staff of Postal Inspectors who investigate and enforce postal laws and regulations. Their investigations include schemes to defraud, extortion cases, mail losses through theft and robbery, and related offenses. A large portion of their time is devoted to cases involving the use of the mails to transport obscene literature and other materials.

The Department of Interior has four units charged with the investigation and enforcement of federal laws. The Fish and Wildlife Service enforces the laws involving migratory game birds, fish and wildlife restoration acts, and international agreements on interstate transportation of wildlife. The Bureau of Indian Affairs maintains order and suppresses illegal liquor and drug traffic on Indian reservations. The Bureau of Mines investigates and enforces regulations concerning mine accidents, explosions, and fires. The National Park Service maintains a staff of National Park Rangers, who perform police services in the National Parks throughout the country.

The Department of Agriculture enforces more than fifty laws that protect the farmers and consumers. That agency is also responsible for national standards in weights and measures in cooperation with the local and various state agencies.

The Department of Health, Education, and Welfare is involved in police-type enforcement work in the areas of purity and standards of food, drugs, cosmetics and standard labeling laws.

One of the newer investigative arms of the Department of Health, Education, and Welfare is the Bureau of Drug Abuse Control. The special agents of this bureau enforce the laws that involve those drugs that are not regulated by the Federal Bureau of Narcotics. Those drugs include some of the dangerous newer drugs that have been used more extensively during recent years than the narcotics, including the barbiturates, amphetamines, and the hallucinogens, or LSD and its counterparts.

INDEPENDENT AGENCIES WITH FEDERAL JURISDICTION

In addition to those agencies that are directly related to the Executive arms of government, there have been numerous quasi-government agencies that operate with the full force and effect of law enforcement agencies, except that those commissions and boards enforce most of their rules by means of administrative actions. A representative sampling of those agencies include the following:

1. The Civil Aeronautics Board investigates all civil aircraft accidents and regulates civilian air traffic.
2. The Civil Service Commission is responsible for preemploy-

ment and other personal investigations, and administration of the federal Civil Service laws.

3. The Federal Communications Commission regulates interstate commerce by means of the many communications media. Their personnel are responsible for enforcement of the Communications Act, which provides for licensing and regulating of operators and broadcasting stations. In cooperation with an internationl committee, the FCC designates frequencies to various applicants, and works to assure maximum compatibility among the many licensees.

4. The Federal Trade Commission is responsible for looking into—and taking appropriate action when necessary—incidents of unfair competition and deceptive practice in interstate commerce.

5. The Securities and Exchange Commission prosecutes malpractice cases in the securities and financial markets.

6. The Interstate Commerce Commission regulates common carriers in interstate commerce and is also involved in the investigation of railroad accidents.

AGENCIES RELATED TO THE POLICE

In the police "system," or "non-system," there are numerous agencies that are involved in the process of arrest, prosecution, adjudication of cases, and post-arrest disposition. The following agencies comprise an important part of that process.

DISTRICT ATTORNEY

The District Attorney is an elected official, an officer of the county, and the chief county prosecutor. In some jurisdictions the District Attorney may handle both civil and criminal cases. In other counties the District Attorney handles only criminal cases, and a county counsel is employed to handle the civil cases.

Except for misdemeanors, the District Attorney's office is generally responsible for determining—upon examination of the report and other inquiry into the matter as he deems appropriate—whether or not to seek a complaint charging an individual with a crime, what charge will be filed against that person, or if he will be charged at all. In some jurisdictions, city attorneys are involved in the prosecution of city ordinances and some misdemeanors. In some jurisdictions the Grand Jury is utilized extensively to hear testimony and examine evidence presented by the District Attorney to determine whether or not a prosecution will be pursued by way of an indictment.

The District Attorney is the legal advisor to the county grand jury. Other responsibilities include the initiation of proceedings against inebriates, the mentally ill, narcotics addicts, and nonsuport of minor children cases. Many District Attorneys employ their owr staffs of investigators who continue investigations of the more serious cases to assure a more completely administered investigation to assure a more successful prosecution. In some jurisdictions, the District Attorney may operate his own intelligence unit to combat organized crime.

THE COURT SYSTEM

There is some difference between the states in the court systems. The information in this section is based upon the system as it exists in California, and should be used as a guide in other states.

Supreme Court

Six associate justices and the chief justice make up the supreme court. They are each appointed by the governor when the opening arises, serve for a number of years (12 in California), then run for reelection against their own records without·opposition at the end of their terms. The supreme court reviews cases on appeal from the appellate courts, renders decisions on questions of constitutionality, and reviews automatic appeals on all capital offense convictions which involve the death penalty.

District Courts of Appeal

The appellate courts are divided into districts, each functioning separately in different parts of the state. Each division has three judges, one serving as presiding judge. The judges are appointed by the governor and run for reelection against their own records without opposition. Their jurisdiction includes appeals of judgments by the superior courts, and the first review of cases destined for the supreme court.

Superior Court

There is one superior court in each county. The judge is appointed by the governor when a vacancy occurs between elections or when a new division is created that necessitates the appointment of an additional judge. The jurisdiction of the superior court includes: (1) juvenile court, (2) all felonies and certain high misdemeanors in some states, (3) civil suits involving claims for over $3,000 (California), (4) appeals from lower courts, (5) probate court, (6) court of conciliation, (7) divorce court, (8) court of equity, (9) writs of habeas corpus, (10) reciprocal enforcement of support laws throughout the U. S., and (11) sanity and alcoholic commitment hearings.

Municipal Court

Each county is divided into judicial districts in which there are municipal or justice courts, depending on the size of the district (based upon population). Jurisdiction of the municipal court includes: (1) misdemeanors committed within the county and in the judicial district, (2) civil actions not exceeding $3,000, (3) small claims (under $200), (4) preliminary hearings in felony criminal matters to determine whether the matter will be brought to trial in the superior court. This procedure is used in lieu of the grand jury indictment in certain states, or concurrently with only certain cases going to the grand jury.

Justice Court

The justice court serves a district with a population containing less than the minimum to qualify the district for a municipal court. Justices are elected in the same manner as superior and municipal court judges, except that vacancies between elections are filled by appointment by the board of supervisors instead of the governor. The jurisdiction of the justice court includes: (1) certain misdemeanors for which there is fine and/or imprisonment, (2) civil cases of lesser amounts than are required for a higher court, and (3) small claims.

Small Claims Court

This court is one of concurrent jurisdiction, and will be found as a part of either the municipal or justice court of the judicial district. The small claims must involve a certain maximum amount of money ($200 in California), and is a "do-it-yourself" court, so classified because attorneys are not allowed to argue on behalf of their clients.

THE CORONER

With a background similar to the history of the sheriff, the coroner comes to modern law enforcement from ancient times. Today he is an officer of the county and may be found in virtually all parts of the country either as coroner or medical examiner. The coroner's ancestor was called the coronator, and he represented the king of England at public hearings. In the United States, his principal jurisdiction involves the determination of causes of death, and care and custody of the remains and personal effects of deceased persons.

The office of coroner or medical examiner may be combined with that of sheriff, tax collector, public administrator, or any other public office that may be combined with his office by law. The coroner is a county officer, and in California he fills the office of the sheriff when it is left vacant. The coroner need not be a medical doctor or have any legal knowledge to be elected, but the coroner in some jurisdictions has been replaced by a medical examiner, who is a doctor, and in many others the people have elected doctors to the office.

The coroner is required by law to investigate and sign the death certificate in all of the following circumstances in California, according to the government code: ". . . all violent, sudden or unusual deaths; unattended deaths; deaths wherein the deceased has not been attended by a physician in the ten days before death; deaths related to or following known or suspected self-induced or criminal abortion; known or suspected homicide, suicide, or accidental poisoning; deaths known or suspected as resulting in whole or in part from or related to accident or injury either old or recent; deaths due to drowning, fire, hanging, gunshot, stabbing, cutting, exposure, starvation, alcoholism, drug addiction, strangulation, or aspiration; death in whole or in part occasioned by criminal means; deaths associated with a known or alleged rape or crime against nature; deaths in prison or while under sentence; deaths known or suspected as due to contagious disease and constituting a public hazard; deaths under such circumstances as to afford a reasonable ground to suspect that the death was caused by the criminal act of another, or any deaths reported by physicians having knowledge of death for inquiry by the coroner."

The coroner may examine the body at the place of death and take custody of the remains for the purpose of identification or determination of the cause of death, and may exhume a body, cause a post-mortem examination or autopsy to be made, or hold an inquest to inquire into the cause of death. After determining the cause of death, the coroner signs the death certificate. If an inquest jury finds that the death was caused as a result of a criminal act of another person, he shall properly notify the appropriate law enforcement agency and the prosecuting attorney in accordance with state law. In cases when the identity of the killer is known and he is not in custody, the coroner may issue a warrant of arrest.

The purpose of an inquest is to determine cause of death and the relevant facts attendant to the death. When the inquest jury finds that the death was caused by criminal means and they accuse an individual of the crime, it is merely that—an accusation. Any criminal charges and conviction or acquittal must be brought before the courts in the same manner as any other criminal charge.

STATE JUSTICE DEPARTMENT

The attorney general is the chief law officer and ministerial officer of the state court system, the chief counsel in all litigation involving the state, and the chief administrative officer of the state department. The attorney general prepares and disseminates opinions relating to the interpretations by his office of the criminal law and, in the absence of written or case law the attorney general's opinion has the same force and effect as law.

In addition to providing assistance in the investigation and prosecution of criminal cases in the state, the attorney general represents the state on appeals from the lower courts to the appellate jurisdictions at state and federal levels, and his office processes extradition and interstate rendition proceedings for persons who have fled from the state—or have left the state—to avoid prosecution.

Some states have agencies under the supervision of the attorney general and the justice department that are similar to the California Bureau of Criminal Identification and Investigation. The Bureau is a service agency created for the primary purpose of assisting local law enforcement agencies in the state in the (1) identification of criminals, (2) control and supervision of certain types of offenders, (3) location of missing persons, and (4) technical and scientific analysis of evidence.

The state law requires all sheriffs, chiefs of police, and marshals to forward daily to the Department of CII fingerprints of persons arrested and copies of investigation reports of certain crimes committed in their respective jurisdictions (felonies, sex offenses, narcotics and dangerous drugs cases), together with a detailed description of the stolen property, if any.

It is the responsibility of the Department of CII to coordinate and correlate this information, to attempt to identify the responsible criminals by their *modus operandi* (method of operation), and to promptly forward to the contributing agency any information which may assist them in identifying and apprehending the responsible parties.

A bureau of statistics may be a part of the justice department or similar state agency. If such a state agency exists, its general responsibilities should include the compilation and analyzation of information relating to criminal activity in the state, crime trends, achievements of law enforcement, and the results of prosecution.

THE POSTARREST PROCESS

Corrections

After a person is arrested and charged for a specific offense, he is brought to trial to answer to his charges. If he is found not guilty, or if the case is dismissed or the subject is not held to answer to the charges, he is released and no further action taken. But what of the process if he is found guilty? There are three functions in this process that are related to law enforcement: probation, incarceration, and parole.

Probation

Probation is a suspension of a sentence giving a period of freedom in the community in lieu of jail or prison time, and the individual's freedom while on probation is conditional for a specific period of time. Probation may actually be granted in the form of a prison sentence that is suspended and replaced by a short term in a county jail followed by a period of time under supervised freedom. The terms of probation are enforced by probation officers, and usually include the following provisions:

1. Observance of all laws.
2. Keeping and developing good habits.
3. Keeping a good work or school record.
4. Associating only with approved persons.
5. Marriage or divorce only with the approval of the probation officer.
6. Abiding by all of the restrictions imposed by the judge who granted probation.

The probation department is an arm of the courts, and probation officers are peace officers. The officers are primarily concerned with supervision of those persons who are placed on probation by the courts. Their jurisdiction includes both juveniles and adults and, in some states, the probation department may maintain the juvenile homes for the custody of delinquent and dependent children, or for children who have no one willing or able to care for them.

Another very important function of the probation officer is to investigate the backgrounds of convicted persons and to present comprehensive reports to the trial judges so that they may be better prepared to mete out the appropriate punishment. The report may be sufficient to show that probation should not be granted. In that case, the defendant is sentenced to jail or to prison.

Institutions

Juveniles are detained in a variety of places, but they are not considered as having been convicted at any time. The philosophy of the juvenile courts has been to return the child to his parents as soon as possible whenever practicable. First and minor offenders may be returned home with no incarceration, or they may be remanded to the custody of county probation officials or a state institution.

When the court remands the juvenile to custody for his first time, he may go to a local juvenile home or a camp of some type. Subsequent incarcerations for the juvenile repeater may result in his being sent to a state institution or camp for a longer period of time, and then eventually home again for probation or parole.

Adults are sentenced either to a city or county jail, or to a state or federal penal institution for a prescribed period of time. Jail sentences are set by the judge for a specific period of time, and the defendant serves that time, less good behavior and earned time off for such voluntary acts as donating blood. Some states have "straight" sentences for felony imprisonment in state institutions that are prescribed by the judge in the same manner as one would be sent to the county jail. Other states, including California, have the "indeterminate sentence" that provides for the judge remanding the subject to prison for "the sentence prescribed by law," and which is later established by a corrections board or similar committee.

The purposes for sentencing a convicted person to prison include the following:

1. The people desire a changed man or woman to emerge after serving a period of time in prison. Their habit patterns

should, according to this philosophy, be sufficiently different after isolation from the law-abiding society during which they have had the opportunity to develop new skills and improve their academic education so that they will seek lawful outlets to satisfy their needs and desires.

2. Segregation from society is a means whereby the offender can be separated from his victims for an extended period of time, and during that time he cannot commit his crime again.
3. The victim and the people in the community want retribution and revenge.

The indeterminate sentence is a procedure whereby the sentencing judge merely sentences the individual to prison. The penal code prescribes the punishment as "one to ten years" for example. Once in prison, the subject is placed under the jurisdiction of the department of corrections. A board of review, comprised of persons usually appointed by a governor, reviews the subject's case and establishes a more definite time within the broader limits as originally prescribed. For example, a man sentenced to "one to fourteen" may have his sentence set by the board at three years before his case may come up for review and consideration for parole.

The convicted person may leave prison at the end of his completed sentence and be done with it. But there are other legal ways that he may leave. One method is for the president or governor of the state to grant him a pardon, which causes the person to be released with full civil rights restored. Another method is a commutation, or reduction of sentence by executive order. Amnesty is a pardon applied to a group of prisoners by executive order, and it is seldom used to any great extent. The most common method for exit is by parole.

Parole

Paroles are granted by federal, state, or county boards from the various institutions. Following release from prison, the parolee from federal or state prison is placed under the supervision of a parole officer. A county jail parolee may be placed under the supervision of a probation officer. The role of the parole officer is basically the same as that of a probation officer in most cases.

The distinction between probation and parole is that in the case of parole, the individual is considered as "still in custody," and only on leave from the institution during the period of time he is on his good behavior. He lives under the threat of immediate return to prison if he does not live according to the strict rules that are prescribed for him. The conditions of parole are also similar to those for the person on probation, but the two should not be confused. Probation refers to the term spent by the individual in lieu of a term of imprisonment. Parole follows imprisonment, and is merely considered as a continuation of that prison sentence while outside the walls of the institution.

Exercises and Study Questions

1. Discuss the police "system" and the "nonsystem" concept as you and your instructor see it in your community.
2. What is the exact relationship of the Federal Bureau of Investigation to the police department in the city where you live?
3. List the state police and investigative agencies that perform law enforcement functions in your state.
4. What is the largest private police agency in the U. S.?
5. What was the purpose for the Coal and Iron Police in Pennsylvania? When and why were they disbanded?
6. What are three alternate ideas that have been suggested to relieve or reduce interforce conflicts of the several federal agencies with overlapping jurisdictions.
7. What is your opinion of the autonomy of local police departments? Should there be more, or less, local control?
8. Give at least three examples of hypothetical cases involving concurrent jurisdiction.
9. Discuss the condition known as "martial rule" and its relationship with local law enforcement agencies in the jurisdiction where it is in effect.
10. *Recommended Semester Project*: Visit or write to a state law enforcement or investigative agency in your state and request as much information as they will send you concerning its organization, jurisdiction, and operating procedures. With that information, plus what additional information you may obtain about that agency from local sources, including newspaper clippings, write a paper about that organization.

Suggested for Additional Study:

Write to each agency in which you have a special interest for further study. Many federal, state, and local agencies provide brochures on request and are eager to explain their purposes and their operation.

Smith, Bruce: *Police Systems in the United States* (2d ed.; New York: Harper and Brothers, 1960). This book explains the many police agencies throughout the country in considerable detail.

6

Basic Police Department Organization

MUNICIPAL POLICE ORGANIZATION

The United States is a republic, composed of fifty sovereign states, each with is own executive, legislative, and judicial branch of government. Operating under its own constitution, and in accordance with its own laws, each state is responsible to its own citizens and residents for providing sufficient instrumentalities of government to assure them of good order in the community, good health, and adequate protection, among other things for which the government is established. As described in Chapter 5, the primary law enforcement agency is the municipal police department, with the rural and unincorporated county areas policed by the sheriff.

With very few exceptions, the municipal police agency is directly responsible to the city government and its administrators. The elected chief of police is now a rarity, and has been replaced by the professional police administrator who is appointed as head of the department by his immediate superior. Some cities have charters that provide for a council-manager form of government, and the police chief is directly responsible to the city manager or administrator. Some cities have a commission form of government with the police chief immediately under the supervision of the police commissioner, an elected public official. Other cities require that their chief of police report directly to the mayor, and still others have a group of citizens who are appointed by the mayor to serve for a specific period of time as members of a police commission. In those cities, the police chief is directly responsible to the commission. In almost all cases, the civilian director or committee to whom the police chief reports establishes the broad general policies under which they believe the police department should be managed. They

111

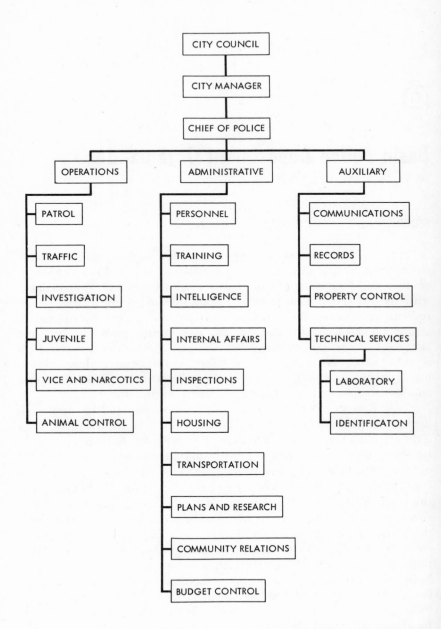

Courtesy Edward J. Allen, Chief of Police

TABLE OF ORGANIZATION, SANTA ANA, CALIFORNIA, POLICE DEPARTMENT.

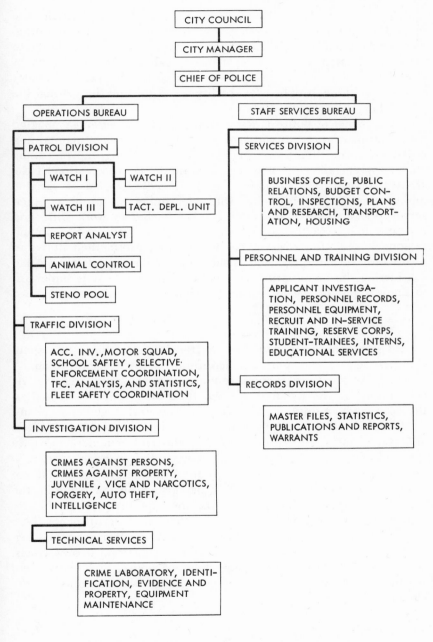

CITY COUNCIL

CITY MANAGER

CHIEF OF POLICE

OPERATIONS BUREAU

STAFF SERVICES BUREAU

PATROL DIVISION

WATCH I   WATCH II

WATCH III   TACT. DEPL. UNIT

REPORT ANALYST

ANIMAL CONTROL

STENO POOL

TRAFFIC DIVISION

ACC. INV.,MOTOR SQUAD,
SCHOOL SAFTEY , SELECTIVE·
ENFORCEMENT COORDINATION,
TFC. ANALYSIS, AND STATISTICS,
FLEET SAFETY COORDINATION

INVESTIGATION DIVISION

CRIMES AGAINST PERSONS,
CRIMES AGAINST PROPERTY,
JUVENILE , VICE AND NARCOTICS,
FORGERY, AUTO THEFT,
INTELLIGENCE

TECHNICAL SERVICES

CRIME LABORATORY, IDENTI-
FICATION, EVIDENCE AND
PROPERTY, EQUIPMENT
MAINTENANCE

SERVICES DIVISION

BUSINESS OFFICE, PUBLIC
RELATIONS, BUDGET CON-
TROL, INSPECTIONS, PLANS
AND RESEARCH, TRANSPORT-
ATION, HOUSING

PERSONNEL AND TRAINING DIVISION

APPLICANT INVESTIGA-
TION, PERSONNEL RECORDS,
PERSONNEL EQUIPMENT,
RECRUIT AND IN-SERVICE
TRAINING, RESERVE CORPS,
STUDENT-TRAINEES, INTERNS,
EDUCATIONAL SERVICES

RECORDS DIVISION

MASTER FILES, STATISTICS,
PUBLICATIONS AND REPORTS,
WARRANTS

ORGANIZATIONAL CHART OUTLINING WORK DIVISIONS DISCUSSED
IN THIS CHAPTER.

represent the people in the community and actually determine the general tenor of law enforcement in their respective communities. The chief of police is delegated the authority and responsibility to determine exactly how his department shall get the job done as efficiently and effectively as possible. He manages the department and selects those people who qualify to assist him in getting the job of law enforcement accomplished.

Each chief of police is responsible for organizing and managing his department so that it will accomplish its objectives of maintaining order, preserving life, protecting property, preventing and repressing crime, apprehending the violators, assisting in the prosecution of the accused, regulating non-criminal conduct, and a myriad of variable duties attendant to the police role. He studies his problems, then surveys the manpower and materiel that he has to work with, and proceeds to divide the work, assign the supervisors and command personnel who will carry out his orders and perform their duties in accordance with the law and regulations of the department. When considering the organization of a police department, it is important to know a few of the following principles of organization.

Organizational Plan

The organization should be separated into divisions of responsibilities and special purposes according to some logical plan. A pyramid-like structure is most common and the most effective. At the bottom of the pyramid are the functional units, composed of the people whose duties are similar and who work together as teams. These smaller units are grouped together into divisions or bureaus and placed under the leadership of sergeants and lieutenants who are the field or working leaders and the commanding officers respectively. One or more of these units are grouped into larger units and are under the leadership of the next higher person on the pyramid, the captains. In the smaller departments, the captains may be directly responsible to the chief of police. In the larger departments there are greater numbers of people working over a wider span of geography, and their pyramids may include inspectors and deputy chiefs. Some organizations have assistant chiefs of police, and when there is only one assistant chief, he serves as the chief of police in the chief's absence.

Definition of Responsibility and Authority

The lines of authority and commensurate responsibility must be defined as clearly and directly as possible. This is most frequently illustrated by means of organizational charts, some of which are quite elaborate. It is most important to remember that an organization is made up of people whose efficient interaction with other people actually make the plan work, whatever it may be.

Span of Control

Regardless of ability, knowledge, experience, or any combination of the three, there is a limit to the number of subordinates that a superior officer can effectively supervise. This is known as span of control, and the increased size of any unit will automatically necessitate an increase in the number of supervisors. Of course, the type of work involved affects the span.

One Supervisor Principle

In a police organization, as in any work situation, there must be only one person in the organization to whom each employee reports directly. There will be a series of progressively higher ranking supervisors up through the pyramid, but each in succession, and the principle should not be violated except for emergency situations. In times of emotional stress an individual will perform in such a manner that is most familiar to him. His standing in the organization in relationship to the others should be clear-cut and well known to all of the persons who have to work together. This is known as unity of command.

ORGANIZING THE DEPARTMENT

The chief of police will probably never have the desirable maximum number of personnel to provide police service for his community. His task is to take the number of personnel that he actually has at his disposal and to provide the best possible service with the tools and the people at his command. He first divides the work of his personnel into logically separated work units. One of the first considerations is to regard manpower assignments on the basis of time factors. The basic operating unit is the patrol, or uniformed division. The men and women who comprise this unit are on duty at all hours of the day and night, providing continuous service one hundred and sixty-eight hours a week, fifty-two weeks each year. Because of the nature of this unit's needs, the greatest number of personnel will be assigned to it. Depending upon the other needs of the department, additional units may also have personnel working on a similar basis, such as traffic enforcement officers and investigative personnel.

The next consideration for the chief in organizing his department is the area to be provided with service by his organization. The size of the entire jurisdiction must first be considered, then the geographical subdivisions or patrol districts each have to be adequately covered. A third consideration is the type of work to be performed by a specific unit, such as traffic or vice enforcement, juvenile control, crime follow-up investigation, record-keeping and office functions, training, and patrol. Numerous other factors are involved in the organizational plan, and they are adequately covered in the reference books and recommended study material listed at the end of this chapter. Let's take a look at the duties and responsibilities of some of the divisions of duties of the officers and civilian personnel of the average police department.

Patrol Division

This is the primary operating unit of the police department, in smaller departments, the only unit. Actually, the patrol unit provides the basic police services as the "backbone" of the organization. All other units are secondary and supplemental in nature in

Photo courtesy Chicago Police Department

POLICE MOBILITY EXTENDS TO THE CITY'S WATERWAYS AS WELL. THE CHICAGO POLICE TASK FORCE MARINE' UNIT'S SEVERAL BOATS PATROL THE RIVERS AND LAKEFRONT.

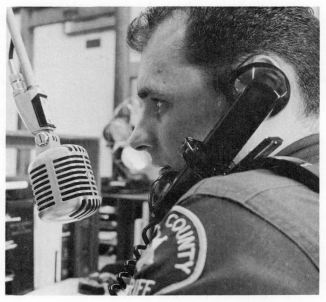

Photo Courtesy Orange County Sheriff's Department

A DEPUTY SHERIFF, PATROL DIVISION, RECEIVES THE INITIAL
COMPLAINT AND ASSIGNS A FIELD UNIT TO HANDLE THE CALL.

relationship to the basic unit. Patrol is responsible for providing continuous police service in all phases of the operation that can be performed efficiently and effectively by officers in uniform, and additional assignments in civilian clothing. The officer in civilian clothing need not be a detective, or a person assigned to what would normally be considered a "plainclothes" assignment. For example, an officer may receive information from a concerned citizen that a gambling operation is in business at one of the bars in the city. The officer reports the situation to his superior officer, who determines that the matter demands immediate attention. The supervisor may call in one or two of his men from the field who are not known to the gamblers, assign them to change into civilian clothing and sit in at the game to secure sufficient evidence for prosecution, then make the arrests.

The patrol division is primarily responsible for preservation of the peace and tranquillity of the community, and law enforcement. Additional duties of the division include (1) patrol of specific districts and observation for odd or unusual occurrences, (2) miscellaneous field services that may include rendering assistance or first aid to persons, (3) answering calls for service and help, (4) processing complaints, (5) investigation of persons or situations which concern law enforcement and crime prevention, (6) preliminary investigation of crimes and accidents, (7) collection and preservation of evidence, (8) arrest of criminal and traffic law violators, (9) testifying in court, and (10) preparation of reports.

The patrol division is comprised of patrolmen and their field supervisors, lieutenants who provide overall supervision from the office usually called the watch commander's office, and captains and higher ranking officers in the larger departments. In the medium and large police departments, usually more than half of all of the personnel may be assigned to this important operating unit.

Traffic Division

The next major operating division of a police department that participates in uniformed patrol on a city-wide and round-the-clock basis (some departments assign members of this division to work only during daytime hours when traffic is at a peak) is the traffic unit. Under the direction of a staff level officer in most departments —lieutenant or higher—the traffic division provides field service to assure a free flow of pedestrian and vehicular traffic throughout the city with a minimum of congestion and to prevent traffic accidents through traffic law enforcement.

The commander of the traffic division is responsible to the chief of police for the overall departmental accident prevention and traffic enforcement program. He compiles statistics and conducts those studies necessary to plan and implement traffic safety and accident programs. He and his staff outline the selective traffic enforcement program that the traffic specialists assigned to his division will carry out, and provide information concerning the department's traffic needs that are to be carried out by the patrol and other divisions.

The various duties of the traffic division include all or most of the following: (1) selective traffic enforcement, (2) follow-up investigation of traffic and aircraft accidents and prosecution of accident-causing offenders, (3) traffic flow control, (4) parking regulation enforcement, (5) pedestrian intersection control, (6) investigating and reporting traffic hazards to the appropriate agencies, (7) enforcement of regulations concerning buses, ambulances, and taxicabs and operators of those vehicles, (8) direction or coordination of school and bicycle safety programs, (9) traffic safety education in cooperation with various other safety agencies, and (10) cooperation with the traffic engineer in studies and recommendations concerning traffic engineering problems.

The size of the traffic division, as well as any other unit within the organization, depends upon the specific needs peculiar to each individual police department. The factors involved in determining the size of the traffic division are the number of miles of streets in the jurisdiction, the number and severity of accidents reflected in the accident records, the attitudes of the chief of police and his superiors toward the traffic problem in relation to the other needs of the department, and the degree of specialization that the chief determines the department will operate within. The larger the department, the more need there is for specialization in the various police functions, including traffic. In the smaller and medium-sized departments, it is most desirable to delegate the majority of police functions to the patrol division and to train their officers to be proficient in as great a variety of duties as possible. In a department whose chief believes in the latter philosophy, the traffic division will be comparatively smaller than in the department of a chief who believes that only a specialist can perform the job proficiently.

Investigation Division

The primary purpose of the investigation division is to conduct follow-up investigations of all crimes and related incidents—other than traffic problems—that have not been cleared or completed previously by the patrol or other divisions. Other assignments relegated to this division include a variety of investigations that require an officer who is not in uniform. Officers assigned to the patrol division may work occasionally in civilian clothing, but the officers assigned to the investigation division work in civilian clothing as a matter of routine so that they may move about inconspicuously and with some degree of anonymity.

Under the direction of a division commander who holds the rank of lieutenant or higher in most police departments, the officers of the investigation division (1) interview victims and witnesses, (2) apprehend and interrogate persons guilty of—or suspected of—violations of the criminal laws, (3) examine crime scenes, (4) secure criminal complaints and warrants of arrest, (5) testify and present evidence in court, (6) recover stolen property, (7) assist the prosecuting attorney in the courtroom presentation of criminal cases to which they have been assigned, and (8) prepare investigative and statistical reports.

Juvenile Division

The juvenile unit in a police department may be a separate division under the direction of a staff-level officer, or it may be one of the sub-divisions of the investigation division. The division of responsibilities that necessitates a juvenile unit is the category of persons to be dealt with on a regular basis—juveniles. The nature of the investigative work is no different, nor any of the other aspects, except for the different laws developed during the last fifty years or so that pertain specifically to juveniles.

Juvenile officers have the same duties and responsibilities as those listed for the officers assigned to the investigation division with the following additional duties: Under the supervision of the unit supervisor or division commander, the juvenile unit is responsible for maintaining continuity in the department's policies relative to the disposition of cases involving juveniles as victims and suspects. This is accomplished, of course, through the appropriate levels of command throughout the pyramid structure of the department. This unit maintains liaison with the juvenile court, the probation department or youth agency, the school systems in the jurisdiction, coordinating councils, and other agencies in the community directly concerned with juveniles and delinquency prevention.

The officers assigned to the juvenile unit may be assigned cases on the basis of the age of the perpetrator regardless of the type of offense, and all cases in which the victim is a juvenile. Or the case assignment may be for specific offenses, such as sex crimes, malicious mischief, and other incidents involving juveniles, such as incorrigible children and runaways. Additional duties may include assisting in community youth activities, making public appearances, and generally working with children in an effort to prevent delinquency and to encourage the children to obey the laws and respect the rights and property of other people. Their patrol duties may include inspection of places of amusement and other places where children congregate to assure the prevention and repression of unlawful or anti-social juvenile activities.

Vice and Narcotics Division

The vice and narcotics unit may be a sub-division under the investigation division in some departments, and in other departments will be found as one or two separate units in the organization. The degree of specialization depends upon the vice and narcotics problem in the community, and the value judgment of the chief of police as to how much time and energy his department can devote to these important tasks in comparison with other equally important tasks. Because of the extremely sensitive nature of the work in the vice crimes, which are directly related to the moral and ethical standards of the people who live, work, and play in his city, the chief may place the vice unit in the pyramid structure where the supervisor or commander of the unit reports directly to him. When such an arrangement is established, it is clearly pointed out that the vice unit has no supervisory authority over any other units, particularly when it involves higher ranking officers.

Primary functions of this division include the investigation and prevention of gambling, prostitution, illegal use and sale of narcotic and dangerous drugs, and other forms of vice law violations, giving particular attention to the places where commercialized vice may be conducted. Additional duties may include cooperating with the state liquor control agency—if any—in the enforcement of laws concerning the management of establishments where alcoholic beverages are sold, and other violations of the law involving the sale or possession of alcoholic beverages. Because of the secretive nature of vice law violations, the vice unit must conduct many of its investigations with the aid of undercover agents and paid informants.

Animal Control

This particular function is one that involves licensing and control of animals in the community. The employees assigned to such a detail are usually civilian non-police personnel, but they may be assigned to the Police Department under the direction of the Patrol Division for supervisory control purposes. Officers are frequently called upon to assist the animal control personnel in the performance of their duties, although this is not a basic police function.

Auxiliary and Administrative Units

The divisions of work assignments that we have discussed in the first part of this chapter are the basic operating units of a police department. Virtually all other duties are either administrative or auxiliary—or supplemental—to the operating divisions. The auxiliary functions normally include such functions as communications, records, property control, technical services, as well as the crime and identification laboratories, or any combination of those units. The administrative functions include such assignments as personnel, training, intelligence, internal affairs, inspections, housing, transportation, plans and research, community and public relations, and budget control. Let us look at the auxiliary units next.

Communications

This unit may be assigned to a separate unit commander, but in the smaller and medium sized departments will be found either as a part of the records unit or a rotating assignment under the supervision of the patrol division. This unit is responsible for supervision of all department communications activities, including fixed and mobile radio equipment, teletype, telephones, complaint desk, private board exchange (PBX), and messenger service within

Photo courtesy Chicago Police Department

CHICAGO'S STREAMLINED, MILLION-DOLLAR COMMUNICATIONS CENTER, PICTURED ABOVE, IS BASED ON A COMPLETELY NEW PRINCIPLE: DIRECT AND COMPLETE INTEGRATION OF POLICE RADIO WITH REGULAR TELEPHONE SERVICE. THE CITY IS DIVIDED INTO EIGHT RADIO COMMUNICATION ZONES. ANY CALL TO THE POLICE EMERGENCY NUMBER IS AUTOMATICALLY CHANNELED TO A DISPATCHER WHO CONTROLS SQUAD CARS ASSIGNED TO THE ZONE FROM WHICH THE CALLER IS TELEPHONING.

the department as well as between the police department and other related agencies.

Records

The records unit in an organization is the memory of the police department, and the one unit that provides an auxiliary service around which the rest of the department revolves. The functions of this unit or division include the following: (1) maintaining a central index file concerning all police incidents and activities, (2) processing and appropriate handling of incoming and outgoing correspondence, (3) providing a report reproduction service for the other divisions of the department, (4) maintaining a clerical pool for utilization by other divisions, (5) compiling statistical data, and (6) performing any other record-keeping or information service that will assure the efficient operation of the department.

Property Control

This unit is usually a section of the records division of a police department because of the record-keeping nature of the work involved. The property section is responsible for the administration and control over the procurement, storage, inventory, distribution, and maintenance of all supplies and equipment necessary to the operation of the department. It is also responsible for the custody and disposition of all property held by the department for the purposes of evidence or safekeeping.

Technical Services

The technical services unit of the police department is another auxiliary function that complements and aids the operating units of the organization. It consists primarily of the criminalistics and identification functions of the department, although some departments may have separate units for each function and assign other names to those units. The basic functions of this unit include the following: (1) scientific and chemical analysis of evidence, (2) processing and classification of fingerprints and other traces left at the crime scenes, (3) photographing and fingerprinting persons suspected of, or arrested for, the commission of crimes, and for certain government employment applicants, (4) crime scene investigations, (5) developing and printing photographs, (6) maintenance of supplies and equipment necessary to the efficient operation of these activities,

Photo courtesy Orange County Sheriff's Department

TECHNICAL SERVICE, OR LABORATORY SPECIALISTS FRE-
QUENTLY RE-VISIT THE CRIME SCENES TO COLLECT AND
PRESERVE ALL AVAILABLE EVIDENCE.

(7) serving in an advisory capacity to the other divisions to assure the proper collection and preservation of evidence and other crime and accident scene investigative duties, and (8) cooperating with the training division in the instructiton of officers in the proper procedures related to the scientific and technical services provided by this unit.

Now let us review some of the administrative functions. In the small department, most of these duties may be performed by the police chief himself, or the work may be done under his personal supervision. As the department grows, each of the divisions of work may be given divisional status under the direction of a full-time supervisor or staff-level commander.

Personnel

Some cities have a separate personnel agency or civil service board that has responsibility for the recruitment and selection of employees for all of the city departments. In the absence of such an agency in the city, the police department's personnel unit may be directly responsible for those activities. If such a city agency does exist, the police personnel unit is responsible for maintaining a close working relationship with the city agency in personnel recruitment and selection. The final selection, of course, should be the sole responsibility of the chief of police or a staff officer personally designated by the chief.

The primary duties of the personnel unit include the following: (1) investigation of the character and background of employee candidates prior to a preemployment interview, (2) maintenance of current and accurate service records on all employees of the department, (3) maintaining payroll records, (4) coordination of the department's personnel evaluation program, (5) issuance and maintenance of uniforms and personnel equipment, and (6) internal investigations into alleged misconduct of the department's employees upon complaint, and case assignment.

Training

The training unit is responsible for the general coordination of the department must be constantly working to assure both are not actually conducted under that division's direct supervision.

Photo courtesy Police Science Department, Orange Coast College

TRAINING IS A CONTINUOUS PROCESS. THE INSTRUCTOR IS DEMONSTRATING THE EFFECTIVE USE OF THE POLICE BATON.

The purpose for this requirement is to assure a maximum in uniformity of training and performance by the many employees of the department. Continuity and uniformity are essential to the effectiveness of a modern and professional police agency. The training unit of the department must be constantly working to assure both elements.

The basic functions of the training unit include the following: (1) coordination and presentation of training programs to qualify all department employees to efficiently and effectively perform their duties, (2) dissemination of training and information bulletins and instructional material to all divisions, (3) maintenance of training and educational records of employees, (4) counseling and advising employees and students in police training and related educational services, and (5) coordination of the police reserve corps (if any).

Intelligence

The purpose of this division is to perform whatever investigations as are necessary to keep the chief of police completely informed as to the movement and activities of organized criminal activities, and to prevent the existence of organized crime or organized vice activities in the city.

Inspections and Internal Affairs

The functions of this unit, or two units, is to assist the chief of police in the actual management of the department. Inspections of personnel and their activities are essential to the smoothly functioning operation of a police department. The duties of this unit include the supervision and coordination of inspection activities concerning all department personnel, equipment, and facilities. The objectives are uniformity with a minimum of confusion and duplication of effort by more than one unit within the organization. Special investigations may be assigned by the chief of police to inquire into allegations of immoral or unlawful involvement of department employees.

Housing

Maintenance and proper care of the buildings and office facilities used by the department is the responsibility of this unit.

Transportation

The officer in charge of this unit is responsible for making all necessary arrangements for transportation in cases of extradition, prescribing the mode of travel according to the circumstances. He also makes arrangements for extraditions and interstate renditions, including the processing of legal documents involved.

Plans and Research

This unit is an advisory unit which institutes such planning and conducts such research as may be directed by the chief of police or a member of his staff. The unit should make such continuous studies as may be necessary to maintain a high level of efficiency in the management of the department, and such studies may include the following: (1) administration and management procedures, (2) forms and reporting procedures, (3) crime and accident statistics analysis, (4) tactical and procedural plans, (5) manuals of procedure and regulations, (6) supplies and equipment, and (7) preparation of various surveys and reports.

Budget Control

The budget control function is handled by the chief of police or under the immediate supervision of the chief or one of his staff officers. The duties attendant to the assignment include preparation of the annual budget and its revisions, and administration of the department's fiscal matters in cooperation with the finance and purchasing departments of the city government. This is a very important function, particularly when one considers the fact that the annual budget of a city police department may be one of the largest of any public or private organization in the entire city.

Community and Public Relations

At no other time in history has there seemed to be such a tremendous interest in the duties and responsibilities of the police. The people have a right to know what their police department is doing to protect their interests and to maintain order in the community. The chief of police has a duty to keep the public informed. In order to assure a maximum of favorable results in this important activity, the chief may assign an individual or an entire division of officers to perform the function of community and public relations. The size of the unit again depends upon the size of the department and the need for the specialized work to be done.

This division is responsible for the coordination of all community and public relations activities and programs conducted by the department. The unit provides a speakers' bureau, maintains liaison with the press and other communications media, studies public opinions and attitudes regarding the activities, attitudes, and appearances of the department and its personnel. The unit serves as advisor to the chief of police in all matters related to the problem of community and public relations.

Now that we have dealt with the organizational principles and other aspects of organizing a police department, study the organizational charts, bearing in mind the basic principle that every police department is distinctly different and has its own personality. The chief of police is responsible for the most efficient operation possible with the personnel and equipment at his disposal. The true test of the effectiveness of the organization is whether the organization produces the desired results.

COUNTY SHERIFF AND RELATED COUNTY OFFICES

The county sheriff is responsible for the same law enforcement duties as the chief of police is in his jurisdiction, which usually is limited to the unincorporated areas of the county, but may include some of the cities on a contracted basis. The sheriff in some counties, particularly in the city and county of San Francisco, may have duties that include those listed below but with almost none of the duties carried out by the police department in the same jurisdiction. We will look at the expanded organization of the sheriff's department, bearing in mind that up to this point the sheriff's organization is basically the same as the average police department.

Jail Division

Although this unit was not listed as one of the basic police department divisions, some departments do maintain their own city jails. All county sheriffs are charged with the responsibility for maintaining their respective county jails, and it is most desirable for the police departments—particularly those in the county seats—to make use of the county jail to avoid duplication of effort. It is both administratively and economically sound that the distance to and from the jail consume not more than a few minutes.

The jail division is responsible for the custody and security of those persons who are held both prior to arraignment and trial, and the committed prisoners. Additional facilities, such as a jail

Photo courtesy Orange County Sheriff's Department

A SHERIFF'S RESERVE SEARCH AND RESCUE TEAM IN ACTUAL OPERATION.

ward of the county hospital, a minimum security rehabilitation center, honor ranch, or labor camp may be operated by the sheriff as part of his jail system.

Civil Division

The sheriff is bailiff of the superior court in his county, which may include many divisions in the larger counties and require a large staff of deputies. Manning the courts is just one of the branches of the civil division. Other functions of a civil division include the service and execution of legal processes and orders of the court. These include the service of warrants, the arrests of persons named on the warrants, and collection of monies attached by court order from business establishments.

Marshal and Constable

These officers serve as bailiffs in the municipal and justice courts and perform the same duties for those courts as the sheriff does for the Superior Court. Their departments are less complex and may be divided into subdivisions of what corresponds with the Civil Division of the Sheriff.

IN ADDITION TO HIS LAW ENFORCEMENT AND RELATED DUTIES
THE SHERIFF AND HIS DEPUTIES SERVE AS ATTENDANTS AND
BAILIFFS IN THE COURTS.

STATE AND FEDERAL LAW ENFORCEMENT AND INVESTIGATIVE AGENCIES

The jurisdiction of the state and federal agencies is limited in scope because of their highly specialized nature. Because of the large areas they have to cover, the divisions of the agencies are generally geographical divisions throughout the state, or the country, depending upon whether the jurisdiction is state or federal. At the headquarters of the agency, usually in the capital city, the agency may be divided into several headquarters divisions. Such divisions include records, laboratory, training, public information, administrative, and the primary operating unit by any of a variety of names. The heads of the organizations are usually appointees of the president or a governor, who serve at the pleasure of the man who appoints them. They, in turn, may appoint their immediate subordinates from outside the agency when they assume command, but in most of these organizations their division and area commanders and other personnel are career members of the organizations.

SUMMARY

Every organization is formed and operated according to a plan. The lines of authority and responsibility must be well defined, and the various supervisors and commanders must be given authority commensurate with their responsibilities so that they are empowered to carry out their directives and instructions. In each department, regardless of whether it is local, state, or federal, it is imperative that certain principles of organization be recognized and applied. These principles include span of control and unity of command, and presuppose the administrative acuity and dedication of the men who implement them. The most important factor in assuring the objectives of any organization is human relations: people working in unison toward a common goal. The administrator must maintain an esprit de corps within his organization in order that he may secure a maximum of efficiency and effectiveness.

Exercises and Study Questions

1. What is meant by a "pyramidlike" organizational structure?
2. Discuss the relationship between the chief of police, the mayor, and the city manager in a Council-Manager form of municipal government.
3. Define "span of control."
4. What is meant by "unity of command"?
5. What division of a police department is considered the "basic operating unit"?
6. In what way does the sheriff's department differ from the city police department?
7. List and discuss the basic functions of the Traffic Division.
8. What is the primary purpose of the Investigation Division?
9. Are Communications, Records, and Property Control units in a police department classified as *auxiliary* or *line* units?
10. *Recommended Semester Project*: Draw an organizational chart for the police department of the city in which you live. Write an accompanying paper in which you explain the duties and responsibilities of each of the many units, and their relationships with each other.

Suggested for Additional Study:

Municipal Police Administration (5th ed.; Chicago: International City Managers' Association, 1961). A text designed for an upper class level college course in police administration, the book explains the general operation and management of a police department.

Newman, W. H. *Administrative Organization, The Techniques of Organization and Management* (2d ed.; Englewood Cliffs, N.J.: Prentice-Hall, Inc., 1965). This is a very comprehensive book that explains in detail the techniques and principles of organizational management. It deals with the concepts of planning, organizing, assembling resources, supervising, and controlling an organization.

Wilson, O. W. *Police Administration* (2d ed.; New York: McGraw-Hill Book Company, Inc., 1963). Superintendent Wilson of the Chicago Police Department has considerable experience both as a police administrator and as a professor of criminology. His book reflects his intimate knowledge of the management principles and practices gained through his years as a practitioner and academician.

PART **4**

OVERVIEW OF THE PRIMARY POLICE FUNCTIONS

7

Protective and Preventive Services of Patrol

INTRODUCTION

The patrol division is *the* police department. A bold statement? What is your first thought when someone mentions the word "policeman"? Is it a mental image of a distinguished appearing gentleman in a grey flannel suit sitting behind an executive desk? Is it an athletic young man standing in front of an enlarger in a photographic darkroom? Do you think of two or three collegiate-looking men sitting around a conference table? My guess is that you picture none of these, who include a chief of police, an identification technician, and some investigators working out the details of a criminal investigation. Your "policeman" is probably a young man with his jaw firmly set into either a pleasant smile or an inscrutable expression. He is probably issuing a traffic citation to you or one of your friends, or he is sitting in a black and white police car having his coffee break at a local drive-in. He is on foot or in a car somewhere in your city performing any of a number of functions that you have seen policemen perform. And your "policeman" is also probably in uniform. To most people in the community the policeman in the patrol division is *the* police department, and all of the other members of the organization are mere names and faces in the dim background. That is the way it should be so that the people in the community sense omnipresence, but not oppressive dominance, by the uniformed policeman.

The patrol policeman is assigned to one of several different work shifts that span the entire day and the entire calendar in such a way that the police department is never off duty. Days off, holidays, vacations, and other matters that take the man off the street for any period of time for more than a few minutes are scheduled so that there is police coverage in the city without interruption. One day several

Photo courtesy Orange County Sheriff's Department

POLICE ON PATROL.

years ago I overheard a desk officer answer the telephone with the usual "Police Department," followed by the smiling statement, "Oh, that's all right, ma'am. We had to get up for another call a few minutes ago." When I asked about his improper response, he explained that an extremely nice old lady had been so apologetic when she asked that the desk officer send someone around to check around the outside of her house because she thought she had heard a burglar. She had said, "I'm sure sorry to get you out of bed, officer, but I think someone is prowling around outside my house." One of the primary objectives of the patrol division and its officers is to dispel any belief that there are times when the police are not on the job. The knowledge that there is a police patrol on the streets at all times gives comfort to those who wish to be protected and generates a feeling of uneasiness and fear of apprehension for those people who violate the laws.

THE PATROL FUNCTION

Text books and course outlines on patrol techniques and principles list almost endless duties and responsibilities of the police

officer on patrol in his district, or "beat." As the real backbone of
the organization, the patrol officer actually performs all of the primary
and basic functions required of the police department. His objectives
are synonymous with the objectives of the police department, and
include crime prevention and repression, maintenance of order, protection of lives and property, identification and apprehension of
criminal and traffic law violators, and recovery of property. A list of
the officer's duties includes the following:

1. Patrol and observation.
2. Prevention and repression of unlawful activities.
3. Attendance at public gatherings to assure order.
4. Public safety services.
5. Inspections on patrol.
6. Answering calls for service and assistance.
7. Reporting disruption of utilities.
8. Providing information services.
9. Identification and arrest of violators.
10. Developing contacts with residents and businessmen.
11. Providing crime prevention advice to merchants and busi-
    nessmen.
12. Recruitment and development of informants.
13. Protection of crime scenes.
14. Collection and preservation of evidence.
15. Public and community relations.
16. Investigations of crimes and accidents.
17. Preparing reports.
18. Testifying in court.

Before we take a closer look at the officer's duties as listed, let's
consider the average day of a radio car officer so that his many duties
may be considered in their proper perspective. The policeman is
seldom able to develop any work patterns, but is more likely to be
so flexible that he can change from one thought and activity as the
circumstances of his duty requirements and various incidents calling
for his attention occur.

To illustrate, the officer reports to headquarters approximately
a half hour before his duty time to change into uniform and to polish
his leather accouterments prior to roll call and inspection. He reports
to roll call for a half hour of briefing, training, discussion of the
previous day's activities, and his duty assignment for the day. Today,
he is assigned to a one-man unit in a district that contains one of the

city's main streets, an industrial area, small businesses, and a residential area. During the roll call training for the day, the hero of this story learns that the perennial problem of report writing is causing some consternation for the "brass" and the sergeant runs through the basic report writing steps for his sixth time this month. Roll call is over at 11:30 p.m. and his day starts.

After roll call, the officer checks out the keys to his unit, inspects the unit and fills the tank with gas, and at the same time discusses conditions in his district with the officer preceding him in that district who is now going off duty. Our man no sooner calls in that he is on the air than he is dispatched to a traffic accident. En route to the accident scene he observes a strange car parked in the lot beside one of the drugstores in his district. He makes a mental note to check the car out later, because burglars have been active around that particular part of town. The officer arrives at the accident scene and spends the next twenty minutes sifting the facts from the self-serving statements of both drivers, the "I didn't see-its" of the witnesses, and the evidence at the scene. He leaves the scene and returns to the drugstore. The car is gone. He checks the building and then completes his accident report under the street light.

The radio begins to get busy and for the next few hours, our hero's day continues: . . . juvenile disturbance . . . a field interview of two strangers to the district . . . checked O. K. . . . burglar alarm . . . just the wind . . . a disturbance in a bar . . . an argument over shuffleboard . . . patrol a couple minutes . . . phone in reports . . . family fight . . . man came home drunk and had spent week's wages . . . a shame, good wages and an orange crate in the dining room with a broken window—and all those undernourished kids . . . a drunk driver, field sobriety test, into the station for breathalyzer, then to jail for booking . . . to station for reports, but interrupted to check out a man in a building . . . turned out to be a cat . . . back to station and reports . . . lunch at a coffee shop while listening to a friendly shoe salesman who likes policemen after about six highballs and now sobering up . . . check residential area . . . stake-out in a used car lot . . . several thefts in past few months . . . back to the drug store for another check . . . patrol district . . . check abandoned car . . . traffic citation for stop sign . . . field contact with sergeant . . . discussed reports, base-ball, the kids, recent burglaries . . . patrol district . . . follow-up another unit on a car stop . . . final sweep through district . . . another ticket . . . person loitering near school . . . gone after ticket written . . . back to station but dispatched to handle a vending machine theft.

After completing the final investigation, our hero returns to the station to check in his unit, to complete his reports, fill out portions of his daily log that he skipped out in the field, then back to the locker room for his civilian clothes, and he is finally ready to go home . . . or court. Another day has been completed, and the next day will be more of something different rather than more of the same. The day is hectic, unrewarding, nothing seems to have really been worked through to completion, but the officer is proud to be a part of the scene. There is excitement, interest, monotony, disappointment, work, and a little of a hundred more factors that make up the work of a policeman.

The list of a policeman's duties is by no means complete, but it does cover the majority of duties that comprise the policeman's fundamental responsibilities. Let's take a look at these duties in greater detail.

Patrol and Observation

The policeman is trained to assess quickly the various situations on his beat, or district, such as unusual working hours and habits of the people, so that he may determine what is normal for that district. He then looks for the abnormal, or the unusual situations that occur, and he takes whatever action he deems necessary. He looks for people who act in a suspicious manner, doors and windows that are open or broken, automobiles that do not seem to belong where he observes them, and thousands of other items and incidents that the untrained individual would probably not even notice. The patrol routine is actually a deliberate "non-routine," and the officer attempts to devote sufficient attention to all sections of his beat to best accomplish the objectives of police patrol.

Prevention and Repression of Unlawful Activities

The functions involved in the prevention and repression of crime are actually the most difficult to categorize. By preventing crime, the officer is attempting to eliminate a person's desire to commit a criminal act. This may be accomplished merely by a friendly contact with a young and impressionable child whose behavior patterns are still in the formulative stage. A lecture or stern warning may apply to other contacts, and mere presence of the officer in some situations may cause some persons to change their minds about committing criminal offenses. The latter situation may more appropriately be classified in the category of a crime that has been repressed. Crime repression is accomplished by the officer when he reduces or eliminates the opportunity for individuals to commit criminal acts. He does nothing to change the intentions or behavior patterns of the offender, but at least he postpones the occurrence of the crime. The optimum situation in the community, of course, is to maintain such an effective police patrol that crime is repressed so successfully that the overall crime rates are reduced appreciably.

Attendance at Public Gatherings

The role of the police officer at public gatherings is to make his presence known so that everyone present may be safe from violence or disorder, and have the knowledge that the officer will assure his freedom to assemble and speak freely in accordance with the provisions of the Constitution. The officer looks for thieves and pickpockets, shoplifters, and sex offenders who are attracted to crowds. He renders first aid and crime prevention services to all of the people who need his services. His role is not to control the gathering, but to help the people control themselves.

Public Safety Services

When some people need assistance of any type, they call for the police. They know that their request will probably not be denied and that there will be no charge for the service. Officers are frequently called upon to render first aid, to help arrange for care of the sick, the injured, and elderly or very young persons who are lost or in need of some kind of help. Although many jurisdictions have full time personnel who are involved in animal control, policemen are frequently called upon to care humanely for injured, vicious, or stray animals. Destitute persons are steered to the appropriate welfare and charity organizations. Because they are continuously on patrol, policemen are responsible for discovering fires and fire hazards and reporting them to the fire department. Violations of licensing and building codes and other safety laws are brought to the attention of the police, and the officers report those violations to the appropriate agencies, sometimes following extensive investigations. Health and safety of the community are the official concern of the police; therefore, violations of health laws or unsanitary conditions observed in the officer's district will be reduced to reports which the officer forwards to the concerned agency. Other public service functions that involve the policemen are a variety of rescue and emergency assistance situations that call for immediate and capable assistance.

Inspections on Patrol

Inspections for the purpose of security against criminal acts and for fire safety are a routine part of the policeman's list of duties. He inspects business and alcoholic beverage control licenses, public places where women and children congregate, and he inspects residences while people are away on vacation. Under different situations and at different times, the policeman may actually conduct inspections for virtually all other public—and some private—agencies, including the boards and departments of fire, health, street, park, planning, public works, recreation, license, building, and school.

Answering Calls

Whenever a person calls for information, assistance, or some type of public service and he does not know who else to call, chances are that he will probably call the police. Referrals are made when possible, and officers are assigned when the police may assist. The wide variety of calls include suicides, deaths, mentally and emotionally ill persons, childbirth, neighborhood and family disturbances, fires, explosions, floods, other catastrophes, lost and found property, missing persons, runaway children, and barking dogs.

Reporting Disruption of Utilities

Health and safety hazards may be great when utilities are out, and the police officers who discover such disruptions quickly forward the information to the utility companies concerned. Power failures may interfere with the operation of iron lungs, lights in operating rooms, special blood purifiers, and other emergency equipment in addition to thousands of freezers containing tons of perishable foods and the convenience of electric lights in the many homes affected. Leaking or broken water mains may make it impossible for the fire department to extinguish a fire. Fallen wires may result in electrocution or disruption of telephone service.

Information Services

To the tourist, the policeman on the beat is the direct representative of the government and the people of the community. They expect him to provide them with information such as the name of a good restaurant, an all-night drug store, a respectable bar, the distance to the next city and the shortest route to get there; where one

TWO SUSPECTS ARE BEING TAKEN INTO CUSTODY.

can ski, fish, swim, skate; where one can find a certain magazine or newspaper, a special blend of tobacco, and other bits of information in addition to the topography, geography, history, and personality of the community itself.

Identification and Arrest of Law Violators

The policeman in a municipal or county law enforcement agency is responsible for the enforcement of literally thousands of criminal laws that may be found in dozens of code books, such as Penal, Vehicle, Health and Safety, Business and Professions, Education, Fish and Game, Harbor and Navigation, Military and Veterans, and numerous others. The patrol policeman is generally charged with responsibility for arresting and citing for all of them, as opposed to the specialist, who may be required to concentrate on only a specific code book or set of laws. The officer must know the laws, what constitutes the elements of each offense, and what legal and constitutional considerations are involved in the contact with the offender and his arrest.

Developing Contacts

The businessmen, the residents, and the passersby in the officer's district are primarily law-abiding and God-fearing people who wish to know the laws so that they may obey them. The officer should make a deliberate effort to introduce himself to as many people as he can so that he may establish a rapport with them. He should explain the laws and answer any questions they may have about the functions and jurisdiction of the police department. He should advise them on how they may assist the police and how they may most effectively protect themselves against vandalism, theft, or any other type of crime. He should go into the business establishments and advise them on how they may render their places more burglar- and robberproof. He may suggest more night lighting, burglar alarms, better locks, and other devices that tend to discourage the amateur criminal. He may also develop future informants for situations when he may need assistance in the case of later crimes. The officer on patrol is the one man who is most frequently evaluated by the residents and businessmen in the community. He must be constantly mindful of the public relations aspect of his job.

Protection of Crime Scenes

In the majority of crimes, it is imperative that the crime scene be protected from contamination so that evidence may be collected, photographs taken, and the investigation conducted with a minimum of interference from persons who are not directly involved in the investigation. The field policeman is usually the first person on the scene. It is his duty to ascertain if a crime had, in fact, been committed and to immediately protect the scene and preserve it in the same state as when he found it, thereby assuring the most desirable conditions for the investigation. In some departments, particularly the small ones and the *(progressive)* medium sized departments, the policeman who discovers the crime may conduct the actual investigation himself.

Collection and Preservation of Evidence

The very large police agency usually employs a staff of identification and laboratory specialists whose sole duty it is to collect, catalogue, evaluate, analyze, and preserve evidence, and then to present it in court when the person responsible is prosecuted. In some departments, the officer who discovers the crime and/or in whose district it was committed is responsible for the complete investigation which includes the collection and preservation of evidence. He is responsible for forwarding it to the laboratory for study and arranging for its presentation in court. Some departments send selected officers to a short specialized training course for crime and accident scene investi-

Photo courtesy Police Science Department, Orange Coast College

MANY POLICE DEPARTMENTS UTILIZE A "C S I" SYSTEM OF
ASSIGNING PATROL OFFICERS WITH ADDITIONAL TRAINING
AND EQUIPMENT TO PERFORM THE INITIAL CRIME SCENE
INVESTIGATION. IN A "CLASSROOM" TWO OFFICERS ARE
LEARNING THE TECHNIQUES OF BURGLARY INVESTIGATION.

gation. They learn the fundamentals of identification and laboratory
work, and are specifically trained in photography, dusting and lifting
latent fingerprints, searching for and carefully collecting evidence,
and are called away from their normal patrol duties to perform the
crime and accident scene investigations for which they are trained.
The individual proficiency of some of these officers assigned as "CSI
men" (crime-accident scene investigators), or their lack of proficiency
is usually the determining factor as to whether the utilization of such
a system is effective.

Police and Community Relations

Every individual officer is a public relations expert, or he should
be. It is the responsibility of the officer to go out into his district
and to communicate with them on a continual and man-to-man basis.
He should know his district and the people in it as well as he knows
his own home and most of the members of his family, except, of
course, his immediate family. He is practicing public and community

Photo courtesy Anaheim Police Department

AN IDENTIFICATION TECHNICIAN CONTINUES THE TASK OF
COLLECTION AND PRESERVATION OF EVIDENCE AT A CRIME
SCENE.

relations in his district. The responsibility is not the sole duty of the chief of police and there are certain specifically assigned officers with a title that denotes them as public and community relations experts. The officer is responsible for identifying and getting to know the leaders in each neighborhood. He should develop them as cooperative informants on the lawful and unlawful activities in the community. The officer who develops acquaintances with the people in the community who wield the actual power by virtue of their personal or political attributes will often be in a position to know through such acquaintances the temper and attitude of the people in that community. The officer must not involve himself directly in the politics of the community because then he could not perform his duties with maximum objectivity, but he should be intimately aware of the social and political activities in his district. Armed with such knowledge, the officer may then direct his own efforts toward impressing the leaders in the community with his own efficiency and impartiality and that of his department, and he may keep his chief of police informed through the proper levels of supervision as to the department's needs with respect to public and community relations within his district, and possibly throughout the city. Rapport with the community is the key to successful performance of the department in the area of community relations.

Preparing Reports

Although sometimes overlooked in the overall appraisal of the various duties of the policeman, report writing is one of the most important aspects of the work. The officer who performs well in the field but cannot adequately express himself when preparing a report of his performance will have considerable difficulty in convincing his superiors that his performance was any better than his inferior report. The officer must develop the skill to translate his actions and observations into written reports, because virtually every action he takes is ultimately committed to a report in one form or other. Reports are used as the basis for most prosecutions and administrative actions. The morning after a major crime involving the spectacular arrest of the suspect is usually when the prosecuting attorney reviews the reports and plans his course of action for the prosecution. He does not have the advantage of having been at the scene at the time, and will plan his strategy and base his opinions and conclusions about the case upon what he reads in the pages before him. It is imperative that all

Photo courtesy Anaheim Police Department

THE POLICE OFFICER IS A GOODWILL AMBASSADOR FOR HIS COMMUNITY. A TOURIST RECEIVES DIRECTIONS.

of the relevant facts and significant information be accurately re-counted in the report. Commendations are likewise based upon the information presented in reports, as is the meting out of disciplinary action.

Testifying in Court

The ultimate objective in any investigation and arrest is the successful prosecution of the responsible party. Without this culmina-tion of the case, the rest of the activity relative to the case is for naught. The officer rounds out his other good work in the field, fol-lowed by his accurate and complete reports, by presenting himself in court as an objective observer and fairly and impartially testifying and presenting the evidence in the case without prejudice.

INVESTIGATION ON PATROL

Investigations on patrol consume a considerable portion of the policeman's time. There are hundreds of different types of investiga-tions, but let's review just a few.

Traffic Accident Investigation

When the officer approaches the scene of an accident his first action is usually to park in such a way with his automobile displayed strategically so as to protect the people and the automobiles at the scene. He then looks after the welfare of the victims by giving first aid and calling for ambulances or rescue services when necessary. Following the emergency services, the officer then conducts his investi-gation. He locates drivers and witnesses and questions them to glean as much information about the accident as possible. He then inspects the accident scene and collects all relevant evidence. His responsibility is to sift through all the information and evidence and to determine what actually happened at the time leading up to and including the accident. The purpose of the investigation is to determine the cause so as to prevent future accidents, to prosecute persons criminally re-sponsible, and to provide accurate information for follow-up action by the persons involved and their representatives.

Vice Violations

Vice laws involve the social mores of a community, the morals of the people involved and the people who investigate, enforce, pass judgment on, and mete out punishment for such violations. Because of the social significance of vice law violations, they are carried out clandestinely and elaborate precautions are frequently taken to avoid discovery and apprehension. Because of the difficulty in conducting vice law violations, specialists in civilian clothing are usually assigned. Nevertheless, the patrol officers are responsible for all criminal activities on their beats and should be on the alert for any activity that signals the possibility of a vice operation. They look for unusual activities at certain business establishments and homes in the city and report such actions to the specialists, sometimes receiving the assignment to assist in the follow-up investigation of the situation because of their knowledge of the locale or the people involved. The patrol officers are responsible for seeking out and appropriately handling law violations involving liquor laws, gambling, prostitution, narcotics, and dangerous drugs.

Stolen Automobiles

Just the taking of a report of an alleged stolen automobile is not sufficient. Many other factors may be involved in the taking of an automobile. A late payment may cause a repossession by an overly defensive lender; the car may have been involved in a hit and run accident, and the driver responsible may attempt to cover his crime by committing another crime of making a false report to the police. The automobile may have been borrowed and kept a little longer than promised, or the complaint may be made for spite or some other emotional reason. And then there is the automobile that is actually stolen. This is the case in the majority of reported thefts, but a thorough investigation is conducted by the patrol officer to eliminate all the other possibilities in addition to actually investigating the theft and attempting to locate the automobile.

Burglaries, Robberies, and Other Property Offenses

The patrol officer is almost always the first policeman to arrive at the scene of the crime, and it is not unusual for him to actually reach the scene of the crime during or immediately following the commission of the crime. When he arrives, the evidence is fresh and uncontaminated, or at least more so than at any later time during the investigation. The officer should immediately quarantine—or seal off from curious spectators—the place where the crime occurred and its immediate surroundings. Footprints in the soil outside a building or in the very thin film of fine dust on a tile floor are invaluable evidence when found, but once obliterated are lost forever. The policeman who is first to arrive on the scene may handle the entire investigation himself, or other policemen who are especially trained for crime scene investigation may assist him. His investigation will include the location and questioning of victims and witnesses; the preservation, examination, collection, and evaluation of evidence. He may also be required to take photographs and draw sketches and diagrams.

Assaults, Sex Crimes, and Other Crimes Against Persons

There is physical evidence to preserve and collect in crimes against persons the same as in cases of crimes against property. But there is the additional responsibility of administering first aid and providing for medical assistance, and providing for the future protection of the victim against his or her attacker. The questioning of victims and witnesses is not merely the taking of information verbatim and accepting it at its face value. Statements may be confused, incomplete, erroneous, exaggerated, or even completely false. It is the officer's duty to ferret out the facts and to reconstruct the crime as it actually happened.

Investigation of Death

The determination as to whether death has actually occurred when one encounters a suspected dead body is imperative. This is the first duty of the patrol officer who arrives at the scene. He must never assume that a person is deceased without utilizing his training and experience and investigating, then directing his efforts toward preserving the life if the person is not known to be dead. The officer calls for the expert coroner or medical examiner to make the final determination, but he knows how to recognize the positive signs of death. He handles every death investigation as a criminal homicide in the absence of any proof that the death was accidental or from natural causes or other than the criminal act of another person.

Beggars and Solicitors

Although they should not be considered categorically the same because of the distinction between their purposes for being where they are located by the policeman, both of these people should be contacted by the officer to determine their purposes for being where they are. People who go from door to door to sell their products or to solicit contributions for a charitable cause are regulated by local and state ordinances, or they may be prohibited altogether. Beggars are a nuisance and are violating the law in virtually all jurisdictions when they solicit people for hand-outs. Many of the former category have legitimate reasons for their presence in a certain neighborhood, but among the people the officer will contact are some thieves, confidence men, child molesters, residence burglars, and petty criminals.

The policeman will investigate thousands of incidents and situations, and in the majority of cases he will determine that no criminal activity is taking place. But he will not know without investigating. In addition to those already discussed, some additional situations that the officer will investigate include family and neighborhood quarrels to distinguish between criminal and civil wrongs, fires to determine whether arson is the cause, sales and promotional schemes to ascertain whether there is criminal fraud involved, and barking dogs to determine if the dog is just lonely or if he is keeping company with a burglar or prowler. Attractive nuisances, such as open factory buildings, lofts, silos, unattended swimming pools, abandoned wells and mines, holes, and any other object or condition that attracts children must be investigated and the owner contacted for advice on how he may correct the situation. The officer must be suspicious, but he must be able to handle each situation he encounters with such skill that he may arrest the criminal violator, or make his contact with the non-violator majority both inoffensive and conducive to future friendliness and cooperativeness.

THE FIELD INTERVIEW

Second only to the traffic citation, one of the police procedures that is most frequently misunderstood by both critics and friends of the police is the field interview. Various people throughout the community have referred to the procedure as nosiness, harrassment, intimidation, "Gestapo-like," and degrading. Although the field interview procedure could quite easily be misused by overzealous policemen, and I am sure it has been, it is actually one of the most essential tools that the policeman must use if he is to accomplish the protection of life and property. Let's take a look at the procedure and then decide upon its value to the police and the people alike.

Each police officer who is assigned to patrol a prescribed beat, or district, is responsible for the safety of the people and the property within that area. He is expected by his superior officers to use every possible legal and reasonable method that he can to keep the district free of crime, and to arrest those who violate the law. He must get to know the people who live and move about in the district during his tour of duty, and become familiar with the nature of their business. He learns and gets the feel of the normality of his district so that he is then able to determine which of those people and occurrences are out of the ordinary. He can accomplish that part of his job only when he frequently contacts the people he meets and asks them questions as to their identity and the nature of their business.

On a typical routine evening tour of duty a policeman may observe many things that he inquires into. Along about eleven-thirty after all the stores have been closed for the night the officer may see two men between the shelves in an auto supply store who appear to be taking inventory, or a man wearing coveralls crawling underneath an automobile in a closed service station just as the beam from the headlights of the police car turn the corner. A couple of other scenes may be enacted under his watchful eyes, such as two men sitting in a parked automobile in a lover's lane, or an elderly gentleman fumbling with the door lock on his car. Every one of the scenes I have described may be perfectly legitimate, but let's take another look. All four situations were actually encountered by police officers who performed their jobs properly and contacted those people for field interviews. The two men in the auto supply store were actually ex-employees who were stealing merchandise. The man in coveralls under the car was actually the owner who was catching up on some of his work before going home. The two men in lover's lane were addicts taking an injection of heroin, and the fumbling old gentleman was a bank executive who had had too much to drink to operate a motor vehicle, but not quite enough to be booked as a drunk. The officer persuaded him to have a couple of cups of coffee.

Whenever an officer observes any activity, such as those we have just discussed, he merely stops the people who are involved and asks them enough questions so that his curiosity is satisfied and he is convinced that there is truly nothing amiss, although it may have appeared so at first glance. He fills out a field interview card, writing down the name, physical description, and other personal information about the person he interviews. After a brief interview, the contact is over and the officer and the persons contacted go about their business. Of course, there are some exceptions, which include those people who have been reported as wanted criminals, missing juveniles, and even those who are actually in the process of committing crimes when contacted by the policemen. There has been no inconvenience or loss of dignity to the people contacted, just a loss of a few minutes of their time, and a pleasant chat with some of the men who are dedicated to the task of protecting their lives. Juveniles have been warned about the curfew laws, potential victims of serious crimes advised to be on guard against criminals at large, business owners reminded that their property is being watched while they are away. Only the known or suspected criminal is arrested or harrassed. If a convicted burglar is interviewed in a place where numerous burglaries have been committed in the past and the circumstances lead a policeman to believe that the burglar's intentions are criminal, the policeman is performing a service to both the burglar and the property owners by telling the burglar to leave the area or to be considered a strong suspect in the event that any burglaries are later discovered in that particular area.

Once the officer completes his tour of duty and turns in his field interview cards, the work that he has done continues to prove worthwhile. The cards are placed in a master index file and retained for several years. Along with the thousands of other cards that go into the same file, the field interview card serves many purposes. Wanted criminals and missing persons are located as a result of the descriptions of those persons and their automobiles. They are frequently contacted by the policemen when they are in the company of friends and relatives, who may later attempt to harbor them, or who can provide leads to the investigating officers as to their whereabouts. There are many other valuable uses for the field interview (FI) cards, which often provide a later address than one given in the phone book. A long lost relative from the East may be hopelessly searching for a member of his family in Southern California. FI cards can help in a situation, or they may locate a girl friend harboring an escaped convict.

In spite of any criticism and inconvenience the field interview program may produce, it is apparent that we must continue to utilize it. The process is intrinsic to the "police process" of protecting life and property. We only hope that the people and the courts continue to see it in the same way.

Exercises and Study Questions

1. List and discuss the Patrol Division's basic duties.
2. Make a personal contact with a policeman and ask him to recount for you a typical work day.
3. Describe the "patrol and observation" aspect of the patrol officer's duty.
4. What is meant by crime *prevention?*

5. What is meant by crime *repression?*

6. Discuss the principal role of the policeman at the scene of a public gathering.

7. What is the purpose for inspections on patrol?

8. Discuss the role of the individual policeman in public and community relations projects and activities of a police department.

9. Discuss the field interview process as utilized by police patrol. What is your opinion as to its value to modern law enforcement?

10. *Recommended Semester Project:* Request permission from the chief of your local police department to review the daily logs of several patrol officers and to interview at least three officers in person. From your research, prepare a job analysis for the patrol policeman.

Suggested for Additional Study:

Bristow, A. P. *Field Interrogation* (2d ed.; Springfield, Ill.: Thomas, 1967). Professor Bristow of California State College at Los Angeles, a former sergeant for the sheriff of Los Angeles County, has compiled the most complete handbook on this most valuable police procedure.

Chapman, S. G. *Police Patrol Readings* (Springfield, Ill.: Thomas, 1964). A carefully compiled collection of contemporary writings on a wide variety of subjects related to police patrol techniques and concepts.

Holcomb, R. L. *Police Patrol* (Springfield, Ill.: Thomas, 1964). A concise book that covers the primary police patrol functions.

8

The Investigation of Crime

INTRODUCTION

The investigation of crime is one of the basic police functions. The patrol officers are usually delegated the responsibility for the initial phases of the investigation, and in some cases they may carry the case through to its conclusion when they are successful in completing the investigation, and arresting the person responsible for the crime. As noted in Chapter 7, there is a point in the initial investigation where it seems logical for the patrol officer to discontinue his work on the case and for a specialist to take it up. Actually, in many investigations, the efforts of the patrol officer and the follow-up investigator will dovetail. The initial investigation will be completed, and reports in preparation, while the investigator is still on the scene reviewing the case with the victims and witnesses, inspecting the scene of the crime, and mapping out his plan of action.

The investigation division officers may be officers who have received promotions to detective status, or they may have been assigned as specialists by virtue of assignment rather than any special talent. The latter situation is the case in the police department that attempts to develop all of its officers as "generalists" rather than "specialists" and rotates them throughout the various divisions before they ultimately return to the patrol division as senior officers and supervisors. The officers assigned to this division are responsible for follow-up investigations of all crimes and related incidents that are either not cleared by the patrol or another division, or that require additional attention before they can be classified as cleared or closed.

The patrol officers are usually held accountable for the prevention and repression of crimes and other preventable incidents in their respective districts, but because of their responsibilities for main-

Photo courtesy Orange County Sheriff's Department

THE INVESTIGATION IN PROGRESS.

taining a constant patrol in their districts, they should not be responsible for the ultimate clearance of the crimes that do occur in their districts. The clearance responsibility is justifiably that of the investigation or detective division officers. The investigative duties include interviewing victims and witnesses, apprehending and interrogating suspected offenders and the guilty, examining the crime scene, recovering stolen property, securing criminal complaints and warrants for searches and arrests, preparing reports and statistical data, presenting evidence, and testifying in court.

THE FOLLOW-UP INVESTIGATION

The follow-up investigation may commence the day after the initial inquiry, or immediately following the initial report of the incident to the police, or it may begin at any point that time and circumstances permit or demand. Two of the first phases of the follow-up investigation are to recontact the victim and to revisit the scene of the crime. The victim may have additional information concerning the offense, and it is also a good idea from a public relations standpoint not only to commence the investigation immediately but also to advise the victim that prompt action is being taken on the case. Some departments require that their investigators make their recontacts within a maximum of four or five days following the initial crime report. Additional contacts will be made with the victim as the investigation progresses, and they may be required at the end of thirty or sixty days—even though there may be no progress—just to let the victim know that the police are looking after his interests.

The ultimate goal of every investigation is to solve the case and to prosecute the offender. The national average of crime clearances may be matched or exceeded by a particular police department, but even though the rate for one type of crime may be only 25 percent the clearance goal should be 100 percent. It will be virtually impossible to attain such a perfect record, but there should be a continuing effort to improve the rate.

Witnesses previously questioned by the patrol officer may have additional information after the initial shock and excitement of the circumstances surrounding the crime. Additional witnesses must be found and questioned for any knowledge they may have about the crime or any circumstances related to it. By reexamining the scene of the crime it is sometimes possible for the investigating officer to discover evidence or certain bits of information that may have been missed before.

Informants can sometimes provide valuable information about the identity of persons responsible for certain crimes, and for the location of contraband. A good investigator devotes some of his time and efforts to developing reliable informants who help him clear his cases. Some investigators hold the view that a good investigator is only as good as his informants.

When the investigator locates the contraband or the suspect— or both—he then secures warrants for search and arrest and follows up with the search and/or arrest. When he recovers stolen property or other contraband, the investigator arranges for its proper storage and later presentation in court as evidence for the prosecution of the persons accused of the crime.

A very essential part of the follow-up investigation is the exhaustive process of searching various files that are available to the investigator. Millions of fingerprints and criminal records are filed at the headquarters of the Federal Bureau of Investigation, and are available to any police agency that requests the information. Various state bureaus of records and statistics maintain crime and arrest files, and the local police departments all maintain their own files. The possibilities for finding crime suspects to match specific offenses without going beyond the records room are extremely good. Nearly all police agencies of any size maintain a central alphabetical index on persons and places that have ever been listed in the department's reports. Other files may be maintained on the locations in the city where specific types of crimes have occurred, stolen objects and pawned objects both filed by name and type of object, date and time of crime occurrence, and separate files on reported crimes by type and further separated into solved and unsolved categories. Access to these various files, and dissemination of the information they contain, is accomplished by means of teletype and various communications media that provides instant access and exchange with the aid of electronic data processing systems.

The Modus Operandi File

Many criminal records files include a *modus operandi* file. All people are creatures of habit, and the criminal offender is no exception. The burglar may always enter a house by the same type of sliding glass door, an armed robber may repeat the same sentence or deliver the same message on a piece of paper when he commits his holdup. Some thieves seek out specific objects, such as cash or tires, or hubcaps, or a specific type of narcotic. Some people leave trademarks of their personal touch to their crime, such as using only wooden matches instead of book matches. They may always leave their tools on the job so that they will not be caught carrying them by field officers. There is a wide variety of characteristics which provide the investigating officer with sufficient information about the criminals and their crimes to lead to their apprehension. All of these facts that add up to the identification of specific individuals are known as a criminal's *modus operandi,* or "method of operation" (MO). By maintaining an MO file on all crimes reported and later identifying the guilty parties, it is possible to identify the same culprits if they repeat the same offenses. Arrest statistics show that habitual criminals usually do develop behavior patterns and that when they do repeat their crimes, they usually follow the same *modus operandi.* They may vary their MO, believing it caused their arrest in the earlier crime, but they can frequently be identified by other elements of their crimes.

Assignment of Investigators

Investigator assignments are usually on the basis of types of crimes or similarity of duties. The crimes against persons detail will be principally responsible for sex and assault cases. Robbery will be an added classification delegated to the CAP detail because of the similarity of investigative duties, although it is technically classified as a property offense, the object of the robbery being some object of value. Auto thefts are committed quite frequently. One factor involved in the auto theft that plagues the officers who have to recover them is that the great majority of cars stolen are left unattended with the door unlocked and the keys in the ignition lock.

Street crimes, such as theft of auto parts and theft from auto, usually involve another detail of investigators. Although there are many adult professional thieves committing this type of offense, they are generally known as crimes of opportunity and approximately one-half of all persons arrested as "car clouts" are under the age of eighteen. Checks and worthless documents require a large portion of the investigation division man-days. Forging or passing worthless papers and documents is a more sophisticated type of crime that is committed by the elite of criminals, the con men. A check investigator spends endless hours during the normal course of his police duties training and retraining the victims of the fraudulent appropriation and their employees who accepted the checks.

Burglaries are committed by a variety of criminal specialists, and the assignment of the officers who investigate them may be similarly divided. Daylight residence burglaries are more apt to be committed by amateur—or part-time—criminals, while many of the nighttime residence burglaries may be committed by career criminals discussed in Chapter 3. The object of both types—daylight and nighttime—is usually cash, but some small appliances or other valuables found during the search for money are taken. Business burglaries include another variety of burglars: the narcotics addict who breaks into drugstores or doctors' offices looking for narcotics or cash, or both; the skylight or rooftop burglar is usually a professional who plans his crime well in advance and covers his entrance into the places he burglarizes so that he may work for long periods of time without interruption by policemen. Safe burglars become proficient only through experience and training, and they are considered as career criminals.

Teams of thieves may work a certain part of the country or the city and methodically case, or study the place they intend to strike prior to the act. They wait until the police patrol passes, smash a front window, run into a store, grab armfulls of merchandise and run out to a waiting car or truck, and disappear. Some teams of thieves have worked with such precision that they have stolen thousands of dollars worth of goods from a store in two or three minutes.

Amateurs and professionals burglarize restaurants, bars, night clubs, service stations, and other businesses where cash is kept on hand, and their primary object is money. Career criminals may specialize to a greater extent than the amateurs in systematically performed burglaries of places for certain types of office machines, electronic components, clothing, or other specific type of contraband for which they may have a ready market. Furs and jewelry are two items that are less likely to be recovered than any other stolen object except cash.

Investigators working miscellaneous theft details may be assigned to a pawnshop detail. Actually, pawnshops may take less time and attention than all the other places of business in a city that trade in second-hand or salvage goods. Some city or state laws require that dealers who buy second-hand goods or who hold property in pawn while a loan is outstanding to the lendee report their transactions to the police on a regular basis. The purpose for requiring officers to inspect personally property that falls into these categories is to assure that their irregular and unannounced visits encourage the dealers to deal and report honestly, and it is also much better for them actually to observe an item than it is for them to read a cryptic written description of it. The officers assigned to the pawnshop detail are usually also required to keep themselves informed on the many items that are reported stolen, so that they may recognize a stolen item in a pawnshop when they see it.

The responsibility for clearance of reported crimes is that of the investigation division of a police department. The investigators assigned to the division should be assigned in such a manner as to assure the maximum in efficiency, and some agencies do not necessarily follow the pattern outlined in the preceding paragraphs. The individual crime problems of a community will dictate to the chief of police how he shall organize his investigation team. The investigators are usually charged with maintaining liaison with various state, federal, and local agencies similarly responsible for the clearance of crimes. Clearance and liaison are improved by requiring officers assigned to investigation specialties to participate in exchange of information and mutual assistance with organizations composed of check investigators, robbery or burglary officers, and many others.

VICE AND NARCOTICS

The various vice crimes require expert attention. The morals of the community are involved in the enforcement of the laws that are categorized as vice offenses. The legislators of state and local

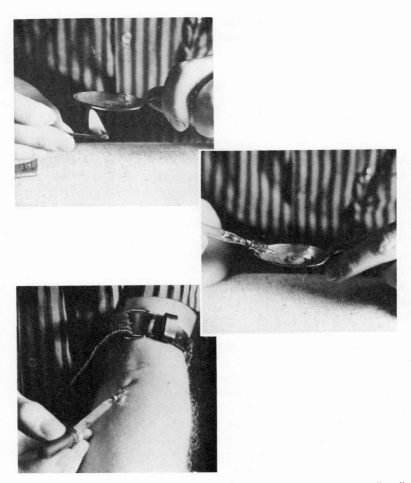

AN ADDICT PREPARES FOR HIS "FIX."

government, by provision of the police power portion of the various constitutions, promulgate the laws that—in their opinion—reflect the conscience of the community. The police responsibility is simply to enforce those laws in accordance with the interpretation by the officers and their supervisors as to the intention of the law. The prosecuting attorney makes the final preprosecution determination—again according to his interpretation of the law as it was intended to be applied. The public morals are again interpreted by the judge or jury in determining guilt or innocence on the basis of the evidence presented during the trial, and finally the judge metes out the punishment for the guilty offender with a view to his interpretation of the public's attitude toward the crime and toward the offender. A crime is a legal definition with a punishment for violators attached for those persons who become so defined as violators.

Police officers are required by the duties of their office to enforce the law, and vice laws are no exception. It is not his responsibility to determine that a certain law is good or bad, then to perform his duties accordingly. He should keep himself fully informed as to what is law and what is not, and how each law shall be enforced, and then perform his duties as he is required by another law to perform. He cannot compromise with himself and decide to enforce only the laws that he considers good. Indeed, there can be no compromise with vice violations, and the policy of a chief of police and his officers should be one of absolute suppression of vice law violations.

There is a matter of priorities involved in the investigation and enforcement of criminal acts, and vice violations are no different. Incidents that occur in the presence of an officer demand action, as

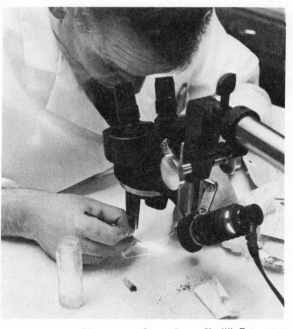

Photo courtesy Orange County Sheriff's Department

LABORATORY EXAMINATION OF A SUBSTANCE SUSPECTED
OF BEING MARIJUANA.

do those that are called to the attention of the officer, either by his own observation, or by complaint made by another. The nature of vice law violations indicates that they are not only unacceptable by law, but they are socially unacceptable to the majority of people whose legislative representatives have either promulgated the law or indicated by their failure to eliminate the law from the statutes that they believe the law still reflects the moral ethics of the community. Certain sophists write and speak on behalf of a mythical "majority" they claim to represent, castigating the police, who enforce the laws. The champion who sincerely seeks to change the laws so that they may truly reflect the morals of the community, in his opinion, should convince his legislative representatives that the view he holds does, in fact, represent that of the majority of people in the community.

The investigation and enforcement of vice laws is usually assigned to a detail or division of officers who may be assigned under the direct supervision of the chief of police, or wherever in the organization he designates. The nature of the work is sensitive, and the chief must be fully informed on all of their activities so that he may be prepared to speak or act intelligently on any matter that should require his immediate attention. The narcotics enforcement detail may be a separate division, or it may be a part of the vice detail, depending upon the community and department's needs. Vice offenses usually include gambling, narcotics and dangerous drugs, alcoholic beverage control laws, prostitution, and related offenses.

Gambling

Gambling of any kind for anything of value is prohibited by law in most states, and further prohibited by individual communities by more specific definition of specific games or devices that are unlawful. Many gambling situations are private affairs among friends or neighbors and may not be brought to the attention of the officers responsible for gambling suppression. Priority of gambling investigations would require that the organized and commercialized gambling operations be given the most diligent attention. Undercover operators are utilized to gather evidence for a successful prosecution, because it is seldom that one of the players or bettors will report to the police the existence of gambling operations at the place where he plays or bets. Wire services that provide inter- or intrastate gambling information for bookies are unlawful and must be suppressed by law and law enforcement in order to reduce the incidence of commercialized gambling on a syndicated basis.

Prostitution

The moral issue of prostitution has been argued for hundreds of years, with opponents and proponents both presenting viewpoints supported by facts. Prostitution is legally wrong and by virtue of the existence of the law that prohibits prostitution, the duly elected representatives of the people apparently hold the view that prostitution is morally wrong. Facts support the views that open prostitution does not cause a reduction of rape and child molestation because the people who are so perverted do not seek the company of prostitutes, and that controlled prostitution where medical examinations are required causes a reduction of venereal disease. It is possible for a prostitute to receive a clean bill of health by a medical examiner in the morning, then to return to work and become infected and—in turn—infect dozens of her later customers before her next medical examination.

The crime of prostitution is difficult to investigate and enforce, because willing participation in a sex act by two adults is not likely to be reported to the police by one of the participants even though one or both of them committed a crime. As in gambling, the investigating officers are compelled to work their cases by priority, and their primary concern with prostitution is to prevent the occurrence or recurrence of the involvement of organized crime in prostitution that may include the syndication of literally hundreds of prostitutes, and to eliminate commercialized prostitution. The officer who investigates prostitution is required to ferret out diligently the violators and to use all legal means at his disposal to assure their successful prosecution. This includes male prostitutes as well as the females.

Alcoholic Beverage Control

State licensing laws regulate business operations where alcoholic beverages are sold. The operator of such an establishment is required to close during certain hours each day, to sell only those beverages for which he is licensed in accordance with the specific provisions of the license, and he is instructed as to the age limitations of persons to whom he is allowed to sell his products. State agencies are charged with the primary responsibility of controlling the licensees, and local law enforcement agencies are similarly responsible for enforcement of the several laws that are involved. Vice investigators are concerned with the incidence of sales of alcoholic beverages to minors, to drunk persons, after-hours sales, the owner allowing the place to become a public nuisance, and the occurrence of other vice activities on the premises.

Narcotics and Dangerous Drugs

At the state level the laws regulating the sales and possession of narcotics and certain drugs that are classified by the codes as "dangerous" are in existence for the purpose of protecting the health and welfare of the people in the state. The federal laws regulating the same substances are also designed to protect the lives and health of the people who are likely to be affected by the illicit production and sale of the drugs. The federal jurisdiction involves tax violations, interstate trade in the drugs and international trade—both legal and illegal. Marijuana and heroin are both outlawed in the United States, neither having any medicinal value. Actually, marijuana, which is the same plant used to make hemp rope, may be grown if the grower possesses a tax stamp and is one of the handful of farmers in Kentucky who are issued the stamps for the purpose of simply perpetuating the hemp plant in the event of some contingency necessitating the domestic production of hemp rope. Cocaine, opium and its derivatives (except heroin), and certain other narcotic drugs including synthetics may be bought, sold, and possessed by doctors, pharmacists, and certain private individuals in accordance with very closely defined and strictly enforced laws.

Doctors may not administer or prescribe the many drugs listed under the laws that deal with narcotics and dangerous drugs without good cause. Druggists and wholesale drug dealers are restricted by law to supply and dispense only those drugs that are medically necessary. Possession of narcotics or dangerous drugs without a valid prescription is a felony or misdemeanor by definition of the law. The police are not primarily concerned with the moral issues concerning use of drugs by adults, but police records show that illicit narcotics use is inseparable from other crimes, such as theft, robbery, burglary, prostitution, pandering, and a variety of other crimes to enable the users to support their expensive habits. Records show that juveniles are supplied narcotics by adult users and pushers somewhere along the deadly supply line. Because of the provable facts that link illicit narcotics usage with the degradation of children who must be protected against their own naivete, with predatory and prurient criminal offenses, and the direct relationship between narcotics trafficking and organized crime, the police responsibility not only encompasses enforcement of the laws related to the illicit narcotics traffic, but they are also responsible for objectively informing the people they serve about the menace of drug habits and narcotics addiction.

The nature of narcotics law violations makes their investigation difficult. On the international level, the illicit narcotics traffic involves the production and exchange of several hundred million dollars worth of the various substances. Great pains are taken to protect the identity of the individuals who comprise the chain of suppliers, and their customers. The continued success of their dealer-customer relationship depends upon their adherance to a code of silence that is punishable by dismemberment or death. Although some voices in some of the larger cities throughout the country belligerently shout that narcotics usage is socially acceptable, that view does not seem to reflect the attitude of the majority, and the narcotics addict is still ostracized by his family and his peers.

Officers assigned to the narcotics detail must diligently seek out informants and undercover operators, and by their own efforts as well constantly gather evidence and information that results in the eventual successful prosecution of the violators. Undercover operators are usually respectable, record-free persons who provide their services on a paid basis, and they may be full time employees of state or federal agencies who cooperate with local police departments for the purpose of accumulating sufficient evidence to identify and prosecute the interstate and international smugglers and entrepreneurs. Informants may be either concerned individuals who acquire bits of information and provide it to the police for altruistic reasons, or may be found anywhere in the social spectrum down to the individual narcotics user or trafficker himself who provides information about competitors or enemies for selfish reasons. The narcotics officers must work adroitly with all of those people in such a manner that he maintains his own high moral sense of values while he goes about his business of investigating and enforcing the laws and their violations.

Pornography and Sexual Deviation

Vice officers may be assigned to details involving sexual deviation and investigating people and places involved in alleged production and sale of pornographic materials. Again it should be pointed out that the police officers assigned to details that involve the morals and personal ethics of the people in the community do not and should not serve as self-appointed or officially appointed censors or moralists. But neither should they wink at certain violations for reasons of personal moral standards that conflict with the intent of the laws as they are written. The police role is to enforce the laws that deal with pornography, or any other form of sexual activity that is legally defined as unlawful. The constitutional guarantees that protect the individual apply to morals offenses as well as to all other criminal law violations, and they must never be compromised under the guise of expediency or efficiency. Policemen are human and they, too, are part of the public they serve. They must be trained to enforce morals offenses with complete objectivity on the basis of what laws have been violated rather than any personal animosity or indignation. Members of the United States Supreme Court have found it difficult to agree on such terms as "prurient," "pornographic," and "immoral." Police officers must sometimes take immediate enforcement action in morals offenses, and their decisions are based upon value judgments on the same subjects.

THE SCIENTIST IN LAW ENFORCEMENT

Criminalistics involves the implementation of scientific principles in the evaluation of evidential items that are in one way or another involved in criminal and other police investigations. The criminalist is usually a graduate in chemistry or will have a bachelor's degree in some related discipline. He will use various methods for the inspection and analysis of various substances known or suspected as blood, semen, alcohol, narcotics, dangerous drugs, or any other bit of evidence that may require analysis. Some of the scientific instruments he will use to conduct his examinations include the spectrophotometer, an instrument that measures the relative intensities of light in different parts of the spectrum, and which may be used to identify positively the elements of a compound and, by comparison with a known quantity, to indicate that a substance is, for instance, a specific narcotic drug. The same substance may be analyzed by the use of chemical reagents and similar conclusions drawn. Of course, the most valuable instrument in the laboratory is the microscope, which is used extensively by the criminalist.

Microscopic examination may be conducted by means of a standard microscope or a three-dimensional type. Photographs may be prepared for study by means of photomicrography, (or microphotography). Types of investigations utilizing the microscope include handwriting comparison, inks, tool impressions compared with tools suspected of having made the impressions, fingerprint classification, comparative analysis, hairs and fibers, ballistics, and mechanical matching of two pieces of evidence to show that they had been connected to one another.

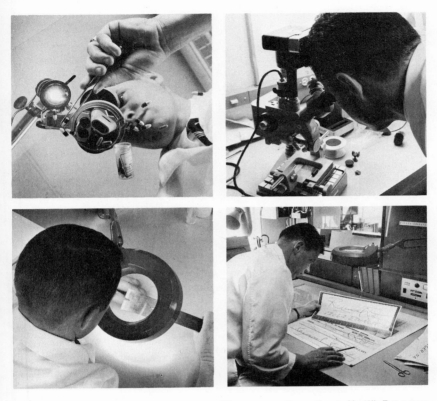

Photos courtesy Orange County Sheriff's Department

THE SCIENTIFIC INVESTIGATION OF CRIME.

The Breath Analyzer

Determination of the percentage of blood-alcohol in the system of a person suspected of driving or being under the influence of alcohol may be made by three commonly accepted methods: blood, urine, or breath analysis. All three methods are valid and reliable, and they are admissable in the courts. The breath analyzer (there are several different types) is the most economical and the least troublesome method, and it can be used to determine the percentage of alcohol in the blood stream by measuring the alcohol content of the alveolar air in the lungs by means of a simple procedure involving light refraction comparisons.

The Polygraph

Sometimes referred to as the "lie detector," the polygraph is a "much-writing" instrument that continuously measures certain bodily processes while the subject of the examination is asked a series of questions. Although a variety of polygraph instruments have been introduced, the most commonly accepted instrument is one with three components that measure and continuously record the subject's blood pressure and pulse rate by means of a device known as a cardiosphygmomanometer, his breathing by means of a pneumograph attachment, and his skin resistance to a very slight continuous electrical charge by means of a psychogalvonometer. The examiner induces the emotional stimuli by asking questions to which the subject answers with a "yes" or " no." The questions ask for an answer relative to facts rather than opinions, and the principle of the instrument is based upon the theory that every person has a conscience (except a sociopath or psychopath). When he answers the question with a truthful response, the subject experiences no emotional involvement. When he lies, he is involved in an internal conflict with his conscience, and certain physiological reactions are stimulated. The normal patterns and any deviations from the normal patterns are then analyzed on the basis of the answers to the questions asked. The examiner becomes the "lie detector" when he gives his opinion of "deception indicated" or " no deception indicated."

Identification Services

The fingerprint expert and the photographer are very essential technicians in the area of physical evidence collection and evaluation. The photographer goes to the scene of the crime and prepares a permanent pictorial record of the scene as it appeared while the investigation was in progress and the pictures were being taken. Short-lived evidence, such as footprints in the thin coat of dust on a tile floor or on wet linoleum will disappear like invisible ink, but the photographs will continue to depict the prints as they were. Many times an investigator will overlook significant bits of evidence or may not see the situation in its true perspective until later when he reviews the photographs. Motion picture photography is excellent for action photography, such as in the case of the administration of a sobriety examination. Videotape for closed-circuit television is another photographic innovation in police identification work that is gaining considerable usage and acceptance.

Photographic records are made of all persons arrested for most crimes by means of the photograph, which usually consists of a profile picture of the subject and a full face forward. When a specific individual is suspected of the commission of a crime and he had been arrested at some time previously, the investigator will mix the photograph of his prime suspect in with eleven or twelve pictures of persons of similar appearance and invite the victim or other witness to look through the photographs and indicate whether or not the picture of the suspect observed at the crime scene is among them.

Fingerprints of all arrested persons are classified and filed in a variety of ways so as to assure successful retrieval in the case of a later need. Some persons who commit crimes will inadvertantly leave smudges or entire finger or hand impressions on some object at the scene of a crime. The impressions are "lifted," or removed from the object by means of a dusting process with a special powder, special transparent tape, and then taped onto a clean, white surface. The impression is examined and then an effort is made to match the latent print with a fingerprint of a person suspected of having committed the crime. A comparison may yield a positive identification.

SUMMARY

The investigation process begins at the moment the call for the police is first received or the discovery of a crime has been made by the patrol officer. He immediately begins the initial phases of the investigation, calling upon the expert assistance of another patrol officer who is especially trained to search for and collect evidence, take photographs, draw sketches, and perform the technical part of the investigation while the originally assigned officer takes information from the victims and witnesses, searches for the suspect, and prepares his reports. The follow-up investigator is assigned to continue the investigation until he exhausts all leads and reaches a dead end or he is successful in clearing the case. It is the responsibility of the follow-up investigator to follow through with the case until it is satisfactorily disposed of in court. Assignment of cases to investigate is usually on the basis of types of crimes, such as burglary, robbery, thefts, and vice. The laboratory services provided by the criminalist and the other specialists, including the identification technicians are vitally important in the overall investigation and should be utilized whenever possible.

The accountability for the solution of crimes that occur in an officer's patrol district should be his, but the ultimate clearance of the case is the responsibility of the officer assigned to the investigation division.

Exercises and Study Questions

1. What division (s) of a police department should have the ultimate responsibility for the solution and clearance of crimes?
2. In your opinion, should an officer be *transferred,* or should he be *promoted* to the classification of investigator? Discuss your reasons why.
3. At what stage of a case should the follow-up investigation begin?
4. Describe a hypothetical follow-up investigation as discussed in this chapter.
5. What relationship to a crime investigation is a police department's records system?
6. What elements make up a "modus operandi" file?
7. What do statistics show about habitual criminals and their likelihood of committing similar crimes a second time?
8. Is robbery classified as a crime against the *person,* or a crime against *property?*
9. What types of activities are considered vice offenses?
10. *Recommended Semester Project:* Write a paper on whether or not one of the following vices should be legalized: gambling, prostitution, marijuana. Support your argument with newspaper clippings and personal interviews with private persons, students, and public officials.

Suggested for Additional Study:

Dienstein, W. *Techniques for the Crime Investigator* (Springfield, Ill.: Thomas, 1965). Professor Dienstein deals with the field of investigation from the viewpoint of a police practitioner and an academician. The book is a must in a working policeman's library.

Kirk, P. L. and L. W. Bradford. *The Crime Laboratory: Organization and Operation* (Springfield, Ill.: Thomas, 1965). The book provides a candid and concise look at the crime laboratory in the police department.

O'Hara, C. E. *Fundamentals of Criminal Investigation* (Springfield, Ill.: Thomas, 1965). Professor O'Hara has prepared one of the most up-to-date books that cover the entire broad field of criminal investigation.

9

Juvenile Control
and Delinquency Prevention

INTRODUCTION

Crime prevention is one of the basic responsibilities of the police department. Prevention is best accomplished by eliminating, or inhibiting, the desire to commit criminal acts. This procedure generally involves police work with juveniles, as adult delinquency and criminal behavioral patterns are fairly well established in the personality structure and beyond the reach of the average police officer. According to law, a juvenile is someone who has not reached a certain minimum age, which varies from state to state but is eighteen in California and many others. Although a minor according to civil law, the eighteen year old may be charged and punished for a crime as an adult. The juvenile may commit the same offense, but his act is classified as "delinquent," not "criminal", and his arrest is usually referred to as a detention.

The philosophy of juvenile control and delinquency prevention is for the police officer to strive for early discovery of the criminal occurrence, identification of the violator, and apprehension as quickly as possible. Swift and sure appropriate punitive action by the juvenile court should be designed to prevent the youth from repeating the same act. Formation of an asocial or criminal behavior pattern may be averted, and we will have made another step toward our ultimate goal, which is crime prevention. In many cases, a juvenile's first disciplinary contact with the police is his last. The chances are that it will be a long-remembered one. The effects of that contact must be positive and constructive.

Photo courtesy Orange County Sheriff's Department

JUVENILE DELINQUENCY PREVENTION.

THE JUVENILE CRIME PICTURE

The Uniform Crime Reports published annually by the Federal Bureau of Investigation consistently show that approximately one half of the total clearances for crimes against property (robbery, burglary, theft, and auto theft) are attributed to juveniles, or persons under the age of eighteen. In the category of auto theft alone, the arrest ratio is about 70 percent juvenile, and a great many of those under the legal age for drivers' licenses.

From approximately 50 to 75 percent of offenses against property go unsolved throughout the country. Because of this statistic, some believe that "it would be reasonable to assume that the unsolved crimes obviously are those committed by older, mature, and experienced criminals—hence, their lack of apprehension." This, however, does not hold true in cities where the clearance rates are consistently as much as twice that of the national average. In those cities, juvenile offenders show approximately 50 percent responsibility for cleared crimes. Based upon that premise, and borrowing the sampling technique utilized by statistical analysts, it would appear more likely that if 100 percent of the reported crimes were cleared, juvenile responsibility would still be at approximately the same ratio.

What does this discussion prove? Can anything be accomplished, except to show that statistics may be used to the advantage of whoever chooses to use them? They do go beyond that point. They prove with a great deal of certainty that the juvenile crime picture is not a pleasant one. Nearly every adult offender who is a recidivist started out on his road to crime while still a juvenile. The answer to the prevention or reduction of adult criminality lies in the framing, or reframing, of attitudes and behavior patterns of children and youths.

THE POLICE ROLE IN GENERAL

Except in large cities, where specialization is a necessity, the principal burden of responsibility for the performance of all police duties and accomplishment of the police mission rests squarely upon the shoulders of the patrol division. The juvenile function is no exception, although ultimate responsibility for the overall accomplishment of juvenile delinquency prevention is charged to the specialized unit or division.

The patrol officer is assigned to a specific district, or beat, which he patrols throughout his tour of duty in a distinctively marked automobile, or on foot, although the latter method is rapidly becoming more rare. The officer nearly always wears a uniform, except when a special problem or assignment calls for plainclothes. When he completes his tour of duty for the day or for the week, his place in the district is taken over by another officer, then another. There is no break in the continuity of patrol; it is constant and consistent. The field officers are always on the streets, available to respond immediately to any call or need for his services. Because of his omnipresent availability, the patrol officer is particularly suited for the role of crime prevention duties.

Whenever a situation occurs that is either observed by the field officer, or that precipitates a call for his presence, he immediately goes into action. If an immediate arrest is to be made, he effects it. The officer interviews the victims, the witnesses and the suspects. He will record all available information concerning the matter and take steps to collect and preserve the evidence. Whenever time and circumstances permit, the field officer may pursue and seek out the suspect and conduct the interview to seek his statements and confessions or ad-

Photo courtesy Santa Ana Police Department

POLICE-JUVENILE CONTACTS SHOULD INCLUDE FREQUENT "GET ACQUAINTED" SESSIONS.

missions. Without leaving his district for any extended period of time—for he is responsible for keeping his district free from accidents and crimes—the patrol officer continues until he can bring the case to a successful conclusion, or a logical stopping point, so that an investigator or juvenile officer can continue and conclude the inquiry.

The uniformed patrol officer is the principal contact between the police department and the public, including the juvenile. The officer on the beat is also responsible for traffic enforcement in his district, again placing him in direct contact with the juvenile, as they comprise a proportionate share of the traffic law violators and principals in traffic accidents. Nearly every other police activity involves juveniles in one way or another, including pedestrian-intersection control, crowd control duties at recreation and sporting events, and so forth. For the present, let us continue with the sequence of a criminal investigation as it involves the juvenile.

THE FOLLOW-UP INVESTIGATOR

A few hours after the discontinuance of the initial investigation, usually the next day, the follow-up investigator is assigned to resume the investigation. In more serious cases, he may be called in during the initial phases of the investigation, sometimes immediately. His task is to take up the investigation where the field officer leaves off, and to dovetail rather than duplicate his work. While the assigned patrol officer is inspecting the crime scene and accumulating data for his report, the follow-up officer—the detail man—busies himself in locating and questioning witnesses, coordinating the collection and evaluation of evidence, and continuing the search for suspects.

Investigative assignments are made in several different ways, depending upon the individual characteristics of each department and the empirical judgment of the administrators. The most common method of case assignment is on the basis of type of crime or incident. An exception to case assignment on the basis of type of crime is the juvenile specialist, who may be assigned to the follow-up investigation on the basis of the age of the person concerned. He receives the assignment if the victim is a juvenile—particularly in crimes of violence and sexual offenses—or if the suspect is known to be a juvenile. A case in which the age of the suspect is unknown is assigned to an investigator of a specific type of crime, such as burglary or auto theft. Then, when the investigation reveals that the violator is a juvenile, the case is turned over to the juvenile division or a juvenile officer. It would seem most appropriate for a theft investigator, for instance, to carry the case to completion once he has started. He may have several similar cases attributable to the same person. One reason for not transferring the assignment would be that such reassignments in too many cases may prove demoralizing to the diligent and tenacious investigator who works the case to a near-conclusion, and then has to turn it over to another officer who will receive the credit for the clearance with a minimum of effort. The more equitable method of handling the case when the violator is identified as a juvenile is to bring the juvenile officer into the case on a cooperative basis so that the case will be brought to a successful conclusion from an administrative standpoint, and the juvenile will be handled properly from a procedural standpoint.

THE JUVENILE SPECIALISTS

Second to the patrolman on the beat, the officer assigned to the juvenile division is a key individual in the police-juvenile problem. In addition to having to be a well-qualified investigator, a specialist with juvenile offenders and the offenses they commit, must have a very sincere interest in children and their problems, an unusual amount

Photo courtesy Orange County Sheriff's Department

JUVENILE SPECIALIST COUNSELS A CHILD AND HER PARENTS.

of patience, and an understanding—but firm—attitude. The juvenile officer is not unlike a good parent, except that he has more experience with more children and he does not become personally and emotionally involved in the life of the juveniles as parents do. In speaking of a juvenile specialist, we are referring to an officer who is specifically assigned to a special detail in the department, in this case the juvenile division, and who is required to devote all his time and energy to that specific job. He need not necessarily be permanently assigned to this job, but should be capable of filling any of a number of other assignments in the organization. Some police administrators do not hold this view, and they may permanently post their personnel to various specialist assignments.

Although it is not administratively or operationally sound policy to reassign a case once assigned to an investigator from another detail, as previously discussed (such as burglary, theft, or auto theft), at the time it is determined that a juvenile is responsible for the offense it is most likely that the juvenile officer will be called upon for advice and assistance. It is the juvenile division's administrative responsibility to guide overall departmental activities in its efforts toward juvenile control and delinquency prevention. For that reason, it is the assigned duty of the juvenile specialists to maintain a close working relationship with all other persons and agencies in the communities that are similarly involved in delinquency prevention and child welfare. All police cannot be all things to all people, but the juvenile officers can, and must, be selflessly dedicated to their assigned special duties. They must know the people and the policies of the juvenile court and the probation department, and their specific attitudes toward individual types of offenses and offenders. They must know the school administrators and the individual teachers, and their policies and practices with respect to the various types of students who are involved in delinquent and near-delinquent acts. It is also imperative for the juvenile officers to have a knowledge of the entrance and membership requirements of youth guidance organizations and similarly oriented civic-sponsored clubs and associations, as well as the people who sponsor and operate them. As a result of this intimate knowledge of the people and the organizations, and daily contact with them, as well as working constantly and directly with both delinquent and non-delinquent children, the juvenile officers are far better prepared to make a determination as to what action must be taken when presented with a specific set of circumstances.

Commencing with the apprehension of a person responsible for a criminal act—or one that would be classified as criminal if committed by an adult--the methods for handling juveniles differ from those involving persons who have attained the age at which they fall within the jurisdiction of the criminal courts. Even the act of taking into custody is given a different name—an arrest is classified as a "detention", and the crime committed by a child is a "delinquent act." An adult offender is either cited and released after signing a promise to appear in court to answer to the charges of the offense, or he is taken into custody and "booked". The determination as to his guilt or innocence is left to the courts, as is the decision as to his penalty. Other than the official's presentation of evidence and testimony in court, there is seldom any further police involvement in the affair, no official concern as to whether or not the offender learns a lesson or gains moral benefits from his getting caught. There are other agencies charged with that responsibility. The picture is different with the juvenile apprehension—the police are officially concerned with what happens after the arrest.

APPREHENSION AND DETENTION OF THE JUVENILE OFFENDER

Whenever a juvenile is identified as the person responsible for the commission of a delinquent act, or for any of a number of reasons is determined to fall within the jurisdiction of the Juvenile Court Law (specific sections of the Welfare and Institutions Code in California), the police officer is very much concerned with the individual characteristics of the violator as well as the violation. The juvenile officer must be intimately acquainted, of course, with the attitudes and procedures of the juvenile court and probation department, but many other factors enter the picture. The police officer represents the father image in the eyes of the child, and the officer's decision as to how he will dispose of the case will have a long-lasting effect upon the life of that child. It is the responsibility of the officer to make the most of each juvenile contact so as to reduce, or totally prevent the probability of the child committing any further transgressions.

Actual detention of a juvenile offender by a police officer may be handled in a variety of ways. Those ways are related to some extent to the policies and practices of the juvenile court and other concerned agencies, but largely to the officer's own discretion. At the time of initial contact, the officer must determine whether he will merely warn the child and send him on his way, or to proceed with the formality of the detention. The current trend is toward

Photo courtesy Santa Ana Police Department

A JUVENILE AUTO THEFT SUSPECT IS BROUGHT IN FOR QUESTIONING.

the latter, as will be pointed out later in this chapter. The former procedure is generally limited to such incidents as routine field interviews and bicycle-riding violations, which are disposed of by taking information from the juvenile, and contacting the parents later in the case of minor law violations. Traffic citations are similar to this procedure, as the violator is cited and released immediately. However, the process is a formal procedure, as a later appearance by the juvenile violator and one of his parents is mandatory.

Of the many choices the officer has when arresting—or detaining—a juvenile, the least punitive is to counsel the child and his parents and release him to his parents with no further action taken, except the completion and filing of appropriate reports that accompany all police actions. This alternative is employed in approximately one-half of all juvenile detentions. It is usually applied in the case of first offenders who have committed relatively minor offenses, and others who may be considered qualified for such handling because of favorable home and other environmental conditions. A second alternative is for the officer to counsel and release the child offender to his parents, then follow up with an application for petition directed to the probation department. The purpose of the application is to call the matter to the attention of the probation department via an official application form that requires some action and a reply from that department. After reviewing the reports and application submitted by the police department, the probation officer responsible may initiate an independent investigation into the matter, or he may make a decision on the basis of the report. It is his prerogative to either consider the matter closed and handled satisfactorily by the officer's actions, or he may petition the juvenile and his, or her, parents to appear in juvenile court before the judge or a designated referee for a more formal disposition of the case. A third alternative for the officer who effects detention of a juvenile is to lodge him in juvenile hall and to file an application for petition. Again, by authority of the juvenile court, investigation into the matter is made by the probation department—custodians of the juvenile hall—and a decision is made by an assigned probation officer whether to release the child to his parents or to detain him until a formal juvenile court hearing. In the event the child is released, the child may or may not be required to return for a confrontation with the juvenile court. This procedure will be covered in more detail elsewhere in the text.

In all of the foregoing situations, the officer's action will be predicated upon many factors, none of which concern the police in the case of an adult offender. Some of these factors involving the juvenile offender are his prior record with the schools and the police, his social relationship within his home and community, the nature of the offense he is alleged to have committed, and his attitudes. Many attitudes are involved: What does he say about his involvement? What are his standards of value? Is he remorseful and do his actions indicate that he is not likely to repeat the offense? Is he defiant and likely to form a delinquent behavior pattern? What is his attitude toward authority—the police and the court? Are there any feelings of resentment, animosity, or remorse with regards to his victim? In some cases, the course of action is clearly indicated by the circumstances. In others, the way is not so clearly defined, and an experienced specialist even is hard put to render a wise and just decision.

As is the case with any other police officer, the juvenile officer must be intimately familiar with many laws. Among the many laws concerning juveniles, the two below are of the utmost importance (California law is cited because of the author's familiarity with the codes of California, and many other states have similar legislation either already in force or pending):

> Welfare and Institutions Code (also known as the Juvenile Court Law) Section 626 specifically prescribes how the arresting officer shall proceed with a detained juvenile. It states: "In determining which disposition of the minor he will make, the officer shall prefer the alternative which least restricts the minor's freedom of movement, provided such alternative is compatible with the best interests of the minor and the community."

> Section 627 of the same code (W.I.C.) requires the arresting officer to immediately take steps to notify the minor's parents, guardian, or responsible relative whenever he takes the child into custody.

The latter of these two sections makes it a must, at least from an administrative standpoint, to make an official record of every such contact to ensure proper handling in each case and to provide the police with an exact record of the situation and all of the attendant circumstances. The procedure does away with many of the informal contacts, such as the "old school" method of "kicking the kid in the seat of the pants and sending him on his way." According to Section 627, this procedure is illegal, and could be called an "abusive police practice" performed in this manner because for some reason the officer did not want to make an official record of the contact. The laws were, no doubt, designed for the protection of the child's interests. The procedures made necessary for assuring compliance with the law may prove detrimental to the child's welfare.

They require a formal record-keeping system of each individual juvenile detention; and the records become a permanent part of the police archives available for review by all authorized persons.

In addition to knowing what is required of him, the officer must also know, and appreciate, the legal limitations that are similarly placed upon the probation department and its officers. Section 628 of the Welfare and Institutions Code describes what action the juvenile intake officer shall take whenever a child is lodged in juvenile hall:

> ... (he-they) shall immediately investigate circumstances of the juvenile's custody (which consists of reading the detaining police officer's arrest report and statements on the application for petition, and sometimes a personal interview with the officer) and immediately release him unless one of the following exists, making it necessary to detain him: a. it is a matter of immediate and urgent necessity for the protection of such minor . . . b. or the person or property of another . . . c. or unless it appears that such minor is likely to flee the jurisdiction of the court . . . d. or unless it appears that such minor has violated an order of the juvenile court.

As pointed out earlier in the chapter, a juvenile who is handled in accordance with the juvenile court law is not at any time legally charged with a criminal offense—except, of course, those who may be adjudged by the juvenile court judge as unfit for juvenile court and remanded to the criminal court—and the court procedure is a civil court proceeding. A child may (1) be remanded to the juvenile court for proper handling of his case, ranging from release and informal probation to being declared a ward of the court and being placed in a foster home; (2) in the more serious and repeat cases, be placed in protective custody under the jurisdiction of the county probation department or the youth authority section of the department of corrections.

The circumstances leading to the official detention of a child may be called to the attention of the court by the police, the schools, or any other qualified officials, and they include (1) protective custody of children who have no one who is either willing or able to properly care for them, (2) children who are in danger—because of environmental conditions—of leading a lewd, idle life, or (3) children who have violated some criminal law. Although the juvenile court law may legally have jurisdiction over anyone under the age of twenty-one in some states (as in California), its use is generally limited to those under the age of eighteen and twenty-one, the juvenile court and the criminal court have concurrent jurisdiction, and adjudication of matters concerning persons over seventeen is almost without exception negotiated with no involvement of the juvenile court.

Obviously, the juvenile control problem of the modern police department is a complex, and extremely important one. For this reason, it is imperative that every department be staffed with at least one officer who is administratively responsible for juvenile control and delinquency prevention in order to assure continuity and a maximization of results.

Juvenile division responsibilities include the following: (1) coordination of the department's policies and procedures regarding juvenile control; (2) maintaining liaison with the various other agencies involved with youth welfare, such as the schools, probation department, juvenile court, and other official and semi-official agencies; (3) preventive patrol of the cities' streets and places where juveniles congregate to prevent juvenile delinquency, and (4) to participate in public relations and public service activities for the purpose of encouraging children to obey the law and to respect the rights and property of others.

None of the duty obligations of a juvenile officer should include social casework or organization leadership during on-duty time. The police administrator cannot justify the expenditure of his officers' time for nonpolice activities, such as serving as recreation or band leaders, camp or club counselors, scout leaders, or "big brothers." Many officers and other police employees do participate in this type of activity as do many other civic-minded individuals, and their efforts are to be applauded. But the work should be accomplished during the officer's own time. The results are more productive and long-lasting when performed on a volunteer basis.

CONCLUSION

Police work with juveniles is no less important than any of the many other specialist or generalist assignments in a police agency; in many ways it is far more rewarding. Effectiveness in dealing with the young people of the community will have a long-lasting effect upon their individual attitudes, and will help reduce the rising juvenile crime rate for many years to come. It is conceivable that truly effective and efficient juvenile delinquency control techniques may be the solution to the problem of the overall rising crime rate throughout the entire country.

The juvenile division in the police department assures some uniformity in handling juvenile situations on a department-wide basis, and there is a definite advantage to the maintenance of such a specialized unit. The supervisor who is placed in charge of the unit and held responsible for maintaining a uniformity of actions and attitudes, should review all department actions involving juveniles. He should take whatever remedial action is necessary to provide the widest possible dissemination of information to all other operating units within the organization.

The tremendous importance of the policeman's role in the lives of children is pointed out in Kenney and Pursuit's *Police Work With Juveniles* (Thomas, Springfield, 1959): "Next to teachers, church and recreation leaders, police officers are meeting more children than any other occupational group. Surely what happens in the police-juvenile contacts is of tremendous importance in the lives of these children." Whatever the nature of the contact, the police officer must be firm and fair. Nothing in his action should detract from a police image that demands respect for the officer and the maintenance of an orderly society that his strength alone can insure.

Exercises and Study Questions

1. What age limits include juveniles?
2. According to the Uniform Crime Reports, what percentage of arrests for crimes against property are attributed to juveniles?
3. At what stage of the investigation should the juvenile specialists enter the case?
4. In class, discuss the type of a man or woman that should be assigned as juvenile specialists.
5. How would you define "juvenile delinquency"?
6. In what ways is a juvenile arrest handled differently from an adult arrest?
7. In class, discuss the advisability of police officers participating in community youth programs, such as scouting, boys' clubs, and athletic clubs as a normal part of their duty assignments.
8. List some of the responsibilities of a juvenile division.
9. Discuss in class: should the names of juvenile offenders be publicized? Why? or why not?
10. *Recommended Semester Project*: Survey the juvenile laws of your state and comment on their adequacy or inadequacy in a written report format. Interview a probation officer, a juvenile police officer, and a juvenile court judge and include their impressions in your report.

Suggested for Additional Study:

Cavan, R. S. *Readings in Juvenile Delinquency* (Philadelphia: J. B. Lippincott Co., 1964). Doctor Cavan, a criminologist herself, has collected in this paperback book of readings an array of exceptionally well-written papers and articles on the subject of juvenile delinquency. The selections serve to define the problem and to advance theories as to its cause and effects. Then, the readings progress toward a study by an imposing list of experts of the prevention of delinquency, the treatment and rehabilitation of offenders, and the several agencies that are involved in delinquency prevention and control.

Kenney, J. P. and D. G. Pursuit. *Police Work With Juveniles* (3rd ed.; Springfield, Ill.: Thomas, 1965). This book was written with the police officer in mind. It covers juvenile laws and delinquency control programs, and a study of police methods for juvenile control.

10

The Traffic Problem
and the Police Role

INTRODUCTION

In 1769, a Frenchman named Cugnot invented a steam-driven vehicle that was one of the predecessors of the modern automobile. A succession of attempts at modification and improvement led to the invention of the Benz in Germany in 1885. By 1895, there were four different types of locomotion to propel approximately three hundred varieties of homemade automobiles in the United States. By the year 1905, there were more than 78,000 motor vehicles registered, including one Packard that made the trip from New York to San Francisco in fifty-two days. In 1926, Henry Ford began mass-producing his Model T Ford, and the trend was begun toward making the automobile an indispensable part of our social and economic structure in this country and in many other countries throughout the world.

While the design and production of the automobile was making considerable progress, and the number of autos and their drivers began to increase, accident statistics began to accumulate. By 1924, the rate of traffic deaths had grown to about twenty-thousand a year. The Federal Aid Highway Program of 1916 was the result of a growing concern on the part of the people in the United States for the quality of roads, and it was under that program that the country's interstate system of connecting highways was created. As a result of the extended highway system and the constantly growing rate of automobile sales, coupled with the phenomenal death rate, President Herbert Hoover called together the first President's Safety Conference in 1924. That conference yielded a uniform vehicle code for the nationwide enforcement of traffic laws by the many thousands of local law enforcement agencies.

Photo courtesy Anaheim Police Department

A POLICE TRAFFIC SPECIALIST.

In the early 1900's it became obvious that some governmental agency or agencies charged with the public safety responsibility would have to be delegated the task of traffic control. Prior to the advent of the automobile, regulation of pedestrians, bicycles, and horse-drawn vehicles on the streets and roads of the towns were handled by the local police agencies. The assignment of the new automobile problems to those same police agencies was both logical and economical. The local police agencies augmented their organizations to include specialists to provide for the safe and efficient movement of automobiles, and enforcement of the many new laws promulgated for the purpose of assuring the greatest possible degree of safety for the people in the communities. Following the adoption of the uniform vehicle code by many states, new state traffic agencies were created to enforce the laws on the state highways and in the unincorporated parts of the state, and the local police continued their traffic control duties in their respective cities and towns.

Some police administrators would prefer to divest themselves of the task of traffic law enforcement. They hope this would reduce the general feeling of antagonism held by people who have received traffic citations towards the men and women who are required to enforce unpopular laws. The recipients of traffic citations and parking tickets are not criminals—except for the serious misdemeanors and all of the felonies included in the vehicle code violations—but are respectable and otherwise law-abiding residents of the community. The officer who stops and cites the popular bank cashier, who is also an active member in three benevolent community organizations, has little chance to capture the heart of the violator and his friends when he performs the duty he must. The officer may be accused of spending valuable time on "petty things" instead of "going out and catching real criminals." He may be accused of being "hard put to get his quota for the day." The officer may, on the other hand, be thanked and apologized to for endangering the lives of other persons who might have been endangered by the violator's act, but the odds are against it.

Many people refuse to accept the irrevocable truth that the automobile as an instrument causing death consistently kills more people in *one* year than all of the other deadly weapons used by criminals over a period of *several* years. More people have been killed in the United States during the twentieth century than Americans have been killed in all the major wars during the past two hundred years. However unpopular, the traffic laws must be enforced, and the police department is charged with the responsibility of enforcing them.

TRAFFIC LAW ENFORCEMENT

In some police departments, traffic direction and traffic law enforcement is handled almost exclusively by the specialists who comprise the traffic division. This is actually unsound, and the patrol officers should be—as they are in a great many departments—held accountable for traffic control in their respective patrol districts and they should be continuously involved in an accident-preventing selective enforcement program.

The commander of the traffic division is required to use accident statistics as a guide and exert his energy and attention toward an effective program to accomplish the objectives of the police role with respect to the traffic control problem: keeping a free flow of traffic on the streets with a minimum of congestion; investigating traffic accidents to determine their causes; and to prevent future accidents through education, coordination with the traffic engineer, and enforcement of the traffic laws with particular attention directed toward those violations that cause the accidents.

Selective traffic enforcement is accomplished by two methods. First, the traffic division commander provides sufficient data to the various patrol division commanders and supervisors so that they, in turn may instruct their field officers as to where they should direct particular attention for traffic enforcement during the course of normal patrol of their districts; second, the assignment of enforcement specialists to the traffic division. The men are specialists by virtue of assignment and do not necessarily spend their entire careers in that detail, but while they are so assigned, they patrol the streets and highways in automobiles or motorcycles. Traffic enforcement officers do not necessarily close their eyes to other infractions of the law, but they direct their enforcement activities toward those violations of the law that cause the accidents at the approximate times and specific locations when and where the accidents occur.

The Traffic Citation

Let us imagine a representative traffic citation. A woman is hurrying home after a hard day's work. There she will have to cook dinner for her husband and children, and do other housework. Her mind is on these concerns. Just as she approaches an intersection,

Photo courtesy Santa Ana Police Department

ONE OF THE PRIMARY PURPOSES OF TRAFFIC ENFORCEMENT
IS TO REDUCE THE FREQUENCY AND SEVERITY OF ACCIDENTS.

the light turns red, but she goes through. Two blocks later, she is stopped by a police car and given a ticket. Her reaction is resentment.

A traffic ticket, or citation, is not a judgment with automatic punishment meted out by a policeman. It is actually nothing more than a notification to a driver that the officer has observed what appeared to him to be a violation of one of the many hundreds of traffic laws, and a formal notice to that effect. The ticket is a summons that requires the alleged violator to appear in court to answer the charge that he committed the violation. It also serves as the suspected violator's promise to appear in court within a required period of time to answer the charge. Finally, the ticket serves as a "complaint" for the issuance of a warrant for the arrest of the violator if he does not appear in court as promised.

The traffic ticket serves many purposes: a notification, a summons, a promissory note, and as a complaint form. But it serves other purposes as well. Those purposes are to provide for punishment of the violator if he is proven guilty and to prevent traffic accidents. The punishment purpose is accomplished in one of two ways: the violator either posts a specified amount of bail money which he can forfeit by simply not appearing in court at some later date, or he may appear in court to answer the charges. If he pleads guilty to the charge, or is found guilty by a judge or jury, he is punished by the imposition of a fine or sentence.

The final, and most important, purpose of the ticket is to prevent traffic accidents and the serious injuries or deaths that frequently accompany those accidents. The police departments compile traffic accident statistics that include an accounting for the locations where the accidents occur, the times of day, and the actual or suspected violation causes for those accidents. Armed with that information, the officers who are charged with the responsibility for reducing the seriousness and frequency of traffic accidents patrol the streets and apply what they call "selective enforcement" techniques. They issue tickets to the drivers whose law violations are similar to those that have resulted in accidents. Although they do not close their eyes to other violations at other times and places, the officers devote most of their attention to the places where the accidents have occurred in the past at the times of the day when they have occurred.

TRAFFIC ACCIDENT INVESTIGATION

There are many purposes for accident investigation. Through careful inquiry and investigation it is possible to determine the many causes of accidents, such as faulty equipment, street or other engineering deficiencies, and driver violations. In the case of driver violations, diligent efforts should be made by the follow-up investigators to seek successful prosecution of the violators. The investigation reports are available for use by the drivers involved in the accidents, the injured parties, and property owners who might be legally involved as the result of an accident, as well as their insurance and legal representatives. The statistics and other factual information compiled with a good reporting system as a base will provide the police administrators, the traffic engineer, and safety coordinators with a wealth of information that will assist them in their enforcement, planning, training, and other accident prevention activities.

Additional purposes for accident investigation include the informational services provided for the motor vehicle administrators who are involved in driver analysis and improvement, and the legislators who must be kept aware of the need for legislative changes, additions, or deletions in order that realistic enforcement may actually be carried out for the purpose of reducing accidents. Public information is a second purpose for accident investigation but it is not secondary in importance. Slogans and clichés about safe driving help reduce accidents, but not to the extent that is accomplished when the police department continually releases information and statistics based upon local situations and facts. The people in the community have a right and a need to know exactly what the traffic problems are and what they can and should do about solving them. Solutions to community problems are not only for the governmental agencies to work out; it is a matter of mutual responsibility. Actually, the police are acting on behalf of the people in the community whenever they are involved in any police activity. It is a matter of mutual goals and efforts to achieve them rather than a matter of choosing up sides and competing against each other.

The accident investigation process should involve the patrol officer for the initial on-the-scene investigation with the assistance of the patrol specialist in crime and accident scene investigation for the collection and preservation of evidence. Some cities utilize the system of assigning specialists to investigate all accidents right from the beginning. The initial investigation involves the location and questioning of drivers and witnesses, preparing sketches and taking photographs, tracing and measuring skid marks, collecting evidence, observing conditions of the road and weather, and accurately reporting the accident in a comprehensive report. The investigating officer may issue citations for violations that he observes, such as faulty equipment and license irregularities. He may arrest persons at the scene for manslaughter or driving while under the influence of alcohol or narcotics. He concludes his investigation by providing for the removal of damaged automobiles and debris on the roadway and taking whatever other precautions are necessary to prevent another accident from happening at the same location.

Follow-up investigation is usually a specialized assignment of the traffic division. The officer assigned should be charged with the inspection of reports submitted by field units, and performing the investigations of a continuing nature such as contacting additional witnesses and injured persons at locations removed from the original accident scene. The accident-investigation officer (or A-I man) will inspect the reports for details, and also serve as the liaison officer responsible for securing complaints for prosecution of the violators who are not cited at the scene. Additional responsibilities include a careful scrutiny of all accident investigation reports that filter through their office and checking for errors in the investigation and reporting process, then notifying the training division and the supervisors of errant officers—through the proper channels of command of course—about the needs for training and correction of errors.

TRAFFIC FLOW CONTROL

Traffic congestion is a major problem in most cities in the United States. Mass production of the automobile, particularly since the middle 1940's, has far outstripped the development of the roads, streets, and highways. The modern freeway is almost obsolete by the time it leaves the drawing board and overcrowded the day it is opened. A sigalert (radio broadcasted notification of a traffic problem) in Los Angeles recently announced that a freeway that had just opened was so congested that travel was slow and alternate routes were advised. Officers assigned to traffic patrol may be delegated full-time responsibilities to devote their complete attention to relieving congestion and maintaining free traffic flow throughout the city.

Officers assigned to this detail constantly patrol the streets which the majority of vehicles traverse, and they clear intersections of congestion, order tow trucks to remove disabled and abandoned vehicles from the flow pattern, look for and report traffic hazards to the appropriate public and private agencies, issue citations to drivers who impede, or otherwise adversely affect the movement of traffic, and generally keep the vehicles moving.

PEDESTRIAN-INTERSECTION CONTROL

Intersections in certain parts of a city must be given police attention, particularly where there are large numbers of pedestrians passing. The pedestrians must be reminded that their time to cross at the intersection alternates with that of the vehicles. The pedestrians must be directed to obey the signals and to walk only where and when it is safe to do so. Drivers also need to be directed at intersections with particular emphasis on stopping before entering the intersection, when the intersection is already occupied, to allow cars to get all the way through so that the traffic on the cross street may move in its turn. Policemen assigned to PIC (pedestrian-intersection control) serve a dual purpose by making themselves available to render assistance in the downtown areas and to provide information about the city to tourists and other visitors.

PARKING CONTROL

In some cities the councils have created legislation providing for parking meters and time-zone parking as a source of additional revenue and to attempt to assure the merchants of a turn-over of vehicles in the limited parking spaces adjacent to their places of business. Other cities have gone into the parking lot business. In all such cases, members of the police department are assigned the responsibility of enforcing whatever regulations may be in existence. Officers may be assigned on a full-time basis to parking control, or they may alternate with intersection control responsibilities.

Issuing parking citations and chalking tires to check later for persons who violate the restrictions of time-zone parking is an onerous task to many police officers who believe they could be putting their talents to better use performing other police duties. Many people become quite hostile toward officers who issue them overtime parking citations, taking the citation as a personal affront and another form of government intervention of their rights to park where they wish. Many police administrators have recognized the fact that young and personable women in neat uniforms not only meet less resistance to their issuing parking citations, but these courteous and diplomatic "meter maids" enhance the police department's public image. In addition to improved public relations, the organization also benefits

Photo courtesy Santa Ana Police Department

A PARKING CONTROL WOMAN "CITES" A VIOLATER.

from increased efficiency in most cases because the women are hired specifically for the job and some officers consider such an assignment a form of punishment.

ACCIDENT PREVENTION

The prevention of traffic accidents is of serious concern to everyone who is involved in law enforcement and traffic safety. Every possible legal and ethical means must be employed to reduce the carnage and destruction of property on the streets and highways. The police administrator's tools and techniques include such items as comprehensive statistics, coordination with the traffic engineer, public information, and a variety of traffic safety programs.

The traffic engineer at one time during police administration history was assigned to the staff of certain police departments. He is an engineer with certain responsibilities to the police department, but his rightful place is in the city's department of streets or public

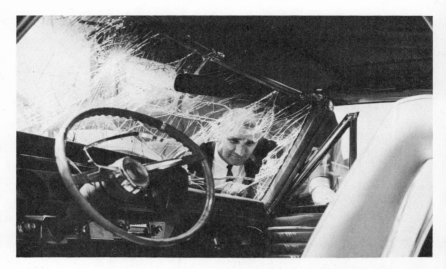

Photo courtesy Orange County Sheriff's Department

A FOLLOW-UP ACCIDENT INVESTIGATOR ASSESSES THE DAMAGE.

works. The engineer relies heavily upon the information provided by the police department, but he also compiles his own information independently by observation and studies. He studies accident records and other data and takes whatever action he can to improve traffic flow and safety. His recommendations may include the installation of new signs and signals, the removal of old devices, installation of new or different lighting arrangements, divided highways, islands, turn lanes, one-way streets, and changes in street design and engineering.

School Safety Programs

Traffic safety programs conducted in cooperation with the school boards prove quite successful, although expensive and cumbersome. Actual regulation of school children while they are in school and en route to and from school are the legal responsibility of the department or board of education. Police departments utilize adult crossing guards to provide protection for the children at major intersections or other hazardous locations adjacent to the schools. Another proven school safety program is the School Boy Patrol. The actual administration of such a program should legally be under the direct supervision of the schools, with training and coordination provided by officers assigned to the program on a full- or part-time

basis. For the police department, the program provides an excellent opportunity for the officers to establish a rapport with young and impressionable students on a personal basis. The result is favorable if the program is conducted properly, and the children develop respect for the police officers that they continue to feel for many years afterward. The boys who participate in school safety programs are selected from the upper grades of the grammar schools and they usually serve one or two years. The program requires the complete cooperation and support of the school officials, because they must provide for their students to miss class time during the times when they must be on duty at one of their duty stations near the schools. In return for their service, the boys are provided special signs, sweaters or jackets and caps, and a field trip or two during the year to a sports event or recreation center to build up their enthusiasm and esprit de corps.

Juvenile Bicycle Enforcement

Parents teach their children to obey the traffic laws when they go out on the streets on their bicycles, but this provides them with a means whereby they may play beyond the sight of their parents.

The children develop riding habits, some good and some bad. In order that he may learn the safe and legal way to ride his bike, it is most desirable that the child be made aware of his riding errors when they happen, and instructed in ways to improve. The policeman patrols the streets on a continual basis and frequently observes children riding their bicycles, and making their errors in skill and judgment. Another traffic safety program that yields substantial and long-lasting results is a juvenile bicycle citation program. The children who ride bicycles are future automobile drivers and it is most desirable that they develop good habits and attitudes before they start driving automobiles.

Basically, a bicycle citation is not issued for the purpose of punishment for the child. The purpose of the citation program is to personally contact the child at the moment he makes his error, or as soon as practicable afterward, point out his error to him, and then to make the fact known to his parents so that they may give him additional training in the rules of the road. The parent notification is accomplished by means of a follow-up letter advising the parents that their child violated a traffic law or bicycle safety rule. The parents are asked to discuss the matter with their child and to attempt to prevent a similar infraction.

As a prelude to a bicycle citation program, the police department may assign officers to speak to school children and to take part in bicycle safety training in cooperation with the school officials and recreation department personnel. They may distribute brochures explaining the rules of the road and other bicycle regulations. Examinations or riding tests may be conducted as a part of the program and the officers may issue "official" safe bicycle rider cards or certificates to the children. When followed by a bicycle citation program, the results are favorable.

SUMMARY

When one analyzes the problem of traffic control, it is apparent that the agency most suitably equipped to cope with the problem on a continual and efficient basis is the local police department. Additional enforcement in the areas of the state outside the cities is handled by the county sheriffs and state traffic agencies. The police responsibility consists primarily of traffic direction, accident investigation, and traffic law enforcement. But there are many additional duties that have been discussed in this chapter and that should be considered no less important to the overall picture of police traffic control. One of the most important factors that will determine the success of any police traffic function is the support of the public. With that factor in mind, it is most essential that the police department's policies and activities be made known factually and continually through a program of public education.

Exercises and Study Questions

1. When and under what program was the country's interstate system of interconnecting highways created?

2. What was the contribution of the first President's Safety Conference in 1924?

3. In class, discuss the principles of selective enforcement and your opinions as to whether such a system is good or bad.

4. In your opinion, should traffic enforcement be delegated exclusively to the traffic specialists, or should all uniformed policemen have the responsibility? Why?

5. What is the responsibility of the Traffic Division commander with respect to the department's enforcement activities?

6. What is "selective enforcement"?

7. Exactly what is a traffic citation and what purpose (s) does it serve?

8. What are the basic purposes for accident investigation?

9. To what extent is the public's support essential to a police traffic enforcement program?

10. *Recommended Semester Project*: Contact the police department in the city where you live. Study their accident charts and statistics. Determine the major causes of accidents and write a detailed report on what specific steps you would take or recommend to reduce accidents in the city.

Suggested for Additional Study:

Baker, J. S. *Traffic Accident Investigator's Manual for Police* (2d. ed.; Evanston, Ill.: Traffic Institute of Northwestern University, 1957) . One of the most comprehensive handbooks available for the study of the traffic problem in general, and accident investigation in particular.

Traffic Law Enforcement Series; Evanston, Ill.: (Traffic Institute of Northwestern University) . A series of training manuals published for inclusion in a looseleaf notebook. The collection provides an excellent collection of source material on traffic law enforcement.

PART **5**

POLICE ETHICS
AND
PROFESSIONALISM

11

Constitutional Considerations of the Police Role

INTRODUCTION

When John Hancock and his colleagues signed the Declaration of Independence on July 4, 1776, it included an extensive list of grievances against the tyranny of King George III. The purpose of the document was to declare the independence of the Colonies from England and the King's oppression. The document also included a statement supporting the new nation's secession from the mother country that in effect stated that governments should not be changed for "light and transient causes," but "when a long train of abuses and usurpations, pursuing invariably the same Object evinces a design to reduce them under absolute Despotism, it is their right, it is their duty, to throw off such Government, and to provide new Guards for their future security." The Declaration reflected the philosophy of the men who fashioned the framework for the newly-formed independent government: "We hold these truths to be self-evident, that all men are created equal, that they are endowed by their Creator with certain unalienable Rights, that among these are Life, Liberty, and the pursuit of Happiness.—That to secure these rights, Governments are instituted among Men, deriving their just powers from the consent of the governed, . . ."

The statesmen who took part in the framing of the Declaration of Independence also set about the task of establishing the new government of the United States of America with the following selfless pledge: "And for the support of this Declaration, with a firm reliance on the protection of Divine Providence, we mutually pledge to each other our Lives, our Fortunes and our sacred Honor." Those same men had very definite ideas as to the rights and privileges of the individual in this great new country, and their relationship with their government "of the people, by the people, and for the people." The purpose of government is to insure all people in the nation that they shall equally enjoy the rights of "Life, Liberty and the Pursuit of Happiness." The right of the government to govern comes from the will of the people, it was also pointed out in the document.

The people in the United States of America have the fundamental right to be free and enjoy their liberties, but also the right to be secure and have protection against others who would interfere with their rights to "Life, Liberty, and the pursuit of Happiness." When the authors of the United States Constitution met, they obviously had those rights in mind, as reflected in the Preamble:

> WE THE PEOPLE of the United States, in Order to form a more perfect Union, establish Justice, insure domestic Tranquility, provide for the common defence, promote the general Welfare, and secure the Blessings of Liberty to ourselves and our Posterity, do ordain and establish this Constitution for the United States of America.

By virtue of police power, the nation's hundreds of thousands of local, state, and federal police officers are sworn to protect the people in the nation and their property, and to preserve the peace to assure the people that they shall pursue their happiness and enjoy their lives and their liberty without fear that either the government or any individuals will deprive them of those rights. The police agencies operate as enforcement arms of the executive branch of government, and the authority of the government originates with the people. The United States Constitution is the supreme law of the land, and consequently the law of each state. The police shall enforce the Constitution, and be governed by it.

THE U.S. AND STATE CONSTITUTIONS

For the purpose of restricting the material to the subject of the text, let us study only those portions of the constitutions that are related to the police role, and begin with the United States Constitution, which is the supreme law of the land.

Sections 8 and 9, Articles I, list many of the powers of Congress so that they may provide for the common defense and general welfare of the United States. Among those laws are to fix the standard of weights and measures, to provide for punishment of violators of laws prohibiting counterfeiting U.S. coins or securities, copyright and patent law, to define and punish for violations of the laws on the high seas, and to provide for organizing a militia and for calling it forth in times when it is needed to suppress insurrections and repel invasions. The Constitution also provides that the privileges of the writ of habeas corpus shall not be suspended unless the public safety may require it in cases of rebellion or invasion. The Congress may also make any laws necessary to carry out the many powers vested by the Constitution in the Government of the United States or any of its officers.

Section 2 of Article IV provides for interstate extradition of a person charged in any state for treason, a felony, or any other crime who flees from justice and is found in another state. On demand of the executive authority of the state from which he fled, the person shall be delivered to a representative of that authority so that he may be returned to the state having jurisdiction over the crime. The same section provides that the citizens of each state shall be entitled to all privileges and immunities of citizens in the several states, which is repeated and broadened in the Fourteenth Amendment.

The various state constitutions are separate and distinct from the United States Constitution. For many years, it was the interpretation of the Supreme Court that the specific provisions of the Constitution, particularly the Bill of Rights, applied only to judicial affairs of the United States courts and not to the individual states. During the past three decades, however, there have been some significant changes. The philosophy during recent years has been that the United States Constitution and its Amendments are to be enforced by state legislation and by the state judicial and police officers. This trend will be particularly noticeable when we discuss later the provisions of the Bill of Rights.

The state constitutions are each original documents and vary in language and total content, but they are basically similar in that they set forth the mechanics for the government, and they also include sections that are similar to the first ten amendments to the United States Constitution, the Bill of Rights. For example, the California Constitution contains a Declaration of Rights in Article I. Some of the sections deal with the following rights:

"Section 1. All men are by nature free and independent, and have certain inalienable rights; among which are those of enjoying and defending life and liberty; acquiring, possessing, and protecting

204 Police Ethics and Professionalism

property; and pursuing and obtaining safety and happiness." This section provides for the police power of the state, and case decisions have held that the exercise of police power by a state is solely for the welfare of the *public* as opposed to individuals. Persons and property are subject to certain restraints and burdens to secure the general welfare of the state.

"Section 2. All political power is inherent in the people. Government is instituted for the protection, security, and benefit of the people, and they have the right to alter or reform the same whenever the public good may require it." Cases related to this section point out that an individual who becomes a member of the society under our form of constitutional government does surrender some of his personal rights, but only to the extent that such relinquishment may be necessary for the common good.

Section 3 declares that the State of California is an inseparable part of the American Union, and the Constitution of the United States is the supreme law of the land. State sovereignty is defined as the role of the states and their relationship with the federal government. "To the Federal Government is delegated the exercise of certain rights or powers of sovereignty; and the exercise of all other rights of sovereignty, except as expressly prohibited, is reserved to the people of the respective states, or vested by them in their local governments."

Section 4 provides for religious freedom, and Section 5 provides that the privileges of the writ of habeas corpus shall not be suspended except when such suspension shall be necessary because of a rebellion or invasion. Section 6 prohibits excessive bail, unusual punishment, and the detention of witnesses in places where criminals are imprisoned.

Other sections of the California Constitution bear a remarkable resemblance to certain portions of the United States Constitution, and are duplicated—in philosophy rather than in exact words or the same location in the documents—in numerous other constitutions. These provide for the right to trial by jury, freedom of speech and of the press, the right to assemble and petition. Due process of law and its administration according to the legal and proper rules is required by the Constitution, as are the right to a speedy trial and protection against unreasonable search and seizure.

POLICE POWER

There is no single document in the United States system of government that provides for police power. The federal police power is described in the Constitution, which lists the specific instances under which powers to make and enforce certain laws, and which is found in Section 8 of Article I. Primary police power in the United States rests with the individual states, which have the inherent power to legislate for the preservation of peace and protection of the public health, morals, safety, and welfare of the community.

The states depend upon the county and city governments and their police agencies to enforce the major portion of the laws enacted by the states, and to pass local ordinances to meet the needs of the respective jurisdictions, providing that the local laws are not in conflict with the state laws. During recent years, many local ordinances have been declared null and void on the premise that specific areas have been pre-empted by state laws and, therefore, the local government cannot enact new laws in those areas because of the conflicting problems involved in their enforcement. Most of those laws have been in the categories of vice and disorderly conduct.

Within the limitations provided by the Constitution, the state legislatures are responsible for defining the police powers in each respective state. What is "public welfare" is for the courts to decide, and the ultimate determination as to whether or not the laws enacted by the legislative police power and enforced by the many governmental enforcement agencies—particularly the police—are reasonable and consistent with the Constitution and public policy also rests with the courts. As it was pointed out earlier in this chapter, use of the police power must be for the public good. The principal control designed to assure the people that there shall not be excessive use or abuse of police power is Section 1 of the Fourteenth Amendment to the U.S. Constitution, which states in part: ". . . No State shall make or enforce any law which shall abridge the privileges or immunities of citizens of the United States; nor shall any State deprive any person of life, liberty, or property, without due process of law; nor deny to any person within its jurisdiction the equal protection of the laws."

THE BILL OF RIGHTS

The first ten amendments to the United States Constitution are better known as the Bill of Rights and were added to the original document just a few months after ratification of the Constitution itself. They include some of the unalienable rights that were alluded to in the Declaration of Independence written several years earlier. They should be zealously guarded by everyone in the United States, particularly the local police departments who have the sworn duty to preserve the public peace and to protect lives and property. One very important fact that should never be overlooked with respect to the Bill of Rights is that along with the rights goes a corresponding set of responsibilities so as to assure liberty to others as well as to self. Madison said: "Liberty may be endangered by the abuses of liberty as well as by the abuses of power." And Oliver Wendell Holmes, Jr. illustrated the premise that all rights are relative, not absolute, and must be exercised within limits, by stating that freedom of speech does not include the right to falsely shout, "Fire!" in a crowded theater.

> Article I. Congress shall make no law respecting an establishment of religion, or prohibiting the free exercise thereof; or abridging the freedom of speech, or of the press; or the right of the people peaceably to assemble, and to petition the Government for a redress of grievances.

Free speech is limited in such cases when such speech or publications are obscene, or tend to disturb the peace, or advocate the overthrow of the established government. The freedom also does not include speech or publications that are designed or intended to incite to treason, rebellion, the commission of crimes, or disobedience of, or disrespect for the law. A person may speak of his intense hatred, but he may not incite others to commit such acts as to riot. People may assemble to picket in a peaceful manner, and shall not be inhibited except when they commit some criminal act, such as trespass on private property, do malicious mischief to personal property, or when their gathering purpose shows evidence of changing its nature to one with the purpose of committing some criminal act. In the latter case, the assembly becomes an unlawful assembly.

The police role with respect to Article I involves one of visiting or observing an assemblage of people to ascertain its lawful nature. The police are responsible for the maintenance of peace, and there may be good cause for the officers to remain present or nearby to assure the continued peaceful and lawful nature of the assembly. Published material is of no official concern to the police unless there is a violation of the law involved. The police are not censors, nor should they be. It is merely the responsibility of the police to enforce the law as it is written and intended. Pornography is illegal filth, but just exactly where the separation lies between what is pornographic and what is acceptable is a matter of interpretation, and the interpretations vary with the changing times, and the interpreters.

Article II. A well regulated Militia, being necessary to the security of a free State, the right of the people to keep and bear Arms, shall not be infringed.

The courts have held that the right to bear arms means that a person has a right to possess firearms, and to use them in defense of self or property. The courts have also held that the states may make whatever laws they deem necessary to regulate the possession and carrying of firearms, such as the prohibition against aliens or felons possessing or carrying guns. Carrying certain weapons concealed, or mere possession of certain other types of weapons, such as machine guns without specific legal cause or compliance with other regulations is not unlawful for the various legislative bodies to prescribe or proscribe. When the public safety demands it, the police have a duty to search persons known or suspected of having weapons on their person or in their possession, to confiscate the weapons, and to arrest the persons for violations of the laws.

Article III. No soldier shall, in time of peace, be quartered in any house without the consent of the owner, nor in time of war but in a manner to be prescribed by law.

This article of the Bill of Rights was intended to prohibit the quartering of military troops in private residences, in the manner practiced by the British Army in the American Colonies. It would apply equally to any police agency that would entertain any inclinations of a similar nature.

Article IV. The right of the people to be secure in their persons, houses, papers, and effects, against unreasonable searches and seizures, shall not be violated, and no Warrants shall issue, but upon probable cause, supported by Oath or affirmation, and particularly describing the place to be searched, and the persons or things to be seized.

The article was originally designed as a protection against abusive practices that had been the rule rather than the exception for the British Army, and from which the framers of the Bill of Rights sought protection. The purpose for such a rule was explained in 1948 by the Supreme Court in U.S. v. DiRe, 332 U.S. 581, 595: ". . . the forefathers, after consulting the lessons of history, designed our Constitution to place obstacles in the way of a too permeating police surveillance, which they seemed to think was a greater danger

to a free people than the escape of some criminals from punishment."
The provision requiring an affidavit for a search warrant was designed
to prevent the practice of police "fishing expeditions."

A key word in the article is "unreasonable," which is sometimes
erroneously used synonymously with the word "illegal." The officer's
actions in situations involving searches must be based upon "probable" or "reasonable" cause, and those two words may be used
interchangeably. For many years, until 1961 actually, the states
each had the complete freedom to make their own rules on search
and seizure, and were not directly involved with the specific wording
of federal rules. Although some states had previously had state
supreme court rulings that applied the federal rule as to the reason-
ableness of searches and seizures, it was not until 1961 when the
United States Supreme Court ruled in Mapp v. Ohio, 367 U.S. 643
that, as a matter of constitutional law, the federal "exclusionary
rule"[1] applied to the several states as well as the agencies of the
federal government. The states may continue to rule on their own
specific cases, but they shall not violate the standards in the Fourth
Amendment, so stated the court.

John Edgar Hoover, Director of the Federal Bureau of Investigation and defender of positive police practices under the law, wrote
in the *Iowa Law Review* (Winter 1952): "Law enforcement, however,
in defeating the criminal, must maintain inviolate the historic liberties
of the individual." Judge Lewis, of the Tenth U.S. Circuit Court of
Appeals, wrote in Anspach v. U.S. (305 R. 2d48, 1958): "But the prevention and detection of crime is not a polite business and we see
no need or justification for reading into the fourth amendment a
standard of conduct for law enforcement officials which would leave
society at the mercy of those dedicated to the destruction of the very
freedoms guaranteed by the Constitution. The 'pursuit of happiness'
referred to by Justice Brandeis in Olmstead can be destroyed by
idealistic theory that shuns the deadly realism of crime."

> Article V. No person shall be held to answer for a capital, or other-
> wise infamous crime, unless on a presentment or indictment of a
> Grand Jury, except in cases arising in the land or naval forces, or in
> the Militia, when in actual service in time of War or public danger;
> nor shall any person be subject for the same offense to be twice put
> in jeopardy of life or limb: nor shall be compelled in any criminal
> case to be a witness against himself, nor be deprived of life, liberty,

[1]The exclusionary rule referred to in this instance is that evidence that is
acquired by means of an unreasonable search shall be "excluded," or held in-
admissable at the trial.

or property, without due process of law; nor shall private property be taken for public use, without just compensation.

The self-incrimination and "due process" clauses of this article are those that affect the police on a more regular basis than the other clauses. The "due process" provision is a reference to the normal and legal procedure, which may not be by-passed for any purpose. Federal police agencies were the first to be instructed and required not only to respect an individual's right against self-incrimination, but they were also required to orally admonish him as to his rights against making any statements that could be used against him in a court of law. This federal rule became known as the McNabb-Mallory Rule, based upon two cases in 1943 and 1957, respectively.

A series of cases in various states eventually led to what is now known as the Miranda Rule of the U.S. Supreme Court, rendered by that body on June 13, 1966. The rule applies to the admissibility in court of a person's statements made during a custodial police interrogation, which means a questioning session during which the subject being questioned was the suspect of a criminal case and the investigation had focused on him at the time. The Supreme Court ruled that the Fifth and Sixth Amendments shall directly be applied to all the states, and that the police shall comply with the rule in the case of all custodial interrogations. The subject must be advised as follows, and he must understand the meaning of what he is being told:

> You have the absolute right to remain silent. Anything you say can, and will, be used against you in court.
> You have the right to consult with an attorney, to be represented by an attorney, and to have one present before I ask you any questions.
> If you cannot afford an attorney, one will be appointed to represent you before you are questioned, if you desire.

The subject may then waive these rights, and the waiver must be made "voluntarily, knowingly, and intelligently." The Court's rule requires that the officer proceed only after asking the subject: "With these rights in mind, are you ready to talk with me about the charges against you?" The subject must then reply with an oral affirmative before the officer proceeds. After the interview begins, the subject is given continued protection against himself and any statements he may make, by the Court's direction: "If, however, he indicates in any manner and at any state of the process that he wishes to consult with an attorney before speaking there can be no questioning. Likewise, if the individual is alone and indicates in any manner that he does not wish to be interrogated, the police may not question him. The mere fact that he may have answered some questions or volunteered some statements on his own does not deprive him of the right to refrain from answering any further inquiries until he has consulted with an attorney and thereafter consents to be questioned."

> Article VI. In all criminal prosecutions, the accused shall enjoy the right to a speedy and public trial, by an impartial jury of the State and district wherein the crime shall have been committed, which district shall have been previously ascertained by law, and to be informed of the nature and cause of the accusation; to be confronted with the witnesses against him; to have compulsory process for obtaining witnesses in his favor, and to have the Assistance of Counsel for his defence.

The speedy trial provision is met by the police officers' taking the suspect before a magistrate without undue delay, and filing charges against him. State laws require that the subject of an arrest be specifically advised of the crime for which he is being charged, except that in some cases this advisement may be waived when it is understood exactly why the arrest is being made, such as when an officer arrests the defendant during the actual commission of a crime, or following a pursuit immediately following the act. The witnesses against the defendant are presented in court to give their testimony, and at that time may be cross-examined by the defendant or his attorney.

At the outset of the investigation when an identification may be made by a witness from behind a screen or other device which hides the identity of the witness from the suspect, such a procedure is in the best interest of the safety of the witness and it is not a violation of the defendant's rights under authority of the Sixth Amendment. His attorney may utilize an "early discovery" rule that many states have that allows the defense to demand, and receive, copies of statements made by witnesses in a specific case.

There are times when the identity of confidential informants are the source of information that may lead to the institution of an investigation, and for public safety reasons—such as sustaining the life of the informant—the informant is never identified. In this type of case, however, there must be evidence independent of the informant's information that will stand on its own merits and sustain a conviction of the defendant.

> Article X. The powers not delegated to the United States by the Constitution, nor prohibited by it to the States, are reserved to the States respectively, or to the people.

Article Ten provides for the primary police power to be vested in the individual states, which are sovereign in our system of government in the United States.

THE COURTS AND THEIR RELATIONSHIP
TO LAW ENFORCEMENT

The American system of criminal jurisprudence is based upon codified laws. There are criminal codes of a wide variety that cover all those acts or omissions that the elected legislators have deemed essential to rule an orderly society. New laws are added with increasing regularity, and old ones are changed or rescinded. Such a system of laws, with prescribed punishment for each offense, serves to "put people on notice" as to what their society expects of them in good conduct, and what they may expect in the way of punishment should they violate the rules. It also provides the police with a set of guidelines that they must follow in their orderly process of law enforcement.

The part played in the system of jurisprudence by the courts is most important. Three major premises comprise the Doctrine of Judicial Supremacy in the American system: (1) The courts, and only the courts, may make the final determination as to what is law and what is not, (2) the courts may require—through legal means at their disposal—adherence to lawful conduct, by the administrative branch of government, and (3) the courts may invalidate a legislative action on the basis of unconstitutionality. This doctrine refers to the Supreme Court, but the general principle is carried down to the lowest court at state level. A state legislature may enact a law that a city council heartily endorses, which reflects the attitude of the community. As a result of such endorsement, the city administrator may convey the message to the police chief, who orders his officers to enforce the law to the "letter of the law." When a defendant appears in court, a "not guilty" decision or a suspended sentence may reflect an attitude on the part of the court that the law is either unfair or unjust. The defendant might be found guilty and sentenced, then appeal to a higher court, and on up through the various higher courts to the state or even the United States Supreme Court. The Supreme Court might then decide that the law is unconstitutional and, therefore, invalid. This does not mean that the law was *illegal,* because it was promulgated by legal process, and all of the subsequent police and court action was likewise legal, but once the decision is rendered by the Supreme Court, the law is no longer enforceable.

The court hears testimony and takes an affidavit to determine whether or not to issue a warrant of arrest, or a search warrant. The lower court in a felony case will hear testimony and receive evidence and decide whether to "bind the case over," or remand the defendant to the higher court for trial. In a jury trial, the jury determines fact and truth, and the judge determines what is lawful. In the absence of a jury the judge determines both fact and law. On the basis of a violation of "due process," or a technical error, or other action on the part of the prosecution—or the police—that denies to the defendant any of the constitutional safeguards the judge may declare a mistrial and the criminal may go free, because he is innocent until *proven* guilty. This is a fundamental responsibility of the court, as well as determining guilt or innocence and prescribing punishment for the guilty.

The Supreme Court

State sovereignty is great, according to the United States system of government as it was intended by its founders, and with respect to that sovereignty the final arbiter in a case or controversy in any state is that state's supreme court. Only under certain circumstances shall the case be studied and decided by the United States Supreme Court, and the primary qualifications must be that there is a diversity of citizenship of two or more states, or there must be a federal question involved.

Although the Supreme Court is involved in a few administrative and supervisory functions as head of the federal judicial system, the principal role of the court is to decide cases. "Original" cases may be taken directly to the Supreme Court, and this is the type of case that usually involves issues to test or challenge the constitutionality of a rule or law. The second type of case decided by the Supreme Court is the appeal from lower federal or state courts. These cases involve the same type as those that are listed above, as well as suits to enforce laws or treaties of the United States, cases involving diversity of citizenship, and suits to enforce the United States Constitution.

The Supreme Court of the United States consists of a chief justice and eight associate justices. They are appointed by the President with the advice and consent of the Senate, and they hold office for life during their good behavior. There can be no question as to the tremendous influence that the Supreme Court has upon not only the judicial system and law enforcement, but upon the entire populace of the nation. Not only must the members of the court be great jurists, but they must be master statesmen as well. The Constitution is the supreme law of the land, and the Supreme Court serves to interpret and perpetuate its principles.

SUMMARY

At no other time in the history of the United States has the Constitution played such a leading role in the process of law enforcement. The police officers walk a thin tightrope while preserving the peace and protecting life and property. They, too, must operate within the law and according to the provisions of the Constitution and the Bill of Rights. They have no time to ponder the finer points of constitutional law, and they must act with speed and decisiveness when the occasion arises. When they effect an arrest of a person or a search of his person or property, they must be acting upon good faith and reasonable cause, or by authority of a warrant that must be based upon information from a reliable source and with good cause.

The freedom of man is sacred, but liberty is relative and there are certain obligations to other persons and their liberty as well. Each person must meet these obligations if his own liberty and safety are to be preserved and protected. The police power within the United States which is not specifically delegated to the federal government by the Constitution is inherent within the individual states. They have the right and the duty to legislate for the preservation of peace and protection of the public health, morals, safety, and welfare of the community. The police agencies and their officers are responsible for enforcing the police power, but with wisdom and proficiency, so as to do the most efficient job within the guidelines established by law and the decisions of the Supreme Court.

Exercises and Study Questions

1. Commit to memory (again) the Preamble to the Constitution.

2. Define "police power."

3. The police are the enforcement arm of which branch of government?

4. Of what significance is the Fourteenth Amendment?

5. What is "due process"?

6. List and discuss at least three examples of abuse of the right to free speech.

7. Of what significance was Mapp v. Ohio to local law enforcement agencies?

8. What is the Miranda Rule?

9. What is meant by the term "Judicial Supremacy"?

10. *Recommended Semester Project*: List and discuss the major decisions of the U. S. Supreme Court during the past fifteen years. Describe the case in point, and discuss the implications of each decision regarding all future police actions.

Suggested for Additional Study:

A political science textbook of your choice. Study the Constitution and the Bill of Rights, and the courts in the American system of jurisprudence.

The Bill of Rights, A Source Book for Teachers (Sacramento, Calif.: Dep't. of Education, 1967). A well-prepared paperback sourcebook for study of the Bill of Rights. It discusses the origin and historical development of the Bill of Rights, and analyzes current and past problems attendant to the application of the guarantees provided by these most important ten amendments to the Constitution.

The Policeman's Public Responsibilities and Private Rights

INTRODUCTION

The police role is one of the most difficult to perform in a free society. There are literally thousands of laws to enforce by means of persuasion when possible, and force if necessary. The policeman must zealously protect all of the people whom he serves, including those who break the law. The accused is innocent until proven guilty even though the officer may have actually witnessed an act that he knows to be a crime. The United States and individual state constitutions provide that the accused shall have the right to "due process" in all proceedings against them. All persons are assured of their inalienable rights to "life, liberty, and the pursuit of happiness," but there are certain obligations that go along with those rights so that the same rights of others are not infringed upon. The policeman should not be so predominant that he interferes with the general design of life and personal interactions, but without him civilization as we know it would disintegrate.

The policeman has a public image that he must maintain at all times whether on the job or at a private social function. He *is* the police agency that he represents. When he drives his patrol car down the street, all eyes may be upon him when he approaches a stop signal to see if he obeys the same laws that he enforces. If he has friends over to his house for a party, his neighbors may look to him to set the example for them to follow, such as to keep conversation, radios, and the like low enough so that the neighbors are not disturbed, and to be sure not to appear intoxicated in public. Although he is no less human than his neighbors, they may sometimes be startled when they discover that he can display "normal" human qualities.

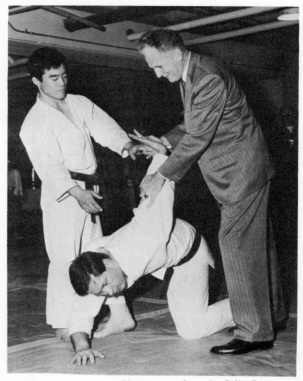

Photo courtesy Santa Ana Police Department

SANTA ANA POLICE CHIEF EDWARD J. ALLEN DEMONSTRATES
TO KARATE CHAMPION FUMIO DEMURA OF JAPAN HIS OWN
KNOWLEDGE OF THE ART AT AN OPEN HOUSE CEREMONY.
THE CHIEF'S "PRISONER" IS ACTUALLY ONE OF HIS OFFICERS.

CODE OF ETHICS

In 1956, the California Peace Officers Association adopted a well-written "statement of policy" Code of Ethics. National police organizations have since adopted the code, including the International Association of Chiefs of Police (IACP), and it is universally accepted as the Law Enforcement Code of Ethics.

AS A LAW ENFORCEMENT OFFICER my fundamental duty is to mankind; to safeguard lives and property; to protect the innocent against deception, the weak against oppression and intimidation, and

the peaceful against violence and disorder; to respect the CONSTITU-
TIONAL rights of all men to liberty, equality and justice.

I will keep my private life unsullied as an example to all; maintain courageous calm in the face of danger, scorn, or ridicule; develop
self-restraint; and be constantly mindful of the welfare of others. I
will be exemplary in obeying the laws of the land and the regulations
of my department. Whatever I see or hear of a confidential nature, or
that is confided in me in my official capacity, will be kept secret unless
revelation is necessary in the performance of my duty.

I will never act officiously or permit personal feelings, prejudices,
animosities or friendships to influence my decisions. With no compromise for crime and with relentless prosecution of criminals, I will
enforce the law courteously and appropriately without fear or favor,
malice or ill-will, never employing unnecessary force or violence and
never accepting gratuities. I RECOGNIZE the badge of my office as a
symbol of public faith, and I accept it as a public trust to be held
so long as I am true to the ethics of the police service. I will constantly
strive to achieve these objectives and ideals, dedicating myself before
God to my chosen profession—LAW ENFORCEMENT.

The private lives of policemen are no different from a constitutional standpoint than that of any other citizen. The control over an
officer's private life should be exercised by the officer himself. Because
of the sensitive nature of police service, most police departments
require their officers to conform to certain legal, ethical, and moral
standards off duty as well as on duty. Reasonable rules of that nature
have been tested in various courts and hearings and have withstood
the tests to date.

Officious actions by policemen should be avoided with determination. His demeanor should be pleasant. The most effective way one
can be sure that personal prejudices will not influence his actions is
for him to overcome any strong prejudicial attitudes that may mani-
fest themselves in inadvertent actions or statements in times of great
emotional stress.

THE POLICEMAN'S PUBLIC IMAGE

To the many "publics" that he serves, the policeman is looked
upon through different eyes and emotions. To the child who is hungry
and lost, the policeman is a strong and friendly benefactor; to the
criminal he is a villain; to the average citizen he is any thing from a
"nice guy" who has an interesting, but difficult, job to do, to a "good-
for-nothing" indolent boor. He can create his own reputation and

that of all other policemen by his own thoughtless or deliberate improper conduct. The policeman must not be a thief. He must be *obviously* honest in every transaction he makes and in his conversations he should never indicate that he has any inclination to commit any type of theft or fraud.

Generally, policemen receive fair salaries. If they are not, they should be increased. An officer who seeks special discounts or gifts of anything—including refreshments—is a "moocher". One never gets something for nothing, and the policeman is particularly susceptible to compromising himself and his official position by accepting any gratuities.

When an officer picks up anything in a store or shop and does not pay for it, he is to the observer a "typical apple-snatcher." Officers should never shop while in uniform, but should handle such personal affairs while off-duty.

One who acquires any type of social or work position in which he exercises any authority or power over others has a human tendency to impose his power upon others, although it may not be real power at all. Public *service* is a *service* function.

Laziness is a quality that an officer must avoid developing or displaying. He must be well rested and enthusiastic about his work. Officers must never drink alcoholic beverages while working, except for plainclothes undercover assignments when the role-playing situation requires it, and should avoid a before-work alcoholic beverage before reporting to work. While on duty and in uniform, the policeman should visit places where alcoholic beverages are sold on police business only, and he should never drink anything at all while in such a place.

A policeman's morals must be impeccable and beyond reproach under any conditions. The officer who attempts to arrange for dates and companionship while on duty, using his official position to impress or attempt to blackmail a woman to accompany or entertain him, is not suitable for the work.

Personal prejudice is a personal matter until it is reflected in the person's official actions. The bigot who identifies himself as being a member of any organization or business that advocates anything but objective law enforcement is not fit to be a policeman.

"Police brutality" is a common accusation even when such actions do not occur. Any act which an officer performs that results in actual injury to a person, or an insult to his self-esteem triggers such an accusation. There can be no doubt that some officers in unusual situations may resort to excessive or unnecessary physical

Photos courtesy Santa Ana Police Department

OPEN HOUSE PROGRAMS PROVIDE A GOOD OPPORTUNITY TO
PRESENT THE POLICE ROLE TO THE PUBLIC UNDER FAVORABLE
CONDITIONS.

force or psychological abuse. Such actions must not be allowed and, when committed, they should not be allowed to go unpunished. Police brutality involves a predisposed attitude and an intentional excess action. Police officers should do nothing to convey such an attitude.

A policeman should be a gentleman, even at the risk of being considered "old-fashioned" or "square." Courtesy is free, and a smile takes no extra time. An officer must be liberal with both.

For a policeman to repeat a rumor even to deny it tends to give credence to the lie that it may be. Any rumors he hears about his fellow employees or any person who may be acting in violation of the law must be investigated as to the source of information and its credence, and then handled according to policy and procedure requirements.

Self confidence is an attribute. Egotism is an undesirable quality for a policeman.

There should be only one truth when a person swears to tell the "whole truth and nothing but the truth". Any compromise for self-aggrandizement, or revenge, or for any reason whatsoever is even more reprehensible than the act of stealing. Nothing justifies an immoral, illegal, or unethical act such as lying. A police officer must always speak the truth.

POLICE-COMMUNITY RELATIONS

Rapport between the police and the public is the key to favorable results, if the police officers are performing their duties in accordance with the laws and proper procedure. There must be a mutual feeling of confidence and respect on the part of both parties for true rapport to exist. The police reflect the community itself, which is comprised of a variety of people, most of whom obey the law in accordance with the mores of the community. Police officers are products and ingredients of the community as are the people he serves and protects.

The "public" is actually not an appropriate term when referring to the people served by the police. The word "public" implies homogeneity, while there are actually many publics. The American community is heterogeneous, and the publics consist of business groups, religious organizations, political parties, minority groups, professional people, fraternal orders, students, parents, criminals, pressure groups, youth groups, housewives, husbands, senior citizens, and so forth. The "publics" are not static; some may merge to form another,

Photos courtesy Santa Ana Police Dept.

MARTIAL ARTS DEMONSTRATION AT AN
OPEN HOUSE CEREMONY.

and others may divide and regroup. Most people will probably be included in several "publics."

Police Responsibility

The public relations responsibility is to provide police service for all of the people in the officer's jurisdiction. Equal protection and service for all people in accordance with the Constitution and the laws should be the primary objective. All officers and employees of the police agency should make a deliberate effort to demonstrate their adherence to the policy of striving to accomplish that objective.

Officers and their supervisors should be responsible for knowing the people in their jurisdiction, and making themselves and their purpose known to those people. They must make a continuous and deliberate effort to become acquainted with as many people as possible and to maintain a good rapport with them on a fair and impartial basis.

Speakers' Bureau

The police chief and his staff should make frequent appearances before various service clubs, church groups, fraternal organizations, and any other citizen groups, that will provide him with a forum. There must be a free-flowing channel of communication between the police and people he serves. He must frankly and honestly discuss police policies and actions, and he must get feed-back to assure him that he is performing the police task in the best interests of the public.

The speakers' bureau may prepare programs and send a list of topics to the various program chairmen to stimulate their interest in their police department. General topics, such as the department's progress, traffic enforcement, juvenile control, protection against check passers, and similar presentations can be complemented by more

Photo courtesy Santa Ana Police Department

RADIO PERSONALITY BOB HARKE AND LIEUTENANT C. W. JORDAN GO ON A TOUR OF THE POLICE FACILITIES BUILDING DURING A RADIO DOCUMENTARY.

stimulating although perhaps less informational programs. Demonstrations of pistol shooting, the lie detector, the police baton, or weaponless defense are both entertaining and instructive. The observers get involved in the demonstration and may develop a better feeling for the police task. They also see the officers as friendly and average people.

Information Services

The news media have a responsibility to the public they serve, and they zealously seek out the news and enforce their right to a free press. Rather than considering them as a hostile camp, it is incumbent upon the police officer to cooperate with the representatives of the press. This is usually accomplished by making all news releases available through certain individuals and offices within the police department so that the officers in the field will not be required to interrupt their work to answer inquiries from the press. Such an arrangement assures the press of complete and "uncontrolled" news. Of course, certain facts about crimes and suspects cannot be released because of the need for secrecy during an investigation or the protection of the accused, who is innocent until proven guilty. Prepared news releases covering various police activities of the department, such as a training program or individual achievements of officers, should be presented to the newsmen for their use. There are items of news and information about a police department that the public should know and that reporters would like to pass on. Brochures, pamphlets, and progress reports are also valuable public relations aids, but should not be used with restraint of cost.

Public Involvement

One program which is quite productive is that of inviting community leaders to ride as observers in a police car for a night. The results can be rewarding for the police, because very few non-policemen have ever experienced at first-hand, the policeman's role. Law students, attorneys, councilmen, teachers, police science students, mayors, and judges are just a few who should be exposed to the policeman's field duties. Liability waivers are usually necessary in order to avoid legal repercussions.

One of the most common statements a policeman hears from the people whom he contacts is "I don't want to get involved." The people should get involved in the matter of law enforcement. It is everybody's business. With only one or two policemen per thousand population, the police are powerless without help, particularly the local leaders who shape the attitudes of their neighbors. The officers should establish a free-flowing channel of communication between themselves and the leaders to provide for a common understanding of their relative tasks in the community. There should be a continuous effort to prevent the formation of an invisible, but insurmountable wall between the police and any segment of the community.

Grievance Procedure

Complaints and grievances must be heard and acted upon with objectivity and impartiality. There must be a procedure for complaint about questioning any police action. There must be no intimidation or harassment that would upset the procedure, and the complaint should be heard with courtesy and respect. The complaining party should be advised that an investigation will be conducted. Complete and accurate reports should be prepared and followed up with a thorough inquiry into the matter. The officer about whom the complaint has been made should have an opportunity to present his accounting for the incident and be accorded the same rights and privileges as any other citizen. The officer who is found to be blameless should be cleared of the charges. The officer who is found to be at fault should be dealt with swiftly and decisively. Only the officer who acted properly or who made an error in judgment and acted improperly—although in good faith—should be exonerated. An officer who clearly has violated the law or a regulation through negligence or willful misconduct should be subjected to negative disciplinary action in the form of a reprimand or dismissal and/or the filing of criminal charges. Whether or not to inform the complainant about the ultimate disposition of the matter is a decision to be made by the chief administrator of the department. Whatever he may choose as a matter of procedure, there should be some form of feed-back to the public so that they may be assured that their grievances are being acted upon quickly and surely.

Civilian Review Boards

In the absence of a workable system that provides persons who wish to complain or question police activities there will be frustration and dissatisfaction. Real and imagined grievances will accumulate and generate a general distrust and dislike for the police. Police review boards may seem to people as the only way to cope with the problem.

What is a police review board? The term does not adequately

describe the many variations of the same general plan. First, it should be understood that it is not an official part of the police department. Many departments provide very successfully for such a grievance procedure through the office of the chief of police, or a personnel or internal affairs unit. Such a review board may be a quasi-official agency with board members appointed by the mayor or other public officials, but it is generally not a board comprised of professionals in the field of law enforcement or related occupations. Nor is it a police commission that is an official branch of government composed of nonpolice citizens of the community who regulate the board and general policies of the police department by committee, and to whom the chief of police is responsible.

The police review board is a committee, of a private or quasi-official government nature, organized as an ad hoc group for the specific purpose of acting upon citizen (or resident) complaints against acts of unnecessary force, aggression, or some other improper performance of the community's police force. The board may meet regularly, or as the members determine the need, depending upon its particular rules of procedure. The board may employ investigators and legal advisors, and conduct its own investigation of complaints it receives and suspected violations of police ethics or rules.

The board hears witnesses, seldom including the alleged violating officer, examines evidence, reviews reports, and inquires into the matter—some boards pay informants and assure them anonymity—and use any means they deem proper and efficient. The boards then decide the case under inquiry and make recommendations to the police administrator as to their findings and whether or not the case needs his action to investigate and to mete out disciplinary action.

There are some questions that must be answered relative to the purpose and methods of a police review board whenever consideration is given to the establishment of such a board.

1. Is there already in existence an agency composed of conscientious citizens whose duty it is to investigate complaints about inefficient or improper actions by government offices, such as the grand jury?
2. Are the courts so crowded that civil recourse is slow or virtually impossible?
3. Are the courts effective in hearing cases and rendering fair and just decisions?
4. Does the police department have a procedure that provides for free access to the chief or a direct representative to report misconduct or other improper behavior of the officers?

5. Are the elected representatives, such as the city council, who have investigative and subpoena powers, accessible to their constituents to listen to, and act upon grievances?

6. Will such a board duplicate any other agency or process already in existence?

7. Would the review board have official subpoena powers?

8. To whom would the board be answerable to assure its objectivity and honesty?

9. Who are the people who comprise the board, what are their qualifications, and how are they selected?

10. What remuneration or other incentive motivates an individual to be a member of the board?

11. How will the board hear and investigate cases? (a) Will the declarants be required to testify under oath? (b) Will there be any cross-examination to verify statements or will all statements be accepted at face value? (c) Will the alleged offending officer have a right to face his accuser, produce witnesses, and be able to answer the allegations under oath? (d) Will the hearings be public or private? (e) Do all people in the community have access to the board without delay?

12. What legal authority would a review board have to request, demand, or recommend action by the chief of police?

13. Does the board usurp the authority of a chief of police presuming it to be able to handle his responsibility to manage the police department?

14. Does the *stated* purpose of a police review board coincide with the *true* purpose of such a board: equal protection under the law and effective law enforcement?

THE POLICEMAN'S PRIVATE LIFE

The policeman is a private citizen. He is a husband, or fiancé, a brother, or a father, a baseball fan, a bowler, an average next door neighbor. The policeman was born, schooled, trained; and he will live and die eventually. When he doesn't have his uniform on, the chances are you would not be able to distinguish him from the other young men who live on the block who work for the bank, or service station, or a law firm. The policeman's private life should be just that, private. But there is one problem—he's a cop.

The officer off-duty lives in a modest home in a middle-class neighborhood. Like any other man of his age, he lives as a bachelor, or as a married man with a family. He participates in sports, seeks entertainment, entertains friends and is entertained by friends, attends classes at college, has a beer or cocktail occasionally, and goes about his business of seeking happiness in his own personal way. The policeman may be off-duty when he is not on the job, but he is always a policeman. His neighbors and friends judge the entire police department on his personal actions. They drive more carefully in his presence, drink a little less, make less noise, and obey the law because a policeman is in their presence. The childern are warned that the policeman down the street will get them if they misbehave. His own children know him as a father and a policeman and it doesn't make a difference to them because of constant intimate association. But the children on the block may not want to play with the policeman's son or daughter because their father is a cop. And everyone watches the policeman to see how he behaves. If he scolds or punishes his children, he's mean. If he argues with his wife, he's cruel and probably a wife-beater. If he drinks he's a drunk, or at least approaching alcoholism. He is always a policeman, but he is a normal human adult who lives a normal life. There are restrictions, of course, that he must impose upon himself if he is to effectively perform his job when he is on duty.

Religion and Politics

While on duty the officer is obligated to remain neutral and avoid discussions of a political or religious nature. The Constitution assures everyone of the freedom to worship as he chooses and to vote for whomever he chooses. This includes the policeman, but he is "government" in the eyes of many. Any aggressive leadership on the part of the policemen, particularly when it involves attempting to convert another person's religious or political philosophy to that of his own, may be construed as a form of governmental duress.

Organization Membership

The policeman should take an active part in the social and civic affairs of his community, such as civic groups, religious clubs, fraternal organizations, parent-teacher groups, Boy Scouts, boys clubs, and a variety of other activities. He should deliberately avoid restricting his off-duty associations only to other policemen and their families. This would result in tunnel vision and a self-imposed barrier between the policeman and the other people in the community. The officer has freedom of choice, but he compromises his effectiveness as a policeman if he affiliates himself with a special interest or pressure group that actively attempts in any way to promote bigotry or prejudice against any particular segment of the population. The officer has the constitutional right to speak freely on issues and his principles, but when he does speak, his listeners who know him as a policeman will tend to interpret his statements as an expression of the philosophy of the police department. Any subsequent police action he may take may be misinterpreted as a reflection of that presumed philosophy. Instead of arresting a man because he has been driving while under the influence of alcohol, he is presumed to be a Whig arresting a Tory on a trumped up charge.

Outside Employment

The policeman receives his authority as a peace officer from the jurisdiction that employs him. He is an agent of that city or other political entity and cannot sell or lease that power to private employers. Working as a bouncer or private guard is a conflict of interest occupation. What about other work? Should the policeman be involved in off-duty employment? Some police administrators say no. Others are either indifferent to the matter, or approve of the practice. Those who oppose outside off-duty employment do so for several reasons:

1. The work week was reduced to forty or forty-eight hours to assure the officer adequate rest.
2. The pay should be adequate without taking outside employment.
3. Conflicts of interest are involved and the officer may find himself working for two masters: law enforcement and the other job.
4. Virtually every other type of work except teaching police science or related subjects are inconsistent with the police role because of the necessity for union membership, regularly scheduled hours, or other employer demands.
5. There is the possibility that the officer could be enticed away from his police employment for higher wages or other benefits not available to policemen, such as week-ends, holidays, and nights off.

SUMMARY

The policeman is a public personality. Like a television personality or a school teacher, the policeman is a community personality who must maintain an image the people expect of him. The officer's private life is his own as an individual, but the public's as a policeman. He must learn to live moderately, within his means, and obey all the rules of society. On duty, the policeman's image is one of honesty, integrity, industry, loyalty, and all the qualities that one expects to find in the model citizen. The policeman must fearlessly execute his duties in the best interests of the community he serves. He has a code of ethics and he should abide by its tenets in a professional manner.

The police responsibility in community relations is to provide equal protection for all the people in his jurisdiction without displaying prejudice toward any ethnic, religious, or political group. He must know the people and the leaders in his district and to strive diligently for a continuous and free-flowing personal interaction and communication between the police and the many publics they serve.

Police officers are chosen from among the ranks of the people they serve. Human weaknesses of hatred, bigotry, disloyalty, dishonesty, and many more are characteristics of modern society. The policeman must rise above such failings, and must enforce the law by example as well as by the performance of his routine duties.

Exercises and Study Questions

1. Commit to memory the Law Enforcement Code of Ethics.

2. Discuss the freedoms of the average citizen as compared with the freedoms of a policeman. Is there a difference, and, if so, what is that difference?

3. List and discuss at least five personal characteristics that a policeman should not possess.

4. List five character traits that a policeman should possess.

5. Define "police brutality."

6. What is the police responsibility in community relations?

7. Discuss the responsibility in police-community relations.

8. Describe a procedure for handling grievances and complaints by the public about police procedures or specific acts of misconduct that you believe would be workable.

9. Discuss your opinions of a police civilian review board. In class, divide the class into proponents and opponents and discuss all the aspects of such a board or committee.

10. *Recommended Semester Project*: In a form that would be utilized by a police chief to his city council, outline a five-point plan for a workable police-community relations program in your community.

Suggested for Additional Study:

Earle, H. H. *Police-Community Relations: Crisis in Our Time* (Springfield, Ill.: Thomas, 1967) . This book is an excellent source when studying the role of the police in community relations. The author is a division chief of the Los Angeles County Sheriff's Department, and he and his department have had considerable experience in this important, and sometimes explosive, problem.

Hollingsworth, D. *Rocks in the Roadway* (Chicago: Stromberg-Allen Co. 1954) . A fifty-four page paper-back booklet that delivers a message relative to the police attitudes and conduct. The book should be required reading for every policeman and student preparing to enter the police service.

13

Police Professionalization

INTRODUCTION

Police work is a profession. So say some of the police practitioners, instructors, and writers. But is it really a profession? Do proclamations make it so? What qualities must a group of people possess in order to be termed professional? What factors are necessary to qualify an occupation common to many people as a profession? It appears that great strides have been made toward the professionalization of police service, but the final objective has yet to be reached.

The law enforcement agency owes certain obligations to the policemen if they are to be truly regarded as professionals, and they are obligated to the agency for which they work. The police department is a community service organization. The people who comprise the organization must be selfless and dedicated to their work. This is one of the qualifications of a member of a profession.

PROFESSION DEFINED AND DISCUSSED

Textbook and dictionary definitions vary, but there seems to be a general agreement on certain factors that distinguish a particular occupation as a profession. Those factors include:

1. A common body of specialized knowledge. Police science, or administration of justice, or criminology departments in many colleges enjoy respectable positions in the curriculum structure. The student may earn baccalaureate and master's degrees in specialized police academic disciplines, and earn a doctorate in public administration with emphasis on police administration.

2. Minimum educational requirements prior to entry into the profession. Most police departments do not qualify under this category

Photos courtesy Orange County Sheriff's Department

TRAINING AND PROFESSIONALIZATION ARE SYNONYMOUS.

because no college education is required prior to entry into the service. The majority of police departments require graduation from high school as an educational minimum, while others will accept high school equivalency or lesser qualifications. A few departments require two to four years of college. In California, and certain other parts of the United States, it is possible to establish such requirements, although the graduating students are not sufficiently plentiful. Such a requirement would be impossible in some states with colleges offering no police science programs. The President's Crime Commission recommended in February, 1967 that the minimum academic qualification for all policemen should eventually be a baccalaureate degree. When that minimum is met on a nation-wide basis, the second professional qualification will have been met.

3. Free exchange of information between individuals and their departments. Trade secrets are personal possessions in the opinion of some police officers and administrators. Professionals may develop their own particular technique, but general procedure should be standardized. The specific needs of the community should dictate the actions of the policeman, rather than the individual actions of different officers. Professional journals, such as *Police, Law and Order, Journal of Criminal Law, Criminology, Police Science,* and various other media provide a common ground for discussion of police techniques. The California Commission on Peace Officer Standards and Training is one of several similar organizations that provide for uniform minimum training standards and approve curriculums. Zone schools of the Federal Bureau of Investigation and regional institutes are conducted frequently throughout the state, and in a number of colleges in the country. All these types of training provide many policemen an opportunity for an exchange of information. Police literature, once limited in scope and quantity, is now available to a much greater degree.

4. Careful and rigid preemployment screening. Many police departments now employ very exacting methods for selecting those candidates who are best qualified, and employ less than 5 percent of the applicants. Some state agencies or commissions, such as in New York, Illinois, or the Commission on Peace Officer Standards and Training in California are charged with the responsibility for establishing minimum recruitment standards. Enforcement of such standards is accomplished by the commission through the contribution of funds matched by the agency cooperating with the commission. These funds pay the salary of recruits while they attend the academy. In order to participate in the program, a police department must subscribe to

certain employment standards which may require medical and psychiatric examinations, physical agility, written and oral tests, and thorough background investigations. Compliance with the commission's rules is a matter of free choice, but funds are withheld unless the police department does comply.

5. A code of ethics. The Law Enforcement Code of Ethics has been adopted by many police departments and organizations throughout the United States. Regulation of the men and women affected by the code of ethics is accomplished by the various police chiefs, sheriffs, and other department heads by means of enforceable rules and regulations.

6. Recognition by the public. This factor is in various stages of progress throughout the country.

AGENCY RESPONSIBILITY TO THE INDIVIDUAL

Employing law enforcement agencies should be required to contribute their share toward the professionalization of the police service. They should comprise the following elements:

Photo courtesy Anaheim Police Department

MODERN QUARTERS ARE ESSENTIAL TO PROFESSIONALIZATION.

1. Competent leadership. The executive administrators of the political unit that seeks to professionalize its police force must employ and support a well-qualified and competent police chief. The chief must be at least as well educated as the men and women he will lead, and his experience must indicate both successful performance as a police administrator, and an attitude conducive to the encouragement of academic progress and experimentation which accompanies professional development.

2. Adequate facilities. The place where the policemen will perform their field operations must be modern and well-equipped. The back rooms or basement of a city hall or similarly inadequate facilities stifle the employees in their work performance both physically and psychologically. A functional, spacious, and well-lighted building should be mandatory.

3. Proper equipment. Emergency vehicles must be capable of performance which can meet their emergency needs. They should be equipped with adequate lights, sirens, first aid supplies, and any other equipment that may be necessary. Uniforms must be attractive and kept in good repair, and the other accessories both servicable and effective. Weapons and ammunition should be standard and capable of serving the purpose for which they are intended.

4. Training and educational assistance. Schedules should be flexible so that officers who wish to may continue their college and specialized training. Financial assistance in the form of tuition and textbooks is provided by some police departments. A few departments pay their officers overtime for the hours they attend classes. Training is a mutual responsibility of officer and department alike: the officer's, to seek and apply the training, and the department's to provide it. The officer must be continuously training in the many techniques he must perform, and in the many procedures that his work involves. The training must be competent and continuous.

5. Recognition. Individual officers should have a team spirit and work diligently to present an image of a police department which is performing the tasks at hand. Private gain should not be emphasized, but within the organization there should be realistic incentives and rewards that will encourage the officers to earn recognition for extra efforts toward improvement of techniques in performing police work. Change for real improvement is most desirable and should be encouraged.

6. Remuneration. Professional people must be paid wages appropriate to professionals. The wages of a day laborer cannot be paid to an officer who is expected to dedicate himself to the police role.

Doctors, attorneys, and other professionals are paid handsomely for their services. Policemen should be paid comparably.

THE INDIVIDUAL'S RESPONSIBILITY TO THE AGENCY

"Devotion to duty" should describe the policeman's attitude and actions. If he is to earn for himself and his fellow officers the status of a professional, he has certain obligations to his employing agency, and to the service itself.

1. Positive attitude. The chronic complainer and the drone have no place in professional law enforcement. The officer's attitude must be one of optimism and enthusiasm. By his own enthusiasm, he will generate the same feeling in the people with whom he works.

2. Industriousness. The officer should be able to work on his own. Success in any profession requires intelligence and energy. Law enforcement is no exception.

3. Loyalty. The professional policeman must be loyal to his God, his country, and to his community. The public good is the primary concern of the Constitution; his concern should be the same.

SUMMARY

The police service is advancing toward the status of a profession. Although law enforcement cannot be classified as a true profession because of the diverse stages of development in various parts of the country, there are some individuals and some police agencies that can be classed as professional. Policemen do not become professionals by proclamation. The prerequisites are a common body of knowledge, pre-entry education, free exchange of information, careful and rigid pre-employment screening, a code of ethics, and recognition by the public as professionals.

Police professionalization involves mutual responsibility of the agency to the officer and of the officer to the agency. It is a two-way street, and a long journey to the final destination.

Exercises and Study Questions

1. What are the factors that distinguish a *calling* as a *profession?*

2. Discuss your opinions as to whether or not there should be a free flow of communications between all policeman, or should specialists be entitled to their "trade secrets"?

3. List five items that a police department should provide for its officers.

4. In your opinion, should the agency assume the financial burden for the college education of its officers? If so, in what manner and to what extent?

5. What should an officer do to fulfill his responsibility to the police department for which he works?

6. Discuss "loyalty." What does it mean to you?

7. Discuss in class: Is police work a profession?

8. Visit your local police department. Are the facilities conducive to professional law enforcement?

9. If you were to enter the law enforcement service today—or if you are already so employed—would you consider yourself qualified for the term "professional"?

10. *Recommended Semester Project*: Write a paper on the subject "Police Professionalization," or "Why Police Service Will Never Become a Profession," or a similar subject with whatever viewpoint reflects your personal opinion.

Suggested for Additional Study:

Wilson, O. W. *Police Planning* (2d ed.; Springfield, Ill.: Thomas, 1962). For any officer or police administrator who intends to participate in any police planning activity, this book will serve as a workable guide and assure a greater probability of success to the person who uses it as a guide.

14

New Horizons in Police Selection, Training, and Management

INTRODUCTION

Progress in law enforcement is essential. This chapter cannot encompass all of the innovations in police administration. Management of a police department is similar in many respects to management of any of the larger business enterprises in the community. There is a significant difference, however. The police "business" is one that directly involves the liberty and safety of every person served by the police organization. One of the most critical factors in the management of a police department is the recruitment and retention of qualified personnel. Another critical factor is that of training the men to perform their jobs adequately. In this chapter, we will discuss some of the trends and newer procedures involving personnel, training, and police management.

PROGRESS IN PERSONNEL METHODS

When a chief of police is asked to list three major problems confronting law enforcement today, his list will usually include the problem of recruitment and retention of qualified personnel. The problem is critical. The President's Commission on Law Enforcement and the Administration of Justice (short title, "President's Crime Commission") concluded in early 1967 that it would require fifty-thousand men to fill the authorized ranks to full strength in all the police departments in the United States for that year alone. As the population continues to grow, so grows the need for police employees.

Position Evaluation and Classification

One technique employed by progressive police agencies to meet manpower needs more effectively is through job reclassification. The principle is to study thoroughly the many police tasks and to determine what positions can be filled by nonpolice personnel without reducing the effectiveness of the police function. This is not intended as an economy measure—although lower salaries for the reclassified positions may be a result—but is designed to keep as many policemen and policewomen on their jobs in the capacity for which their appointment is intended. The result may also be an increase in efficiency in some cases.

Parking Control

Issuing citations for overtime parking in timed zones and in metered spaces can be effectively accomplished by the employment of women for the job. Although male civilians may accomplish the task just as quickly and competently, the meter maids prove to be a definite public relations asset.

Records Clerks, Stenographers, and File Clerks

Policemen have been replaced to a considerable extent in many office duties such as records-keeping, filing, and other jobs that can be performed with much greater efficiency by people hired specifically for clerical functions. Many hours of a policeman's work week may involve the preparation of reports. Some of these hours can be put to better use with the assistance of capable stenographers and clerks.

Property and Evidence Control

There are many decisions made by people handling evidence and recovered property that may determine the ultimate fate of persons charged with crimes. A chain of continuity is essential to show that the same evidence taken from the suspect, or collected at the scene of the crime, is that which is being presented at his trial. Improper handling of evidence may cause its contamination or destruction, and may consequently be the cause of an unsuccessful prosecution. Releasing evidence or property to the victim of a crime too soon after a trial, and then to find that a re-trial is ordered by the court may result in the total loss of the evidence for the second trial. The job calls for a responsible person performing a multitude of tasks for which he is responsible, with diligence and perseverance, and who intends to continue at his job for a considerable length of time. Rotational assignment of policemen to the detail is not administratively wise because of loss of continuity, and assignment of a policeman who is either temporarily or permanently disabled is far less efficient than a permanent appointment of a civilian to fill the job.

Communications Operators

"Only policemen can understand the field problems of other policemen" is a valid argument. It is used in defense of the retention of nearly every task within a police organization by policemen with special interests in that particular task. The radio is the lone patrol officer's partner, and when he is in the field by himself in a one-man patrol car or motorcycle he learns to rely heavily upon the people at the other end of his radio transmissions. Many police departments utilize civilian employees as switchboard operators, and as radio operators. Because of the need for radio transmission and procedure decisions that only a policeman is capable of making, one or more officers are assigned to the communications center to coordinate the activities of the civilians. Complaint desks may be manned by policemen so that many calls for information or service can be adequately handled by telephone, or a determination made as to what police action should be taken. The actual routine of dispatching and receiving radio calls and operating the switchboard can be performed quite capably by well-trained and closely supervised civilian personnel.

Identification and Laboratory Personnel

The criminalistics and identification specialties require a considerable amount of additional training and formal education; that of criminalistics requiring at least a baccalaureate degree in chemistry or related disciplines. The nature of work involved in both details requires a considerable amount of additional study and practical experience before the individual may qualify in court as an expert. Although some police experience is desirable for the personnel assigned to these tasks, it is not absolutely essential and it may be wiser for the administrator to consider persons with no prior police experience, particularly when those persons can prove their specialized proficiency.

Student Trainees

Employment of college students in criminology or criminalistics or related law enforcement specialties who need to earn extra income is another way some departments find qualified personnel. Such employment of students should be on a part-time basis and should not be used by students simply as a means to support themselves while getting an education for eventual employment in other occupations. The purpose of the position would be primarily to prepare the student for his eventual role as a policeman, and secondarily to make use of his academic training to accomplish a variety of tasks which would otherwise have to be performed by the policemen they assist. Tasks that can be quickly learned and effectively performed by these young future policemen may include special research projects, darkroom technician duties, property control assistance, records, communications, and a variety of desk duties that officers assigned to various specialized divisions must perform. Student trainees may be required to agree that they will apply for a police position when they reach their twenty-first birthday or when they acquire their degree, whichever occurs latest. In addition to their academic standing, candidates for student trainee jobs may be required to go through the same screening process required of policemen. Successful candidates would be reasonably assured of employment by the agency of their choice.

Minimum Recruitment Standards

In some states, special commissions or boards have been formed to handle the establishment of minimum recruitment standards. Other states will follow suit, no doubt, because of the improved results of such a program. In states where there is uniformity in minimum qualifications for policemen, it is possible to establish a certification program similar to that of licensing in certain professions and occupations. Once such a system is utilized on a state-wide basis, the next step may be "lateral entry."

Lateral entry, or lateral transfer from one police department to another is virtually impossible in many departments because of the disparity between their recruitment standards. Inroads have been made in some parts of the country, and a few police departments will accept policemen from other departments upon their presentation of "basic" or "intermediate" certificates similar to those issued by the California Commission on Peace Officers Standards and Training. Requirements for the certificates are completion of a commission-approved academy program and proof that the officer's selection was based upon a battery of prescribed tests, a thorough background investigation, and certain other criteria. The intermediate certificate requires an additional period of demonstrated satisfactory service.

If an entire state's police departments and sheriffs' departments were to subscribe to a certification program, tests could be administered at several central locations in the state and a single eligibility list established. Departments in need of qualified candidates would request the names of candidates indicating a preference for that particular department or a specific part of the state. Officers seeking a transfer to another part of the state or possibly another state, would also be eligible. Employment of individual candidates would continue to be a matter of agreement between the hiring agency and the candidate.

Promotional lists would be the next step in the lateral transfer concept. An officer may be well-qualified for the next higher rank, but not be able to advance because of all the higher ranking positions in his own department being filled. Other departments have the problem of not having qualified persons to fill higher ranks. Under a system of this nature, state-wide promotional examinations would be given regularly and eligibility lists established. As in the case of entrance employment, promotional employment would also be a matter of mutual agreement between the employing agency and the officer seeking the position. There would be no usurpation of power. As a matter of loyalty to their own employees who seek a higher position within their own departments, it would be possible for the employing agency to specify in their requirements that their first preference would be for their own officers should they place high enough on the eligibility list.

Recruitment

In its report in early 1967, the President's Crime Commission recommended that there be provision for three levels of entry into the police service. The Commission stated that such a plan would alleviate the recruitment problem and serve to fill some of the thousands of existing unfilled police positions, more than fifty thousand at that time, and which increase every year because of population growth in many parts of the country.

The Commission's recommendation outlined the first of the three levels of entry, the Community Service Officer. The CSO would be at least eighteen years old and probably less than twenty-one, although he could be older. He would wear a uniform, but would be unarmed. This man would perform primary functions, according to the Commission, of maintaining a close working relationship with juveniles, perform minor community service tasks, and generally assist the two higher ranking levels of officers. Upon attainment of his twenty-first birthday, and satisfaction of certain educational requirements, the CSO would be eligible for the next higher position.

The Police Officer would be required to possess a high school diploma and be twenty-one years old. He must be adjudged capable of continuing successfully in college, and he would be expected to continue a college education on his own time. The Police Officer would be employed with either no prior police experience, or he may have started as a CSO. The officer in this second level would perform nearly all of those duties currently performed by patrol policemen excepting the less critical duties assigned to the CSO. His duties would include responding to calls, routine patrol, emergency services, preliminary investigations, and enforcing traffic regulations.

The third and highest of the three levels of entry would be the Police Agent, as recommended by the President's Crime Commission. He would be required to have at least two years of college, and this would eventually be changed to require four years of college when feasible. The agent would be assigned the more complex tasks because of his superior academic standing—according to the Commission —and those duties would include specialized patrol in high crime areas, community relations, or juvenile delinquency control.

Some police departments have utilized similar categories of assignments, with the exception of the entrance requirements for the Police Agent. The traditional procedure employed by police departments is for all officers, regardless of age or academic accomplishment, to enter at the lowest policeman or patrolman level, and to advance through the ranks from that point. Many departments employ police cadets or interns, whose duties are similar to those of the Community Service Officer, except that the latter woud perform actual public contact and service functions that are currently restricted to policemen. As the cadets and interns perform currently, they serve as aides to the field officers. They perform research and clerical duties, and their field time is devoted almost exclusively to observation only.

The Senior Policeman

An alternate to the creation of the rank of Police Agent is the Senior Policeman, or Training Officer. Not all officers are successful in attaining higher ranking positions. Some do not pass tests with high scores, and others fail the tests. Yet, these same men may be outstanding policemen with several years of valuable experience and technical skill. The Senior Officer should be one who has been rotated through at least one division other than Patrol, and meet certain minimum service and academic requirements. Three or four years of service should be the minimum, and the officer should have completed at least two years of college. The Senior Officer rating should have requirements stringent enough to require that the officer demonstrate initiative and to exert himself to earn the rank.

Upgrading the Uniformed Officer

The uniformed policeman is the backbone of the municipal or county police department. He performs all of the basic police functions; he is the first, and many times the only officer who comes in contact with the public; he is the hub of all other police functions. Detectives, traffic officers, and other officers are no less important, but neither should they be considered any more important in prestige. One method to accomplish upgrading is to create a "senior officer" rating to encourage officers to seek permanent assignment to the patrol divisions as they aspire to plainclothes details.

Another method for upgrading the uniformed officer is to have a planned personnel rotation system. Rotation is particularly good for the small and medium-sized police departments in which every officer is a "generalist," and he performs all police duties during his tour of duty and within his assigned jurisdiction. This system is more efficient, particularly when manpower needs are critical, than one which compartmentalizes the department into a system of specialists. Rotation prepares the officer for promotion as well as his eventual return to the patrol division, where he will perform with considerably greater proficiency than he would if not allowed the opportunity to work in the various divisions.

Personnel Ratings

With the financial assistance provided by the Office of Law Enforcement Assistance (OLEA), a federal grant program, many police departments have begun to conduct many research projects not previously possible with the restricted budgets of most law enforcement agencies, particularly the small and medium-sized ones. Exotic equipment and many sophisticated new techniques have been studied with varying degrees of success.

Additional studies have been directed toward some of those procedures already in existence, including one that has always been problematic: the personnel rating system. The ultimate results will, it is hoped, be a considerable improvement over the rating systems that many departments now use. Transfers, promotions, dismissals, suspensions, commendations, and pay considerations all have direct relationship to the rating system. Careful and objective ratings by well-trained superiors are essential to the efficient management of a police department.

Personnel Selection Testing

Written and oral examinations have been used for many years. Industry has had considerable success in using the personal history of the candidate as a prediction of probable success on the job. Studies are made of officers and other employees who are considered by a consensus of management as successful. Their personal histories are studies, and factors such as age, marital and familial status, prior employment, education, community involvement (service clubs, youth groups, etc.), are all assigned relative weights considered valid because of proven performance by the standards established for the purpose of evaluation. Each new candidate is required to fill out a similar history form, points are assigned each answer, and the total score is used for rank-ordering the candidates in the order of their probability of success in the job for which they are being considered.

Situational Tests

Policemen must possess certain characteristics peculiar to the role of law enforcement, such as inquisitiveness, reasonable suspicion of questionable situations or persons, or a relentless determination to complete a job once it has been started. Situational tests, or role-playing techniques may be applied for the purpose of simulating situations the policeman may encounter at some time during his career. His behavior is observed by qualified persons who evaluate his actions and rate him according to a success-predictability scale.

TRAINING PROGRAMS AND TECHNIQUES

The training of policemen is a critical factor. Many techniques have been applied in law enforcement during recent years as if they were new techniques. Actually, many of the "new" training methods are only new to law enforcement. In addition to the many items listed in the following paragraphs, which only serve as a sampling of the vast variety of techniques available, the police supervisors involved in training utilizes visual aids, motion pictures, displays, and study charts which are all standard training tools.

Role Playing

Developed by psychiatrists as a form of psychodrama, role playing has been utilized with considerable success in law enforcement training, particularly in supervision and human relations classes. Simulated real-life situations are structured in such a manner as to present to the student under controlled conditions many situations they may encounter at some later time when under great emotional stress. If properly trained in such areas as decision-making, (when *not* to fire one's service revolver) or under what conditions force should be used with greater or lesser restraint the officer will develop good habits. His habits will be developed under stress, but *simulated stress,* and he will probably perform similarly in real situations.

Seminars and Symposia

Exchange of information will prove more valuable in some cases than a series of lectures. Members of various. operating units within an emergency service organization such as a police department should know and understand their relative positions and each should be familiar with the duties and responsibilities of the others. Brainstorming sessions in which several people are closeted for the purpose of thinking at random to seek a solution to a problem are very worthwhile, provided there is no immediate need for action. Follow-up conferences and other types of action reinforce the benefits of the brainstorming session.

Zone Schools

Police academies and specialized training by some of the larger police departments has been considered by those agencies as most beneficial. All their training may be designed to meet their specific needs. Recent trends have been toward centralized "zone schools" at one or more locations in the county or state cosponsored by the several cooperating agencies, and to which those police departments send their officers for training. Although individual department heads may feel that some of their powers have been usurped, the result in most cases has been an improvement. Instructors and other resources can be pooled, and a more uniform approach by officers from different departments may be taken when similar situations occur.

Some states have commissions, such as the Commission on Peace Officer Standards and Training in California, previously discussed, which provide for minimum educational standards and some control

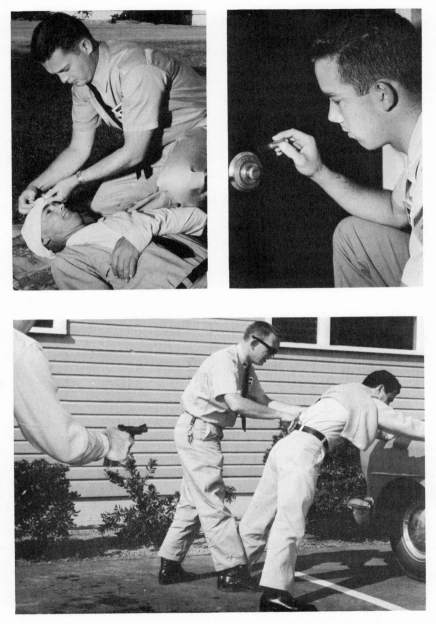

Photos courtesy Police Science Department, Orange Coast College

ACADEMY TRAINING COVERS ALL PHASES OF POLICE WORK.

over the content of the course in accordance with a broad outline. Exchange of information among police agencies, the various academies, and the coordinating commissions results in a greater degree of uniformity in training and subsequent field activities. There is the additional favorable effect of a better understanding of the police function and philosophy of law enforcement. Regardless of what jurisdiction they may find themselves in, the personnel find similar law enforcement tactics and techniques.

CHANGING CONCEPTS IN POLICE MANAGEMENT

The entire field of human relations involves a constantly changing set of concepts. A more humanistic approach to management, or "people-oriented" supervision as opposed to the "task-oriented" trend has been gaining momentum since the depression years of the 1930s. Although a completely democratic management would not be feasible for a police department, there is more employee or subordinate involvement in decision-making and long-range planning in the progressive police department than there was in the more rigid police organization of former times.

Individual motivation is the direct concern of the police chief down through the levels of command to the newest policeman on the job. Intelligent policemen not only want to have a part in decision-making, but they have a need to know *why* certain policies are in existence and what is the purpose for a procedure to be followed according to a prescribed manner.

Community relations is a police responsibility. It should not be set aside by policemen who regard it as the business of sociologists. The responsibility is everyone's *including* the police. In order to cope with problems involving the many people in the community, each with his own special interests, the policeman must attempt to know them, their intricacies, and their idiosyncrasies. This does not necessarily mean that their philosophies are to be embraced by the policemen, but it is important for the policeman to know what those philosophies are and what effect, if any, they will have on the police function.

Policies and procedures must be better articulated than in times when there were considerably fewer rules and court decisions to understand and to follow. Policemen should have sufficient training and guidance so that they may do the best job possible within the framework of the rules they must follow.

CHICAGO POLICE UTILIZE THE LATEST IN MODERN EQUIP-
MENT SUCH AS COMPUTERS IN ITS DATA SYSTEMS DIVISION,
PICTURED ABOVE. DEVELOPEMENT AND USE OF COMPUTERS IN
FIELD OF LAW ENFORCEMENT IS A GIGANTIC STEP IN CRIME
FIGHTING.

Police crime prevention and repression activities need evaluation
and improvement. Considerable strides have been taken in many areas
of law enforcement, but crime rates continue to increase at an alarm-
ing rate. Continuous evaluation of police methods to repress crime
and apprehend offenders must continue, and any new ideas must be
given consideration. Because of the limitations of cost and manpower,
it will be necessary to make extensive use of mutual aid agreements
among the various police agencies with contiguous boundaries.

With the advent and phenomenal progress of electronic data
processing equipment and corelative communications systems, the trend
toward centralization of records and informational services has gained
impetus. Information centers already in existence, such as the central
clearing house of the Federal Bureau of Investigation, and the various
state agencies, have been linked with the many state and county
information centers. The value of almost instantaneous access to
central files and the exchange of criminal information is inestimable.
As the systems are improved upon, local agencies may find that there
is considerable duplication, and it appears that a greater reliance on
centralized files is inevitable. Similar centralization has also been
observed in such areas as laboratory and identification services.

SUMMARY

In a chapter of this nature, it is not possible to cover all the many new and changing concepts in law enforcement. To be too specific about systems and techniques in the operational stage today—particularly when dealing with computers and data processing—would be difficult. The present attitude in police management is to accept new methods, and to encourage a continuous reevaluation of existing methods. When the need for change becomes clear, there should be change, but for the sake of improvement, not for the sake of change itself. Move with wisdom and caution—but move.

Exercises and Study Questions

1. What would you suggest that would stimulate the necessary number of qualified candidates to want to become policemen?

2. Visit your local police agency. From your observations, list at least three types of work now being performed by police officers that could be done by civilians.

3. Should the task of property and evidence control be assigned to a police officer, or civilian personnel? Why?

4. Should parking meter enforcement be assigned to police officers or to civilian personnel? Men, or women? Why?

5. Discuss in class the relative merits of utilizing a student trainee program.

6. Discuss the "lateral entry" and "lateral transfer."

7. What is a community service officer, as defined by the President's Crime Commission report of 1967?

8. In what specific areas do you suggest more and better police in-service training?

9. Describe what is meant by a "more humanistic approach" to personnel management.

10. *Recommended Semester Project*: In a detailed report, list and discuss five procedures or types of police equipment that have been developed during the past five years that have resulted in improved police efficiency.

Index

A

Accident prevention, 193–196
Adjutant general, state, 90–92
Age:
  and crime, 50
  for police service, 19
Agriculture, Department of, 101
Air Force, 100
Air National Guard, 90
Alcohol and Tobacco Tax Division, of
  Internal Revenue Service, 98
Alcoholic beverage control, 163
  state agencies for, 93–94
Alfred, King, and tithing system, 68
Allen, Edward J., 62
Amnesty, 109
Animal control, 121
Anslinger, Harry, 62
Answering calls on patrol, 141
Appellate courts, state, 103
Application form, for police service, 23
Arizona Rangers, 89
Arrest of law violators, 142
Assaults, investigation of, 149
Attorney general, state, 106
Attorney General of U.S., 98
Automobile theft, investigation of, 148

B

Background, of police candidates, 20–21
Background investigation, for police
  service, 31–36
Bailiffs, in England, 70
Beccaria, Cesare, 45
Beggars, investigation of, 149–150
Bicycle control, juvenile, 195–196
Bill of Rights, and the police role,
  205–211
Boards, police, 75
Border Patrol, 99
Boston, Mass.:
  night watch in, 74
  police department in, 73

Bow Street Runners, in England, 71
Breath analyzer, 167
Budget control function, of police
  department, 127
Burglaries, investigation of, 148–149

C

Cadet training program, 10–11
California:
  court system in, 103–104
  State Police in, 90
California Bureau of Criminal Identifi-
  cation and Investigation, 106
Capone, Al, 62–63
Career criminals, 57–58
Career opportunities, in police service,
  21–22
Chief tithingman, in England, 69
Circumstantial offenders, 56–57
Civil Aeronautics Board, 101
Civil defense, 96
Civil division, of sheriff's office, 129
Civilian review boards, 224–226
Civil Service Commission, 101–102
Classical School theory of crime, 45
Classification:
  of information, 13
  of positions, 239
Climate, and crime, 50
Coal and Iron Police, 83
Coast Guard, 100
Collection, of information, 13
Colquhoun, Patrick, 71
Comes Stabuli, in England, 69
Common Law, 53–54
Common sense, in police work, 3
Communication relations, on patrol,
  144–146
Communications Act, 102
Communications operators, policemen as,
  240
Communications unit, of police depart-
  ment, 122–123
Connecticut, state police agency in, 90